Ballet Across Borders

Career and Culture in the World of Dancers

Helena Wulff

BERG

Oxford • New York

First published in 1998 by
Berg
Editorial offices:
150 Cowley Road, Oxford, OX4 1JJ, UK
70 Washington Square South, New York, NY 10012, USA

Berg is an imprint of Oxford International Publishers Ltd.

Library of Congress Cataloging-in-Publication Data
A catalog record for this book is available from the Library of Congress.

British Library Cataloguing-in-Publication Data
A catalogue record for this book is available from the British Library.

ISBN   1 85973 993 8 (Cloth)
       1 85973 998 9 (Paper)

Typeset by JS Typesetting, Wellingborough, Northants.
Printed in the United Kingdom by Biddles Ltd, Guildford.

In memory of my Father,
who introduced me to ballet.

'You see, this place is like a life. It's not just
the stage. This is where we have our relationships,
everything!'

Woman soloist dancer

'I enjoy very much that I have an international
language. On stage, I can talk to anybody without
knowing or actually seeing the person!'

Male principal dancer

Contents

Acknowledgements

This book has grown out of a love for ballet and dance that I kept stowed away for many years. By making an anthropological study of the ballet world, I have been able to combine my intellectual and artistic interests into a research approach that also offers an understanding of contemporary life, work and thought in general.

My gratitude to the many people and institutions that made this study possible is enormous. Simon Mottram, ballet director of the Royal Swedish Ballet during my field study, was an invaluable key informant and introducer who became a friend. A highly intelligent and imaginative artist, Simon often understood intuitively what kind of information or access I needed. Through his many connections, he opened up the transnational ballet world for me. I am in great debt to Simon for being my guardian angel in the ballet world.

I owe special thanks to Eskil Hemberg, director of the Royal Opera House in Stockholm during my field study, and Nils-Åke Häggbom, the ballet director who gave me permission to spend one year with the Royal Swedish Ballet. He also saw to it that I got access to the American Ballet Theatre. Dag Simonsen, ballet producer of the Royal Swedish Ballet at the time, was always supportive and pivotal for my access to the Royal Ballet in London.

Among the people I met backstage at the Royal Opera House in Stockholm, I would in particular like to thank Gunilla Roempke, Jan Willem de Roo, Per Mankeus, Dobrana Mirchev, Viktor Fedotov, Eric Sjöström, Vija Briedis, Marika Lagercrantz and Bo Wulff (not a relative). Per Mankeus, Paul Nelissen, Agneta Stjernlöf-Valcu and Ewa Bjarnholt were also helpful.

A Swedish *The Nutcracker* by Pär Isberg made ballet history in 1995. I have had many enjoyable conversations with Pär, considerate and insightful house choreographer of the Royal Swedish Ballet. Madeleine Onne provided well-articulated information about ballet as a career. Johanna Björnson, Eva Nissen and Hans Nilsson also contributed generously to the study. So did Anneli Alhanko, Matti Alenius, Jan-Erik Wikström and Anna Valev. Elina Lehto and Charlotte Stålhammar shared much information about ballet, as did Christian Rambe and Tiiu Kokkonen, Mikael Fjellström, Henrik Burman, Anders Groth, Kate Lind af Hageby and Alexandra Kastrinos. I also wish to thank Marie Lindqvist, Susanna Englund and Rennie Mirro.

I visited the Swedish Ballet School in Stockholm, thanks to Kerstin Lidström, the director.

I am extremely grateful that the administrative director Anthony Russell-Roberts at the Royal Ballet in London accepted my presence there. The director Sir Anthony Dowell and assistant director Monica Mason also took a kind interest in my study, as did Christopher Carr, Elizabeth Anderton and Jeanetta Laurence. With Britt Tajet-Foxell, consultant psychologist at the British Royal Ballet, I share a concern for dancers' health and well-being. I appreciated Britt's warmth, enthusiasm and hospitality very much. Rebecca Hanson and Niki Katrak were important gate-openers on my way through the networks in the British ballet world.

The young choreographer and dancer, Matthew Hart, told me how he got 'the ballet bug' and helped in many other concrete ways, and also through his positive outlook. So did Benazir Hussein, Ricardo Cervera and Joshua Tuifa. Sylvie Guillem supplied insightful and original views on ballet and ballet culture. Zoltán Solymosi, Viviana Durante, Deborah Bull, Sarah Wildor and Darcey Bussell amply shared their experiences of ballet with me. At the British Royal Ballet, I would also like to thank Irek Mukhamedov, Adam Cooper, Ashley Page, Tetsuya Kumakawa, Fiona Chadwick, Belinda Hatley, Hubert Essakow, Milena Regis and Patricia Roivas.

Adrian Grater at the Benesh Institute in London was very informative about ballet notation. Not that far away from the ballet world in London, the sculptor Antony Dufort (who sometimes makes ballet drawings) provided interesting conversation.

At the American Ballet Theatre in New York, I owe the greatest debt of gratitude to the artistic director Kevin McKenzie. The assistant director at the time, Ross Stretton, was also supportive, as were Terence S. Orr, Michael Owen, Georgina Parkinson, Irina Kolpakova, David Richardson and Florence Pettan.

Johan Renvall was a very helpful first contact at the American Ballet Theatre. Later, Marianna Tcherkassky, Susan Jaffe, Cynthia Harvey, Paloma Herrera and Robert Hill spoke eloquently about ballet. So did Guillaume Graffin, Parrish Maynard, Yan Chen, Christina Fagundes, Lisa Sundstrom, Amy Wilder, Christopher Martin, Laura Martin, Katherine Linden and Vladislav Kalinin. Rebecca Massey and Robert Underwood were especially interested in my study.

Adam Sklute at the then Joffrey Ballet took me to rehearsals with his company and provided information about ballet life in New York.

Despite the fact that William Forsythe harbours a pronounced dislike of representations of his company, he allowed me into Ballett Frankfurt in Frankfurt-am-Main. It is therefore with a particularly deep bow of gratitude and admiration that I thank William Forsythe. His choreography continues to open up unimagined spaces and atmospheres. The administrative director at Ballett Frankfurt, Urs Frey, is very good at his job, and was indeed helpful with the study. Anders Hellström contributed extensively by way of intelligent, tragic, sensitive and witty accounts of the ballet world. Thierry Guiderdoni provided wisdom, zest and elaborate explanations of ballet. Stefanie Arnt, Desmond Richardson, Antony Rizzi, Dana Caspersen, Francesca Harper, Simon Frearson, Anouk Spiess and Bill Seaman were all supportive. I thank them, Nik Haffner, Dirk Haubrich, Bettina Eger, Heiko Frosch, Chris Salter and Philipp Danzeisen for good company, as well, and Matthias Lorenz and Joel Ryan especially. Nicholas Champion helped me getting a certain video tape. Ivar Hagendoorn offered dance enthusiasm and practical information.

A composer of great talent and originality, Thom Willems, introduced me to the world of writing and making contemporary ballet music. This artistic craftmanship is flagrantly neglected in most ballet and dance reviews, as well as in the bulk of dance scholarship. In his computer studio, Thom showed me how electronic sounds are made, and put together with samplings of all kinds of other music and also processed live recordings and silence into crossover collages. This had a momentous impact on my thinking and writing process by gearing me towards issues on 'dance and new technology' that carry over to my next research project.

In Frankfurt-am-Main I was affiliated to the Institut für Kulturanthropologie und Europäische Ethnologie at the Johann Wolfgang Goethe-Universität. I am very grateful to Professor Ina-Maria Greverus for being my loyal host.

Towards the end of my writing period, I did a short site-visit at the Zentrum für Kunst und Medientechnologie in Karlsruhe, where Volker Kuchelmeister was an informative guide.

'The critic's point of view' is illuminated in the study by Clement Crisp, Mary Clarke, Kathrine Sorley Walker and Alasdair Macauley in London, Anna Kisselgoff, Arlene Croce, Deborah Jowitt and the late Dale Harris in New York, and Gunilla Jensen and Bodil Persson in Stockholm. I wish to thank them all very much for contributing to a fuller understanding of the social dynamics around performances. Jane Kramer was crucial for connecting me to the New York critics, and also to Elizabeth Kendall.

The photographs were taken and supplied by Agnès Noltenius, Mats Bäcker and Enar Merkel Rydberg. I appreciate their assistance and thank them very much for granting permissions to publish their photographs. It is also with gratitude that I acknowledge the permissions to publish a revised version of 'Perspectives towards Ballet Performance: Exploring, Repairing and Maintaining Frames' from Felicia Hughes-Freeland, ed.,

Ritual, Performance, Media (London: Routledge, 1998) in Chapter 5, and a revised version of 'Studying Ballet as an Ex-Native: Dialogues of Life and Fieldwork' from Anne Claire Groffmann *et al.*, eds, *Kulturanthropologinnen im Dialog* (Königstein/Taunus: Ulrike Helmer Verlag, 1997) in Chapter 1.

In the university world I am especially grateful to Barbro Klein, Owe Ronström, Mark Graham, Lena Hammergren, Orvar Löfgren, Andrée Grau, Vered Amit-Talai and Moshe Shokeid for being early supporters of this study, and also to Felicia Hughes-Freeland, Gudrun Dahl, Donald Broady, Setha M. Low, Loïc Wacquant, Don Kulick, Thomas Hylland Eriksen and Susan Leigh Foster, who learnt about it later. I wish to thank dance scholar Cecilia Olsson in particular for friendship and penetrating conversations and comments.

The study has benefited from suggestions prompted by papers I have presented at the Conferences of the European Association of Social Anthropologists in Oslo, 1994 and in Barcelona, 1996; the Conference on 'Culture in the Global Marketplace' in Vaxholm, 1994, organized by the 'National and Transnational Cultural Processes' Project; the Conference on 'Organizing the Global Ecumene' in Sigtuna hosted by the Swedish Collegium for Advanced Study in the Social Sciences; the Conference on 'Studying Social Fields' arranged by the Swedish Research Council for the Humanities and Social Sciences in Långholmen, 1995; the annual meeting of the Association of Social Anthropologists of the Commonwealth in Swansea, 1996; the Workshop on 'Transnational Field Studies' at the Department of Social Anthropology, Stockholm University, 1996; the annual meeting of the American Anthropological Association, San Francisco, 1996; the Workshop on 'Personal Identity and National Identity: Time and Space' at the Department and Museum of Anthropology, University of Oslo, 1997; and at the Conference of the Nordic Forum for Dance Research in Helsinki, 1997. I have had many useful responses to papers about the study at guest lectures at the University of Hull; the Institute of Ethnology, Stockholm University; the University of Linköping; the University College of Dance in Stockholm; and at the Johann Wolfgang Goethe-Universität; and also at my home Department of Social Anthropology, Stockholm University.

The study was a part of the programme on 'National and Transnational Cultural Processes', funded by the Swedish Research Council for the Humanities and Social Sciences. This research council also financed two periods of the field study in Frankfurt-am-Main through an exchange programme with Germany.

I am much obliged to my editors at Berg: Kathryn Earle, Sara Everett and David Phelps, not least for their enthusiasm over this book. It has also been a great joy to work with them.

Finally, I would like to thank my niece Victoria Wulff and my nephew Ludvig Wulff very much for good times at children's ballets. Their comments and questions showed me that children switch between taking part in the illusion on stage and deconstructing it more frequently than adults. And that there are many ways to draw the boundary between illusion and reality.

Moving around in the transnational ballet world would, however, not have been as immensely enjoyable, unless my husband and colleague Ulf Hannerz had been waiting for me at home. He provided emotional shelter that I carried with me when I went on tours and field studies abroad, and even kept me company as a field spouse most of the time in New York. Not a ballet-goer, this was still where he was thrilled by *Revelations*, the signature piece of the Alvin Ailey American Dance Theater. Later, Ulf patiently accepted my regimented writing schedule. All along he has been an inspiring discussion partner – especially when I took my own intellectual paths. I am most grateful for his encouragement and endurance; I thank him from the bottom of my heart.

Helena Wulff

Prologue: A Return to the Ballet World

When I was two years old my parents noticed, they used to tell me, that I would dance when I heard music. They then took me to a local ballet school for toddlers, and this was the beginning of fifteen years of intensive practice in classical ballet for me. At the age of seventeen I had to stop because of a back injury. But my body still remembers what it feels like to dance.[1] Learning to dance and dancing are muscular experiences that never go away completely. The feeling is activated, for instance, when I hear music to which I used to dance.

Growing Up in the Ballet World: A Memoir

One Christmas, when I had danced for a few years, my parents took me and my younger brother to see the German children's ballet *Little Petter's Journey to the Moon* at the Royal Opera House in Stockholm. It became our Christmas treat for a number of years, so it is likely that different performances melt together in my recollection. But I remember clearly that on one occasion, when 'The Man in the Moon' entered to a huge thunderclap, my brother became so scared that he had to be taken out by our mother. I was never scared. On the contrary, I was absorbed by the allure of the stage. One year, when we were seated close to the stage, I even had a momentous experience of ballet art, the first and formative one that I believe imprinted a passion for ballet in me. On stage the light was turned down and a black starry sky appeared. Girls dressed in glittering white tutus made their way with the soft music on a low ramp. The girls sat down, each one with her legs gracefully to one side.

I was spellbound. I had never seen anything so beautiful. There is a notion of ballet revelations in the ballet world, a state of mind that can be likened to a religious experience, a conversion. These exceptional experiences of ballet art usually happen to children, but they may strike later in life as well, producing a feeling of such force that it is never forgotten. It can be suppressed over the course of many years, yet it is still there. It seems to arise with some preparation, be it through cultural capital and/or experience of dancing, not during a first visit to a ballet performance. Many dancers, choreographers, critics, ballet fans and ballet sponsors remember one particular moment of ballet splendour that mesmerized them irrevocably. A ballet revelation can be the impetus to pursue a career as a dancer or the beginning of balletomania; but it can make an imprint on any theatre-goer.

A male principal with the Royal Swedish Ballet told me how he as a ballet student used to watch performances from the wings at the Royal Opera House in Stockholm. *The Taming of The Shrew* made a particularly strong impression on him: 'Then I felt – *this* I want to do! From then on dancing became a job, not only a hobby.' As he was standing in the wings that night, he had realized, quite unexpectedly 'how the steps you learn in the studio can be used'. The world of ballet art opened up to him, full of unexplored treasures, and he was overwhelmed by 'a feeling you can never get again'. It all resembles how Agnes de Mille as a fourteen-year-old ballet student in the 1920s saw Anna Pavlova dance and recalls how she 'sat with blood beating in my throat', struck by a sudden certainty that this was going to be 'her life's work' (Gherman 1994: 27). And the ballet sponsor and writer Lincoln Kirstein (1994) was as a child prohibited by his mother from seeing the Ballets Russes in 1916, on the grounds that he might fall apart as he had done at a performance of *La Bohème*, believing that Mimí was really dying on stage. Later, ballet did become 'a luminous magnet' (ibid.: 214) for Kirstein.

As I grew physically from a child to an adolescent, my body was being disciplined – sometimes with aching muscles – by and into the steps of classical ballet, and so was my world-view. I was living in the intensity and discipline of ballet dancing that separates dancing adolescents from non-dancing peers (cf. Sutherland 1976). I was attending a ballet school in Stockholm. My teachers, a Latvian couple, used to be a ballet director and a principal dancer. They had fled in a small fishing boat to Sweden during the Second World War, bringing with them their ballet scores amongst a very few belongings. From these ballet scores they were able to mount original Russian classical ballets (Ralf 1979). They taught us their Russian training, the Vaganova school.

One variation of steps that has stuck in my mind (and body), probably because I realized the historical significance already at the time, was that they instructed us in 'how to do *révérance* to the Tsar', i.e. thanking the audience for their applause with a specially deep curtsy, turning towards the box where the Tsar used to be seated in their theatre.

With the ballet lessons came a decorum of politeness, a chivalry in the studio as well as outside it that echoed courtly manners all the way back to the fourteenth century, when ballet was first practised in Italy, descending through King Louis XIV of France, and (for us, then) especially through the court of the Russian tsars. According to this decorum, men were supposed to be polite to women when it came to ways of greeting, passing through doors, and so on and younger people to older people. Generally people of lesser status showed respect (at least interactionally) to people of higher status, i.e. of greater fame.

In the dressing-rooms we ballet students discussed dance wear, dance shoes and hairstyles for dancers. We were learning an adorned femininity, which is a characteristic of costuming in classical ballets. Importantly, it also becomes a way to dress outside the theatre and studio for ballet dancers when they wear their 'street' or 'private' clothing and 'street' or 'private' hairstyles.

Wearing my hair gathered in a small bun at the back and a light blue leotard, I did the barre exercises standing in the middle of a long line of girls. Our ballet mistress was determined. She wanted perfection. Her dark hair was cut short, and she usually wore a simple dress and red ballet shoes with low heels in order to be able to 'mark' the steps for us. Sometimes she used the best girls to fill in where, because of her age (she was in her fifties), she was too stiff to move. She gave corrections verbally or came up to the girl who had missed the step, and moved her leg or arm the way it was supposed to go. Getting warm and beginning to sweat, we continued doing short variations, such as *pirouettes* (turns) and *jetés* (jumps) in two groups on the floors. Now we danced to Chopin waltzes and pieces by Ravel from the black grand piano. We were anticipating the day when we would be old enough to start dancing on pointe.

Our ballet mistress had complete authority. We never questioned anything; but I recollect wondering in private about the background and the context of the steps. As I gradually learnt French in school, I took a secret delight in making connections between the ballet terms and what they illustrated. That the *pas de chat*, for instance, is a step that imitates the soft leap of a cat, and a *glissade* is a sliding step.

One year we were preparing for a recital, the section with the snowflakes in *The Nutcracker*. Our ballet mistress was not pleased with our dancing. She showed us a particular variation again. It still did not work. By then she was getting irritated; and when it did not really improve the third time either, she lost her temper. It must have been a forceful fit, since it has stayed in my memory for so many years. I was not only scared and disciplined by it, but also impressed.

3

Later, as an adolescent, I got a black leotard, like the other girls in my class. We were also sporting skin-coloured tights and the necessary light blue, home-knitted legwarmers. Now we were doing more advanced exercises, and one of them was to start the momentous pointe dancing. My first pair of pointe shoes were pink satin. It was important to put rosin on the soles of them in order not to slip. We took turns pawing in the rosin box that was placed close to the entrance of the studio. The rosin soon sent out its dry smell, which still fills me with a familiar excitement whenever I get close to it. For dancing on pointe was such a thrill: we were learning to reach into a new, aerial dimension. Clearly, it would take a lot of practice to dance effortlessly on pointe for longer stretches of time. At first it hurt; yet to break through the law of gravitation with the music released a special feeling of delicate euphoria that I have never experienced in any other way since then. Now I think of this exceptional state in terms of Csikszentmihalyi's (1990) concept of flow, an optimal experience where action and consciousness meet.

But I did not only dance myself, I was also taken to the Opera House in Stockholm to watch performances. I saw *Swan Lake* and *The Nutcracker* a number of times, and I acquired a ballet literacy, a habit of 'reading' balletic form and movement. A turning-point occurred, I think, when I was nine years old and my father took me to see *The Moon Reindeer* by Birgit Cullberg. In the intermission my father and I talked about the ballet and I expressed an objection: 'It's a pity that they don't have horns on their heads, since they are meant to be reindeer.' My father then turned to me, exclaiming: 'That's the whole point with ballet! They *dance* the horns!'

My parents recognized that 'ballet is Helena's interest'. When Rudolf Nureyev came with Margot Fonteyn to do *Giselle*, my parents realized that this was a once-in-a-lifetime event and bought a ticket for me. Nureyev and Fonteyn were of course preceded by their transnational reputation as well as by advance promotion for this particular visit. I remember Fonteyn as a fragile and adorable Giselle; but it was Nureyev's Prince Albrecht that made the lasting impression on me. He jumped very high; his technique was impeccable. What really got to me, however, a fourteen-year-old girl on the verge of womanhood, was his overwhelming stage personality. The audience was exalted, unusually loud for a Stockholm audience, and demanded no less than sixteen curtain calls.

A few years later I stopped dancing. It was not until then, when I was unable to dance, that I really understood how much dancing had been a way to breathe for me, and to express myself. Now I did not want to be reminded of ballet; I blocked it out, stopped going to performances, even avoided ballet and dance on television. I buried my love for ballet, and went on to university to train as an anthropologist. I became fascinated by anthropology: here I could explore my interest in people theoretically. Through fieldwork and writing, I saw a potential for personal and intellectual development that satisfied me deeply. I became particularly interested in youth culture and ethnicity (see mostly Wulff 1988; Amit-Talai and Wulff 1995), and later in transnationality (Wulff 1992). With time I discovered aesthetic anthropology, performance studies and the anthropology of dance. There were discussions on occupational cultures. I had started teaching, and enjoyed it, but felt after some time that I needed recharging. I wanted to move ahead anthropologically by way of research. For a while I was thinking of studying writers, perhaps ethnic novelists, but realized that it does not make much anthropological sense to do participant observation with people while they are writing. Then, it dawned on me that I could study another kind of artists – dancers! Their work practices lend themselves very well to observation. And I thought that my previous experience of dancing would make up for the fact that I could not participate in the dancing any more.

As early as 1961, long before reflexivity became a staple concept in anthropology, C. Wright Mills (1961) wrote that scholarly thinkers do not separate their work from their lives but let them spark each other. Most people have to separate their work from their lives, since their work is shallow; intellectuals, on the other hand, can make use of their life experiences in their work.

Doing a study on the ballet world has reminded me of familiar and forgotten sides of my personal 'self'. In a sense, I started out as an 'other', but have become able to reformulate a part of my personal as well as professional 'self' through this fieldwork; clearly the two inform each other.

There are basically two advantages in having some dancing experience when doing a study on dancers. First, a dancing career is a hard one. Moments of triumph, such as ovations and applause, are very short. But since I used to dance, I know something about the pain – and the passion – of dancing that won me the respect and trust of the dancers. Having grown up in the ballet world I possess the kind of social capital that structures the idiom in the theatre, both frontstage and backstage.

Discussing the problem of transferring the mental models of informants to anthropological text, Maurice Bloch (1992: 130) argues for connectionism, the notion that knowing everyday practical skills, and making sense of the world, form networks of mental models that can be connected to each other in complex systems. Being partly linguistic, these models also combine 'visual imagery, other sensory cognition, the cognitive aspects of learned practices, evaluations, memories of sensations, and memories of typical examples'. They are the outcome of activity that is learnt during socialization, managed and remembered not only through language but in fact primarily through 'experience, practice, sights, and sensations'. This, Bloch states, is also how the anthropologist should learn a culture he or she is studying in order to grasp its mental models and translate them into text.

Just like me, Cynthia Novack (1993: 36) practised ballet for fifteen years. She said that this 'kinesthetic reference' stayed with her afterwards. And even if dance may evoke 'kinesthetic identification' in any viewer, for those who start to dance when they are children and dance for many years this becomes a formative experience. Dance is for ever inscribed in their bodies. I was unable to practise ballet the way the people I was studying were doing it, but since I too grew up taking ballet classes – with some of my informants – we have a shared past. There was so much I recognized in what they did and in the ambience in the ballet world. Bloch's discussion could also be framed in terms of the notion of the body and linked to ballet as a non-verbal art form. Many dancers are not very verbal people: they are trained to express themselves through their bodies, they have an extreme body-consciousness. They communicate through their bodies even when they are not dancing. In general, dancers move their bodies more when they engage in a conversation than non-dancers, getting up from a chair, for example, in order to emphasize a point through gesturing with arms and legs.

As Kirin Narayan (1993: 678) points out, 'preexisting experience' of societies we study is restructured analytically mainly by 'locating vivid particulars within larger cultural patterns, sociological relations, and historical shifts'. Returning to a setting as an ex-native or a native fieldworker of some kind, does not mean, however, that everything is known in advance. Reconsidering her two field studies in Jordan, on Circassians and the Wadi, Seteney Shami (1988: 137) realized that she 'knew' those parts of her country in different ways. On both her field entrances she had identified familiar 'ideas, values, and patterns'. Yet she went on to discover many new ones.

There were aspects of the ballet world that I had been ignorant of when I was still dancing. This can be explained partly by the fact that I never was a professional dancer, and that I was quite young when I left. It had not occurred to me, for instance, that most dancers have rather low salaries, nor had I completely grasped the excitement and unpredictability of the creation of ballet art on stage. When I was dancing, I did have a vague feeling that I was doing something that was different, something that not many people were doing or found interesting. I was aware of connections both to contemporary and historical court life as well as to an old-fashioned notion of dancing as an indecent activity. But I did not see how impenetrable the ballet world appears to many people.

When I started talking about my plans to do a study on ballet dancers, and later when I was still doing fieldwork, I got a number of reactions that I had not expected. A middle-aged American male anthropologist was unable to relate to my topic of research, so he got out of the situation through a joke: 'Do you want help with observations?' (The dancers were all assumed to be women.) A middle-aged male European anthropologist warned me: 'They're gay, you know that, don't you?' (Now the dancers were all men.) Both these comments offended me. The first one, because I found it sexist; the second, because even though there is a certain truth in the fact that there is male homosexuality in the ballet world, it is not the entire truth (in some companies, in fact, it is hardly true at all). Neither is it something that ballet people (including me in this instance) care to hear as a first, characterizing comment about ballet. This is not to say that the prevalence of male homosexuality does not matter, because it does – now and then. Just as heterosexuality is one social (and artistic) feature of the ballet world, so is homosexuality. But neither can sexual identity be reduced to sexual acts, nor is sexual identity the entire identity of anyone, regardless of sexual orientation (cf. Weston 1991).

Reflections of the Self in the Other

As I began observing daily classes and rehearsals at the Royal Opera House in Stockholm, I sometimes took the opportunity to cast a secret glance in the mirror at the dancers. It did not take long before I noticed that they were doing the same thing with me. The observer was being observed, and had to adjust her facial expressions and bodily posture accordingly.[2]

They were checking me, who I was, and what I thought of their dance. Later, I was told that the dancers had indeed commented to each other on the fact that the way I was watching them had revealed that I used to dance. Thinking about it, I realized that it is mainly a manner of moving one's body and head as if one were doing the steps.

As I gradually got to know the dancers, I found myself communicating with them through the mirror, chatting during breaks with mirror eye contact, nodding encouragingly and showing that I was following them attentively during rehearsals. And of course, I saw that they were communicating with each other through the mirror, as well as comparing themselves with each other. The coaches also watched the dancers more or less openly through the mirror. Mainly the dancers observed themselves, however, using the mirror for corrections of steps over and over again. In this they may be helped by the coach, or sometimes by other dancers. It was, as James Fernandez (1986) has pointed out, the mirror indicating perfection. Since dancers spend so much time in front of mirrors in the studios and in the dressing-rooms these, along the lines of Ulf Hannerz's (1983) reasoning, become devices in the routines of their management of identity. Contrary to a common belief, the use of the mirror does not have to be antisocial, he (ibid.: 359) says. The dancers' fixations with mirrors are regarded as crucial for their work towards performance, which is a social act by definition. During rehearsal, the mirror is the point of orientation, reflecting the steps that are being corrected time after time. The mirror is placed where the audience is seated during performance, thereby suggesting the reactions of the audience, and of critics, to the dance. When the time of performance eventually comes, there is no mirror: so during the last studio rehearsal a curtain is often drawn to hide it. The dancers need to learn to forget the mirror, to dance without constantly checking what they look like. This usually means that this is the phase at which they move from technique to artistry; it is in a sense the moment when they start to dance. Liberated from the mirror, their steps become more expressive.

This preoccupation with the mirror image of one's body may, however, in the long run at times be too much for the dancers. It was both the fear of gaining weight and getting old that made a Swedish woman soloist in her early forties sigh with disgust in front of the mirror in her dressing-room one morning: 'We get obsessed with our bodies, you know, looking at ourselves in the mirror all the time. You always think you're fat! Mirror sickness!'

Christy Adair (1992) is concerned especially with women's absorption with their looks and how this is exaggerated by the fact that women dancers have been taught to scrutinize their mirror images. According to Adair, women dancers are seldom pleased with what they see in the mirror, and this often leads to unhealthy dieting.[3] On the basis of my field experience I would not put it so strongly, as if it were something most women dancers suffer from; but it is a common problem, and it also affects some men. Another difficulty for dancers, men and women, is ageing. The idea that dancers have to be young, look young, can of course be dismissed as a Western assumption especially prevalent in ballet. This assumption is for instance contested by Jiří Kylián's contemporary ballet company Nederlands Dans Theater 3, featuring dancers over forty years of age.

Doing Ballet versus Watching Ballet

A central dichotomy in the ballet world is the one separating the act of doing ballet from watching ballet: 'You have to do it in order to understand what it's like.' It seems primarily to be the physical exertion of dancing that makes dancers distinguish themselves from the audience in general, and from critics in particular. The vulnerability is another important feature of the stage experience. A leading woman dancer explained to me: 'You're completely naked out there. They see what you have inside!' There is also a subtle boundary between dancers who have danced a particular role and dancers who have not. All this goes into a scepticism of translations of dance to other symbolic modes – be it text, photographs, video or film. Something inevitably gets lost on the way. This elusive quality is, however, still a part of the experience of ballet art – in fact often the heart of it. Watching themselves on video, dancers note that the dancing does not look from the outside like it feels from the inside when doing it (cf. Chapter 6).

The dichotomy between doing ballet and watching ballet can fruitfully be related to Merton's (1972) discussion on insiders and outsiders. His point is that both total Insider doctrine and total Outsider doctrine 'one must be one in order to understand one' (ibid.: 24) are misleading. Merton takes up the notion of monopolistic access to certain knowledge versus privileged access. He develops the argument from the idea that you have to be black to be able to study blacks epistemologically. For in that case, you have to be white to study whites, French to study French society, and a woman to study women.[4] According to this view, only a proletarian can fully comprehend proletarians and a Catholic other Catholics. Merton excludes age status in his enumeration, on the basis that social scientists who live long enough will have passed through all of them.[5] This extreme Insiderism states that the Outsider who has not been socialized in the group and has no direct experience of it, is thus excluded from understanding it. Merton goes on to show the illogical consequences of extreme Insiderism, saying that 'if only whites can understand whites and blacks, blacks, and only men can understand men, and women, women' (ibid.: 22) it follows that some Insiders cannot understand other Insiders, such as white women and white men, and so on. Not only Insiders turn out to be a diverse group, however; so do Outsiders. In line with Merton's idea about people who are *both* Insiders and Outsiders in a social stratification, I was indeed switching between an ex-Insider and an Outsider at the beginning of my fieldwork in the ballet world.

Native anthropology is a contradiction in terms, according to Kirsten Hastrup (1993). Either one is an anthropologist or a native, she points out, identifying them as involved in 'different knowledge projects' (ibid.: 154). The native is operating on a practical level, while the anthropologist in the end moves up to a theoretical understanding where the native's point of view and voice are included in the analysis, but not the equivalent of it.[6]

With modernization and increasing transnational connections there are not only new kinds of fieldworkers nowadays, more or less native (cf. Narayan 1993), but the variation and range of natives are also different. I would suggest that the relationship between the anthropologist and the native has become more complex, at least in certain fields. All natives are not alike in their relationships to the anthropologist, not even in the same field. Natives may well possess an analytical talent – these are the ones who tend to become key informants – and nowadays may even be highly educated people. My anthropological training did not delete my native perspective. It does appear different through the anthropological lens, but not distorted or useless for anthropological theorizing. This is not to say that I see myself as a native, just that my native experience has been very useful for me in this field. In her comprehensive discussion on native anthropology, Kirin Narayan (1993) discards the separation between 'native' and 'non-native' anthropologists in favour of an exploration of shifting, multiplex identities in the field and in relation to theoretical issues.

Not only did I balance my status and experience as an ex-native with the implication of my status as a non-native in the ballet world – I also acquired a new form of nativeness: the form that comes with becoming a part of the setting on a daily basis. Assisting as a dresser on a long tour to Japan with the Royal Swedish Ballet made this even more obvious. With time I was introduced as 'someone from the House', 'our academic' or 'a friend, she loves ballet'. Although my initial strategy was to express my appreciation of the dancing, it did not take long before both dancers and management demanded my honest opinions. Many times outsiders assumed I was one of the dancers (including Hilary Clinton backstage after a performance by the American Ballet Theatre on a tour to Washington, DC).

I could not have managed to cut off my own dancing experience when I was in the field, it was and still is too much a part of my personal self; and even if I could have cut it off, the dancers would have identified me as someone who was more native than most non-dancers, almost one of them. To me, there is an analytical significance in this: some anthropologists may define themselves, and be defined by the people in a particular field, as more native than others. Studying a mostly non-verbal bodily activity, like dancing, that people spend almost all their time doing, is easier with some dancing experience, unless one is an exceptionally skilled ethnographer, and/or has some other bodily experience that resembles dancing, like skating, for example. When the French sociologist Loïc Wacquant (1995b) did fieldwork on boxers in Chicago, he became an apprentice boxer in order to understand this body-centred universe. Catherine Palmer (1996) would undoubtedly not have been able to conduct her fieldwork on competitive cyclists at all, unless she had been one herself. My experience of dancing has facilitated my access to the closed ballet world as well as my data collection; but also, perhaps even more significantly, it has influenced my theoretical thinking and writing (cf. Novack 1992) in my choice of themes and their accentuations.

Access to a Closed World

The notion of the ballet world as a closed world is something dancers agree with, albeit reluctantly. They do not like to be told that they may be missing out on other aspects of life, when they in fact get experiences most people do not. Dancers identify themselves as different from other people – more so than most groups. There are even traditional efforts in the ballet world to hide what is going on backstage, since the work practices are sensitive; dancers are exposed both physically and psychologically in the studio. The image of pain from injuries, constant fatigue and highly strung nerves is moreover believed to tarnish the illusion of ethereal tutus and seemingly weightless steps in polished performances. The ballet world is fenced with security at electronically monitored stage doors where visitors have to sign a roster and get a visitor's tag. Inside the theatres there are signs saying 'No admittance' at doors leading to the stage as well as red lights that are on (or flashing) when there is a change of set going on. Entrance is prohibited at those times on the grounds that there is a risk of accidents when large and heavy sets have to be moved fast, especially during intermissions (some years ago a stage-hand was killed in one of the theatres in my study). The momentous 'pass door' between back stage and the auditorium has a 'Private' sign in most theatres. It is furthermore usually locked during performance. I was given ID-cards to help me get through security (on one tour I got the ID-card of a woman secretary who had not come) and codes to open locked doors and entrances. When there are royals, presidential families and other dignitaries in the auditorium, the security is heightened, with secret service personnel backstage in electronic contact with their colleagues and body-guards who pretend to mingle with the audience. On these occasions, which usually coincided with important premières, the level of anxiety in the theatre was high both among directors and dancers.

Layers of Acceptance, Zones of Access

I started my transnational fieldwork in the ballet world by asking the director of the Opera House in Stockholm for formal permission to spend one year with the Royal Swedish Ballet. When he had discussed my request with the 'leaders' group', in which the dancers have a representative, I met with the ballet director. Everyone was positive about my presence, but I was told not to cause any disturbance in the studio, but just to watch 'like a fly on the wall'. Then I was immediately invited to watch a performance from the wings.

It was in August 1993 that I began my daily contact with the ballet world at the Opera House. With formal access I could observe the company classes, rehearsals and performances from the wings and the auditorium. The canteen was a good place for participant observation, as were parties in the House and in the homes of dancers. I started interviewing dancers and other personnel.

My relationship to the field, observational and participatory as well as dialogical, ran smoothly during the first two months of fieldwork. I passed the usual initiation test by coping with one or two misrepresentations, but also with beliefs that I was a critic or perhaps there to recruit dancers to other companies. A few times, I had to distract both marginal and career-minded hangers-on. I was aware that I had to be extra careful in this setting, where people were trained to act, and illusion may crop up anywhere, sometimes extended from the stage.

A tour to a provincial town during which I shared the dancers' strain and excitement in every detail marked the acceptance break for me; thereafter I moved on to dealing with confidences like 'What I'm going to tell you now, Helena, you mustn't write in your book, but . . .'. Pleased that I had got that far, passed a significant threshold, I was well aware, however, that there was yet another zone that I had to penetrate in order to understand many of the goings-on: the dressing-rooms, which were locked with passcodes. On the three-week Japan tour I assisted as a dresser, and I thus came to spend a lot of time in the dressing-rooms. This made it easier to hang around in the dressing rooms at the Opera House in Stockholm when we got back. I was also invited there by dancers to look at pictures, have coffee or just come in for a chat.

Immersing myself in such an intense and engaging milieu as the ballet world, there were instances when I simply forgot that I was doing fieldwork. Sometimes ballet people reminded me, however, as on one afternoon when I was having coffee in the canteen with a coach I had started to think of as a friend. We were talking about an upcoming revival and the fact that leaders of the technicians in the theatre had been threatening to go on strike. This was quite worrying, since it might mean that performances would have to be cancelled, perhaps even a première, and a lot of rehearsal work would have been in vain. Suddenly, in the middle of a sentence he went quiet, looked inquiringly at me, and said in a sharp tone of voice: 'Are you analysing me?' I could do nothing but threw myself back in my chair and laugh. Scholarly analysis was the last thing on my mind at that moment.

Another comment on my presence at the Royal Swedish Ballet was performed in the sketch 'reviewing' major events of the season from the dancers' point of view at the annual spring party. This is one of only a few opportunities dancers have to release the intensity and strict ranking of their career through structural rituals of rebellion (cf. Gluckman 1982 [1956] and Chapter 5 on practical jokes at last performances). Dressed up as the ballet management, including the coaches and the opera director, dancers made fun of their bosses and fellow dancers. Then 'the ethnographer' made her entrance in the sketch. One of the dancers (incidentally a man) was acting me. Dressed in trousers and a jacket, and with a wig looking like my hairstyle and hair colour, 'I' was standing shyly in the background radiating quiet interest. As the sketch moved on 'I' appeared here and there, sometimes quite unexpectedly, making my way towards the centre of activity, where 'I' found friends.

Increasingly, I noticed that some of my formulations and observations both about ballet and social life in the theatre 'came back' to me from the dancers. By then I had an idea about who was talking to whom about what, and I was able to trace my comments. Without striving for it, I had given the dancers words by verbalizing aspects of crucial ideas in the ballet world in a way that appealed to them.

I was also used as a resource, for keeping track of names of new corps de ballet dancers and for my literary orientation and writing skills. It happened that dancers asked me about the motifs of classical dramas that were staged as ballets, or the lives of authors whose work had been made into ballets, before they were interviewed at press conferences. A number of times, administrators at the Royal Swedish Ballet checked with me when they were writing notes for the dancers or reports to the managements. But even more often dancers borrowed pens from me, since they spend their days dressed in leotards and practice clothes, their handbags, wallets and personal belongings locked in.

The Fragmented Fieldworker: Threat, Supporter, Confidante

The dancers related to me in different ways depending on their gender, age, personality, position in the company and experience of the world outside the theatre. Some of the leading dancers who were skilled at charming dance journalists thought at first that they could perhaps use me to promote their careers. When a couple of them encountered setbacks in their careers, as well as personal problems, they saw me as a threat before they understood that I was not there to reveal declines in famous dancers' careers or family lives. I had to assure them over and over again that I was not an ordinary dance writer, let alone a critic.

Other sensitive issues in the ballet world concern the use of drugs, the prevalence of anorexia or conditions close to it, and AIDS. It took a long time before I asked about them. By then I knew from observations and conversations that there was a low incidence of them. Not surprisingly, there had been a few attempts to distort information for me about these matters.

It also happened that dancers tried to use me as a pawn in intrigues. Once I was talking to a woman dancer and she suddenly got the idea, she said, that 'since Sven has been gossiping about me, I'm going to tell you that he is having an affair with Emma'. She knew that I knew that Sven was married, but not that I already had heard about the rumour she was telling me about. A male corps de ballet dancer, a jovial sort of person who had realized that his prospects for advancement in the company were not very good, enjoyed exhibiting his story-telling talents in the canteen. This was where he really had an audience, especially of young corps de ballet dancers. One evening before performance he was in high spirits, ridiculing an acclaimed woman ex-dancer with the company who still has a prominent position in the ballet world: 'She has used ballet to come up in the world, but in fact she is common!' Turning to me he continued: 'You have to write this!', and indulged in a series of toilet stories about this woman. Encouraged by our roaring laughter, he set out on a new story by triumphing: 'and *this* I know for sure!'

Obviously, I did not get to hear or see everything that happened; but no one else did either. No one in a place of work has access to information about all the goings-on there at a particular point in time. Yet some people know more than others, because of their personalities and positions. In the ballet world a compassionate physiotherapist and a non-threatening assistant to the director may garner all kinds of personal as well as professional secrets.

Marginal in the beginning, I came to move up and down in the social structure, discreetly taking care of confessions from aspiring new corps de ballet dancers, tired principals, and busy ballet directors. I comforted dancers with broken hearts and homesick foreign dancers who missed their families and suffered cultural clashes. At times when a performance had not gone as well as it could have, or even occasionally had been downright disastrous, I was there to talk to. When bad reviews struck, I was sympathetic, just as I was when there were setbacks in casting and upsetting social dramas. Since my informants knew that I was following them with a passionate engagement, they asked me to come to performances or rehearsals they were in. They were also eager to bring me good news about casting and promotions (sometimes before they were announced officially), show me good reviews and inform me about compliments and indications about casting and promotions from the ballet management. Clearly, I learnt about circumstances that were not common knowledge. Some of this does not have an anthropological relevance; other elements I am unable to discuss because of their sensitive nature. I have omitted personal names in most places and particular characteristics of people and circumstances that may be hurtful. It is likely that the people involved will recognize themselves and each other in the study; but my aim has been that outsiders should not be able to figure out who or what events I am writing about – unless they already know about them.

I reached a phase when I noticed that people were relaxed around me, took my presence for granted, and asked where I had been when I had been away for a few days or missed a performance. One aspect of this was the fact that some dancers had developed an addiction to my encouragement. It became especially obvious when one dancer asked me after a performance what I had thought of his dancing. I managed to say something generally nice, but felt terrible, because the truth was that I had not been watching him in particular during that specific performance. Like coaches, choreographers, ballet directors and even critics who watch performance after performance of the same production, I had taken to a strategy of focusing on different dancers at different times in order to register anything new at all in the course of the long run. Sometimes, too, I was concentrating on the set, the costumes, the lighting or how the music worked, or how the conductor connected the dancers and the music.

Since dancing is *the* vital experience for a dancer, especially being on stage, it sometimes happened that dancers urged me to 'take barre with us' or to join them as a an extra on stage; someone even suggested I could stay on in the company by training as a choreologist.

Occasionally, I pretended to know less about a specific matter than I in fact did in order to double- or triple-check it, or get a different perspective on it. This usually worked very well; but at one point, when I had been in the ballet world for quite some time, I was conducting an interview with a male principal I had watched in the studio many times. I posed my questions and he gave interesting and useful answers. But when I asked him to identify different ballet styles, he started laughing: 'Come on, Helena! Don't ask questions you already know the answers to!' I laughed, too, of course; he had broken through my professional shield.

By then I found myself in a situation where I was so much a part of the setting that I noticed that people were uncertain whose side I was on in the shifting structure of camps and conflicts in the theatre. I had been seen socializing with women dancers of my age around forty, young corps de ballet dancers, up-and-coming stars, world stars, ballet directors, sound designers, gay men, stage-hands, famous choreographers. The fact that some of these categories overlapped, contextually and periodically, makes social analysis even more intricate.

With time I could not avoid becoming associated more with some people in the theatre than others. These informants and friends were those I spent most time with, in the theatre as well as outside. We went to plays and the pictures, had dinner at home and in restaurants, watched ballet videos and took walks together. As rewarding personally and professionally as this was, it also entailed that some people, who disliked my best informants, became less accessible to me. It did not really matter fieldwork-wise; in fact it is an ordinary development in successful fieldwork (as in all social process). A situation when this surfaced occurred when I was jokingly taken to task by a male corps de ballet dancer for having had a short, polite conversation with a coach he and his friends disapproved of: 'I saw you talking to Albert! Traitor!' I was slightly embarrassed, but the incident did not harm my relationship with the dancer; we had many nice conversations afterwards and even went out for a drink.

It is often said that fieldworkers grow personally. This is probably because in the field we may be able to accept fractions of our identity that we normally suppress. By encountering new situations we also sometimes acquire capacities we did not possess before. The 'multiplex identity' of fieldworkers that Narayan (1993) delineates in terms of partial and processual racial and cultural nativeness has clearly been underrated. For as we release different reactions from our informants about who we are and what we are doing in their place, they obviously in turn set thoughts and feelings in motion in the fieldworker, activating both open and hidden 'strands of identification'. One of my hidden strands of identification was my dancing experience, which became open through my fieldwork. Open identities of mine were those of a scholar, a woman about forty years old, a Swede, a university lecturer, a wife. Rather than having them mixing into one unit, I was able to activate just one or two of these identities at a time, depending on the context, tying in with different positions in the social structure in the theatre. Thereby I assembled a fuller picture of the power relations than I would have had I been close to one level only. Renato Rosaldo (1989: 194) suggests that the distant social analyst observing down from on high is nowadays replaced by an observer with multiple identities. Rosaldo does not regard the scholarly process as going from a theoretical level and down but 'outward from in-depth knowledge of a specific form of life'.

The Anthropology of Dance and Dance Studies

By contrast with the general approach of dance studies and the anthropology of dance, this study is not focused on what is presented on stage: on movement, or dance analysis.[7] What is happening on stage is anchored back socially, and can therefore be explored anthropologically.

Dance studies tend to be about *dance*, whereas this is an ethnography of *dancers* in terms of the course and culture of ballet careers from ballet school to a professional company. Like all ethnographies, this one is the product of the personal, ethnic and national identity, as well as the age and gender, sexual orientation, academic training and subsequent intellectual development and research interests of the ethnographer.

Dance has been acknowledged by anthropologists for about a century (Royce 1980); but it took some time before the anthropology of dance was established as a subdiscipline. Inspired by the expansion of critical dance studies and cultural studies, the anthropology of dance has lately become increasingly theoretically sophisticated. Influential anthropological thinkers commented early on dance in passing, like A. R. Radcliffe-Brown (1964 [1922]), who reported on dance among the Andaman islanders as a social ceremony. In a 1928 article about dance among the Azande in the Sudan, E. E. Evans-Pritchard stated: 'In ethnological accounts the dance is usually given a place quite unworthy of its social importance. It is often viewed as an independent activity and is described without reference to its contextual setting in native life. Such treatment leaves out many problems as to the composition and organization of the dance and hides from view its sociological function' (1928: 446).

Dance has been analysed anthropologically by way of 'a symbolic, structural, or semiotic approach' (Royce 1980: 31), or as 'cognitive, sensory non-verbal communication' (Hanna 1979: 57–82). The meaning of gender and sex in dance, with respect also to gay dancers, is explored in Hanna (1988). In a review article on dancing culture, Susan Leigh Foster (1992) recognizes that works by Jane Cowan (1990) on Greek dance and Cynthia Novack (1990) on contact improvisation in the United States apply the concept of culture that takes process and diversity into account, and regard dance as an embodied discourse, and the body as culturally constructed. In a recent article by Sally Ann Ness (1997), a Philippine neoethnic ballet is analysed in terms of postcolonialism and transnationalism.[8]

The anthropology of dance has centred on dance in non-Western cultures that yet were quite diverse, and consequently the attempt to find a cross-cultural definition of dance became an early preoccupation.[9] This was an almost impossible task, because of the many different kinds and meanings of dance, from a purely aesthetic activity to one that primarily served some ritual function. Here I am inclined to adhere to Cowan's (1990) view that it is time to leave aside the discussion about one universal definition of dance. In any case, in a study of the world of classical ballet, with its precise conventions and standards, this cannot be a central problem. In contemporary ballet and dance, as in the work by William Forsythe, the boundary between dance and physical theatre (including acting, singing and speaking, as well as steps to silence), is extended, challenging the definition of dance, however. While there has been little attention to classical ballet in the anthropology of dance, it is addressed by Hanna's *To Dance is Human* (1979) and *Dance, Sex and Gender* (1988).[10]

A Multilocal Study

The ballet world is an intense, closed, highly specialized community that has reached across borders since its inception in the fourteenth century at Italian courts. Yet modern technologies of communication and transportation have increased the opportunities for mobility within a structure of old and new centres and peripheries.[11] It is clear that the generic transnationality of the ballet world calls for multi-locale ethnography (Marcus and Fischer 1986; Clifford 1997), or 'multi-sited ethnography', as Marcus (1995) terms it. In the ballet world, there is a constant transnational awareness and communication with other places (cf. Marcus 1989) through guesting, touring, competitions, galas, festivals and new technology, especially ballet video. Personal and professional links reach across the globe. Many ballet people possess both an active and a hidden web (that can be activated) of transnational experiences and connections.

Drawing on ethnography from three national classical ballet companies – the Royal Swedish Ballet in Stockholm, the Royal Ballet in London, the American Ballet Theatre in New York[12] – and from the contemporary company Ballett Frankfurt, which mostly performs dance productions by its artistic director and choreographer William Forsythe, in Frankfurt-am-Main, this book describes and analyses the culture and social organization of these companies. It also traces the connections between them, to show how dancing careers are produced and reproduced in a transnational web of ideas, encounters and communications.[13]

My units of study are demarcated by old and new ballet centres, by dancers' professional and personal networks, and by how dancers and other ballet people move between these localities, which consequently are connected. There is, in fact, a history that goes back to the 1950s of mobility between the three classical companies in this study, and since 1984, when William Forsythe took over Ballett Frankfurt, this company too is included in this particular transnational network. The four field locales were also divided in smaller sites. The theatres were the major arenas for participant

observation except for the American Ballet Theatre, which did not have a theatre of its own, so I spent most of my time there in its studios on lower Manhattan. The homes of my key informants also became recurring sites for participant observation outside the theatres. Altogether I conducted almost 120 interviews, mostly with dancers.

During the time of my field study there was much travelling of dancers, conductors, choreographers, composers, coaches and ballet directors between the companies I was studying. I have thus, without planning it, met some of my informants in two countries (a few even in three countries), which gives a particular depth to the issue of transnationality. Some circumstances unexpectedly made sense in a transnational context. Yet, on the whole it was clear that a transnational approach was necessary in order to do analytical justice to the four companies in their different national settings.

Transnational ballet news, which travels fast and far, especially from ballet centres to peripheries and between ballet centres, concerns new productions, appointments of ballet directors and leading dancers, and breakthroughs, as well as dismissals and resignations. Serious injuries, illnesses and deaths, and details of personal circumstances, mostly about the love relationships of ballet people, also spread quickly. Major commemorating or celebrating galas and ballet competitions are kept track of. The centres are obviously more present in the periphery than vice versa; but when someone from a centre has visited the periphery, he or she is asked to share information with directors and dancers about the dancing, the repertory, and the local work conditions, both as a way to situate individual careers and companies in terms of the transnational competition and for the possibility of openings for guesting and appointments in the permeable ballet world.

The names of some prominent dancers of transnational reputation came up regularly in conversations in the centres as well as in the periphery. The French dancer, Sylvie Guillem, who lifts her leg very high, was often mentioned, and so was the Japanese dancer Tetsuya Kumakawa, who jumps high and turns in the air. The American Gelsey Kirkland, who now gives classes in New York, was remembered as an exceptionally delicate and dramatic ballerina. The legendary dancer Mikhail Baryshnikov, who was Kirkland's partner, still dances in New York, and was admired not only for his dancing but also by many women dancers for his good looks, and was regarded as something of an idol. They told me how they had been infatuated with him when he had been guesting with their company, hovering outside his dressing-room door and even asking for his autograph. There were also some scandalous stories that were common transnational knowledge, such as the one about a ballet director who took big loans to finance new productions and then left the company with a huge deficit. There were some recurring rumours that certain prominent companies were on the verge of bankruptcy.

When my year with the Royal Swedish Ballet was drawing to an end, I asked the ballet management to connect me to the Royal Ballet in London and the American Ballet Theatre in New York. After negotiations through mail, fax, telephone and personal meetings I was welcomed to both companies. Apart from the approval of the directors, their respective unions were agreeable. With Ballett Frankfurt, I obtained permission myself by asking William Forsythe when he was mounting a ballet on the Royal Ballet in London while I was there. Hence I was able to do participant observation and interviews with these companies, as well.

And I was to obtain key informants among them. I watched company classes, rehearsals and performances from the wings and the auditorium, and spent time with dancers and other ballet people in canteens and green rooms and at parties. I also met with dancers outside the theatres, at restaurants and in their homes.

With formal access my processes of informal access started, first in London then in New York and later in Frankfurt. They were quite similar to the one in Stockholm, though shorter. My stay with the British Royal Ballet was divided into two periods: one month in the autumn of 1994 and two months in the spring of 1995. This provided a longer time-span than I had originally thought of, since I was kept informed about events during the three months I was away. My field study with the American Ballet Theatre ran from December 1994 to March 1995, and included a tour for one week to Washington, DC. I was sometimes used as a carrier of transnational information between the companies: dancers and directors asked me about repertories, tours, leading dancers, directors, the rate of injuries, and so on in other companies. I also conveyed personal greetings. During the second year of my field study my data continued to grow denser: later events and processes illuminated early ones, sometimes providing clues I had been struggling to find and now could suddenly discern among my expanding fieldnotes.

Just as in Stockholm, there were misunderstandings in London, New York and Frankfurt that I was a critic, habitual attempts to hide what was perceived as sensitive; yet later I was taken for granted so much that I literally had to ran from last meetings with informants in order not to miss my planes.

In the beginning it sometimes happened that I forgot that I was more used to the ballet world than the people in the field locale I was currently in were to my presence there. Power structures, formal and informal, were not identical everywhere. Local power structures reflected national ballet culture and current alliances and antagonistic camps in daily politics. Since I had watched performances from the wings at the Royal Opera House in Stockholm innumerable times, I took it for granted that I would be able to watch performances from the wings at Covent Garden. After getting a polite: 'No, I don't think that is possible' time after time, I realized that I had asked the wrong person, i.e. someone who did not have as much actual influence as her position seemed to imply. Later, I managed to get permission to watch from the wings from someone who had real power in the House. As I expanded my zones of access to the wings and the dressing-rooms at Covent Garden, I also learnt the tacit House rules, and which ones could be broken by whom in what way. One tacit rule was to sneak through the pass door from the auditorium to the backstage area and walk close to a wall during intermissions when the red light was flashing. (This meant that entry to back stage was in fact prohibited, since a change of set was going on and there was a risk of serious accidents.) One evening I was in a hurry because I was going to make a telephone call during an intermission. I took the short cut and, as I was leaving the backstage area, I encountered not one, but two of the directors of the company. Blushing, I stammered: 'I've learnt to break the rules the way you do!' One of the directors looked amused at my alarm; the other seemed worried, and admonished me: 'Just don't walk across back stage!'

A few times dancers helped me with information or access that I had been denied from a higher level in the power structure. There are important differences among the dancers when it comes to influence in the company; famous principals generally have some say when it comes to casting (their own and that of others), for example. Yet guesting choreographers often upset the power dynamics by requesting dancers for their ballets that the management would prefer to keep down, for example. Rehearsal periods with guesting choreographers are usually intense and conflict-ridden, with the choreographer threatening to leave or take his or her ballet out of the repertory, unless he or she gets his or her way. This process does not hinder success; on the contrary: the tensions that seem to be a necessary part of the process tend to be resolved, and the productions may well turn into acclaimed productions, even hailed as masterpieces by critics.

A woman choreographer of world fame was mounting a new ballet on the American Ballet Theatre when I was there. Her assistant started the work, and I was able to see some of it. After a while, the choreographer arrived herself, and since I was well into the setting by then, I asked her if I could watch a rehearsal. She was not in a mood for that, which I respected, thinking that she would be more accessible another day. But when she said that I should ask the press officer to book me in, I realized that she had not been informed (or cared) about the nature of my permission to be with the company. Nevertheless, I followed her instructions; but the press officer did not find her in an agreeable mood either. When the rehearsal period was about to end, I went to the dancers for comfort. One of the male principals then suggested that I just go into the studio as I used to: 'What is she going to do?' he remarked 'take you out of the ballet?'

Anthropology at Home and Paramount Realities

Kirsten Hastrup (1993: 151) has pointed out that '"home" is a conceptual category with shifting references': since I grew up in the ballet world, doing a field study there was, because of my dancing experience, like coming back home for me.[14] But the concept of 'away', too, has shifting references. My home is 'away' for someone else; and in the present case, the ballet world seems impenetrable and alien to many outsiders.

Far from every fieldworker shares a household with his or her informants, even if some do. Many fieldworkers prefer a hut, a house, an apartment or even just a room of their own to withdraw into for resting, writing notes and tending to their personal cultural identities through correspondence, and so on. One often hears and reads that fieldworkers are visited by informants in their field homes. To be visited by informants in one's own permanent home, as I have been during this field study, may, however, temporarily confuse the ordering of paramount realities, a notion that Alfred Schutz (1967) discusses in his essay 'On Multiple Realities'.

Following Hastrup's idea that native anthropology is a contradiction in terms, this position ought to apply to anthropology at home, as well. No one literally does fieldwork at home in a situation where everything is taken for granted: there is always a momentous *contrast* of one kind or another at work, whether it is produced by differences in place, time, language, ethnicity, religion, age, gender, sexuality, class, education, occupation or any combination thereof.

During the first year of my field study in the ballet world, I worked in Stockholm, where I live. This meant that I did not move geographically, but, indeed, mentally. I continued my life as usual in a number of ways: I even did some teaching at the University. But the difference was that this year I gave priority to my field study: I spent most of my time at the Opera, on tours, or elsewhere with dancers or other people from the House, which was only eight minutes away by bus. And when I entered the House – everything was about ballet. In many other fields one has to chase field situations, to wait sometimes in boredom or anxiety for something useful to happen, or even to initiate events. I just had to go to the Opera House to find myself immersed in the issues I was studying. There were stretches of redundancy, of course, and some days and moments were more rewarding than others. Since repetitive days were important as a way of distinguishing between the ordinary and the exceptional, they were not difficult for me to endure. The exceptional may take different forms: both euphoric, as when the corps de ballet excelled in precision during a première, and tedious, as when they were rehearsing a variation for a seemingly infinite number of times, or just waited for hours on end for their turn to rehearse. The ordinary was of another kind: that is, the daily routine of morning class and rehearsals in the afternoon, uneventful but securely moving ahead.

When I had been in the field for a couple of months, a feeling of a split reality overtook me. There I was, moving between the Opera House and Stockholm University, both intense and closed worlds: two separate finite provinces of meaning, as Alfred Schutz (1967) would have noted, with no connections between them. Schutz was interested in multiple realities and how they may be transgressed, mainly by thinking about inner, fantasy versus outer, paramount realities, which may be more similar to each other than we ordinarily assume. It took a while for me to get used to switching between two paramount realities, one of them harbouring an elaborated fantasy world at times extended from the stage to backstage and even outside the theatre. A frustrating state of not being sure of where reality actually was, kept coming back during the course of my year at the Stockholm Opera. When I entered the last phase of fieldwork, and had about three months left, then I went native, as the saying goes. My mind was constantly at the Opera House, even when my body was in the unreality at the University. This happened, I believe, because the ballet world is an intense, closed world that once was my everyday life, a familiar part of my 'home' at the time: now it was leading to confusions of time and space. In my two previous field studies, the first on ethnicity and youth culture in London and the other on globalizing young Swedes in New York City, I did not have to synchronize the reality of any previous life-world (cf. Schutz ibid.) of mine with my present life-world in relation to those field realities. But it also mattered that I was doing field work in my home city, that I had not moved out of my ordinary life but was zigzagging back and forth between the Opera House and the University.

Tracing Four Companies, Four National Settings

In the overall centre–periphery structure in the ballet world, there are different kinds of ballet centres that to a certain extent are considered hierarchically, although the exact ordering of places varies from different vantage points in the ballet world, as well as over time. New ballet centres come about in large part because individual persons, talented choreographers with an abundance of ideas, have been able to work very hard, since funding has been made available and marketing is efficient. The Americans William Forsythe in Frankfurt-am-Main and John Neumeier in Hamburg, as well as the Czech Jiří Kylián in the Hague, are among the contemporary choreographic innovators who have established new ballet centres attracting dancers from many different countries. The question remains, of course, whether these ballet centres will be institutionalized beyond the periods of presence of these choreographers. There is no major new force in classical choreography at the moment, which means that London, Paris, New York, and to some extent Copenhagen and St Petersburg have kept their positions as traditional ballet centres, each one characterized by what is considered in the ballet world to be a typical national ballet style.

Different peripheries, moreover, have their own most significant centres. This means that one person's ballet centre may be another person's ballet periphery, and vice versa. From the Finnish perspective, for example, Stockholm is a ballet centre. And anyone, except an English dancer, can have an 'international career' in the ballet centre of London. The English dancer has to go abroad, preferably to the United States, for that to happen; whereas Swedish, and even American, dancers can make 'international careers' in London. If they then go back to their own countries, they may be promoted, and usually get to dance more than they did before they left, and in more prominent roles.

Although there was a multitude of manifest and ideational transnational connections between the Royal Swedish Ballet, the British Royal Ballet, the American Ballet Theatre and Ballett Frankfurt, they all had their own company culture shaped and structured by different national cultures, union laws, funding systems and ballet traditions.

The Royal Swedish Ballet, the British Royal Ballet, and Ballett Frankfurt reside in opera houses, which they therefore have to share with opera companies. The notion that 'opera comes first' organizationally, especially in financial and marketing matters, surfaced now and then in Stockholm and London. Not so in Frankfurt, since Ballett Frankfurt in only a little over a decade has been more successful (in reputation and also financially) than the opera company, Oper Frankfurt, both at home and on tours abroad. The director of the opera house, Martin Steinhoff, is a ballet enthusiast and has supported Ballet Frankfurt more than is usually the case in opera houses.

Two Hundred Years of Heritage at the Royal Swedish Ballet

The Royal Opera House in Stockholm is to be found in the city centre of Stockholm on a square by a stretch of water opposite the Royal Palace. It was opened in 1782 by the Swedish 'theatre king' Gustavus III (and later rebuilt and reopened in 1898). The most significant characteristic of the Royal Opera House for visiting dancers is the rake of the stage, which they have to adjust to; but so does the Royal Swedish Ballet when it comes back from tours. There is a lot of gold and red velvet and a huge chandelier in the auditorium, which also has a special Royal Box for the exclusive use of the Royal Family. An additional small stage, called 'the Rotunda' in the House, is used for experimental dance, choreographic workshops and opera and dance productions for children. Backstage facilities are quite up to date, many of them with extensive views over Stockholm.

King Gustavus III appointed the French ballet master Louis Gallodier in 1773 to train an existing dance troupe into a national ballet company. Other European dancers joined, and French, Italian and Danish ballet masters came for longer or shorter periods of time. Charles-Louis Didelot was born in Stockholm, but became a well-known dancer and choreographer abroad. Italian dancer Filipo Taglioni spent a year with the Royal Swedish Ballet, during which time he married a Swedish harpist. After their daughter Marie Taglioni was born, they all left Stockholm. Almost forty years later Marie Taglioni came back, as an exceptional ballerina, to dance sections from *La Sylphide* among other ballets. Her partner was Per Christian Johansson, an eminent dancer who moved to St Petersburg, where he also became renowned as a teacher, important for Russian ballet. August Bournonville danced with the Royal Swedish Ballet in Stockholm twice, as well as working there as producer and director for three years in the mid-nineteenth century. During that time, Anders Selinder was ballet master and director. In the teens of the twentieth century, Michel Fokine worked for short periods as a ballet master and choreographer with the Royal Swedish Ballet, inspiring the company to make remarkable progress. One of the dancers that Fokine taught, Jean Börlin, left the Royal Swedish Ballet and went to Paris, where he made a name for himself as a choreographer and a dancer. Backed up economically by Rolf de Maré, he established a touring company, Ballets Suédois, in the early 1920s, consisting of Scandinavian dancers, many of whom had been corps de ballet dancers at the Royal Swedish Ballet.

After the Second World War, the English choreographer Antony Tudor was hired to revitalize the Royal Swedish Ballet. Birgit Cullberg worked at the Royal Opera House, and in the 1950s Mary Skeaping, dancer, ballet master, and director, was brought in from England. She stayed for ten years, giving a full-length production of *Swan Lake* to the Swedes. Striving for raised standards, she expanded the company and the number of performances. During the 1950s, choreographers Birgit Åkeson and Ivo Cramér created new modern productions, as in the 1960s did Margaretha Åsberg. Ballets by Leonide Massine and George Balanchine, and later by Jerome Robbins, José Limon, Glen Tetley, Kenneth MacMillan, Rudolf Nureyev, Eliot Feld, John Cranko, Jiří Kylián, Flemming Flindt, John Neumeier and William Forsythe have all been significant. The Canadian Brian MacDonald and the Dane Erik Bruhn were influential directors in the 1960s. In the mid-1970s the Royal Swedish Ballet engaged in extensive touring worldwide. Ivo Cramér has directed the company, as well as Gunilla Roempke, Nils-Åke Häggbom (Skeaping and Ståhle 1979; Rödin 1979; Koegler 1987), Simon Mottram, and from 1995 Frank Andersen.

The Royal Swedish Ballet has operated at the intersection of national and transnational ballet and dance, often serving as a transit place for dancers and choreographers of transnational fame. The peripheral status of Sweden, politically and culturally, has probably affected the company's transnational reputation, at times unfairly.

The Britishness of the British Royal Ballet

Dating from 1732, the Royal Opera House, Covent Garden is regarded as the leading opera house in London. The present Victorian building originates from 1858 (Koegler 1987). Centrally located in a busy part of London, it is close to a gentrified shopping mall, Covent Garden, which used to be a fruit, vegetable and flower market, but now mostly caters for tourists, who walk passed the Royal Opera House in large numbers in the day time. Because of the risk of bomb threats in London, the electronic surveillance system at the Royal Opera House, Covent Garden covers the streets around the block. The auditorium is furnished in red velvet and some gold, evoking memories of Great Britain at the height of its Imperial power, as well as those of significant ballet events and renowned dancers and choreographers.

In 1956 the Sadler's Wells Ballet, Sadler's Wells Theatre Ballet and Sadler's Wells Ballet School were given the name the Royal Ballet and the Royal Ballet School by a Royal Charter. Both the ballet company and the school originated from the Academy of Choreographic Art that Ninette de Valois set up in 1926 in London. After some years Lilian Baylis offered de Valois the opportunity of taking the school to the new Sadler's Wells Theatre. Frederick Ashton began choreographing ballets for the company in the early 1930s, and soon for Margot Fonteyn. After the Second World War the company moved to Covent Garden. In the 1950s Kenneth MacMillan and

John Cranko set out to create ballets for the company. When de Valois resigned as director in the early 1960s, Ashton took over, with MacMillan as the leading choreographer until 1970, when he was appointed director. There were to be two companies, the Royal Ballet, based at the Royal Opera House, and a smaller touring company, the Sadler's Wells Royal Ballet. Norman Morris acted as director until 1986, when he was succeeded by Anthony Dowell (Koegler 1987). In 1990 the Sadler's Wells Royal Ballet became the Birmingham Royal Ballet, with a home at the Hippodrome Theatre in Birmingham (Clarke and Crisp 1992).

The Royal Ballet acquired a transnational reputation after the Second World War. Rudolf Nureyev was a permanent guest with the company for many years. Since there is not enough studio space at Covent Garden, the Royal Ballet also rehearses in studios at Barons Court, twenty minutes away by underground. In 1997, Covent Garden closed for renovation. The narrow meandering corridors and run-down facilities backstage were in need of improvement, as was the technology and machinery in the wings, partly for safety reasons.

The rise of the Royal Ballet coincided with the decline of Great Britain as a colonial power. Trying to adjust to less global power, Britons reacted with a mixture of feelings of anxiety and responsibility, sometimes clinging to a heightened nationalism that for instance was manifest when the Royal Ballet went on foreign tours in the 1950s and 1960s. 'We were taught that we were "ambassadors" of Britain, that we had to behave very well', ex-members of the company have told me. This meant in particular evincing at all times a modest demeanour.

The Theatricality of the American Ballet Theatre

The American Ballet Theatre is a touring company without a theatre of its own. It rehearses in old studios on two floors in a large office building located above the bustling urban life on lower Broadway in Manhattan in New York. This world metropolis is still sometimes called 'the Mecca of dance' in the ballet world, although that was an even more common designation in the 1970s and 1980s, during the so-called 'dance boom'. The megastars of the American Ballet Theatre company greet visitors already in the reception area: there are posters of Mikhail Baryshnikov and Natalia Makarova, as well as of dancers who are still dancing with the company.

Originating from the Mordkin Ballet, Ballet Theater, which premièred at New York Radio City Center in 1940, was renamed American Ballet Theatre in 1957, being then directed by Lucia Chase. It had established a reputation based on American productions combined with revived classics, but soon came to cultivate a host of choreographers, not only Agnes de Mille and later Twyla Tharp; works by Michel Fokine, Antony Tudor, George Balanchine, and Birgit Cullberg and Jerome Robbins have also been acclaimed. Celebrated dancers like Gelsey Kirkland and Rudolf Nureyev have danced with the company (Koegler 1987). Baryshnikov was also director of the company for a time. Then Jane Herman came in for a couple of years, and was replaced by Kevin McKenzie in the early 1990s.

Struggling with a less stable economic situation than that of its neighbour and rival, New York City Ballet, American Ballet Theatre has still recruited many megastars as guests and company members, and has had highly successful productions created for the company, among them Balanchine's *Theme and Variations*, Makarova's 'Kingdom of the Shades' from *La Bayadère*, and Twyla Tharp's *When Push Comes to Shove* with Mikhail Baryshnikov. After a period of financial and artistic decline, the American Ballet Theatre is now enjoying a renewed success among critics and audiences, in large part as a result of launching ethnic (mostly Latin American) dancers.

Crossover Collages at Ballett Frankfurt

The new Opera House in Frankfurt-am-Main is named Oper am Willy-Brandt-Platz. It has one stage for drama and one for opera and ballet, although both visiting dance companies and Ballett Frankfurt sometimes also perform on the drama stage in the *Schauspielhaus*. This Opera House was reopened in 1991 after a fire that destroyed much of the earlier building.[15] Here Ballett Frankfurt resides in light and spacious studios, dressing-rooms and offices. The technology around the stage is quite up to date. The auditorium is designed with simple blue chairs, brown wooden surfaces and black iron rails.

William Forsythe started creating dances in his early teens in New York, old Broadway musicals that he mounted as school performances. He was seventeen years old when he took his first ballet lessons at college, and he then continued to Robert Joffrey's school and company in New York. In the early 1970s he joined the Stuttgart Ballet, at first as a dancer; but in 1976 he established himself as a choreographer with the lyrical *Urlicht*. It was the beginning of intense choreographing both in Stuttgart and for other leading companies; in seven years Forsythe created twenty ballets. *Gänge – ein Stück über Ballett* for the then Ballett Frankfurt scored a tremendous success in 1983, and led to his appointment as ballet director in Frankfurt-am-Main. With the help of a regional economic programme to promote culture, especially dance, and the opera director Martin Steinhoff, William Forsythe produced a turn-over of the ballet repertory and the audience in the new Opera House in Frankfurt. One of the dancers recalled that when the classics first were replaced by contemporary, experimental work 'we danced for five people, who were booing' in the audience. The new Ballett Frankfurt then went on to transnational fame.

The transnational breakthrough for William Forsythe came in 1987, typically in a ballet center from which news spread rapidly across the ballet world. The one-act ballet *In the Middle, Somewhat Elevated* that Forsythe created for Sylvie Guillem and eight of the other dancers at the Paris Opéra Ballet was hailed as a turning-point in the history of ballet, connecting George Balanchine's neoclassical style with contemporary vocabulary and rhythms. The electronic score by Forsythe's collaborator, Dutch composer Thom Willems, defined a thundering and hissing theme that recurred in different variations throughout the ballet.

'Desire and rigour' are qualities that William Forsythe says that he is looking for when he chooses dancers for his company. As Robert Joffrey did, Forsythe has gradually put together an ethnically mixed ballet company of many personalities in contrasting shapes, sizes and colours. It gives him a rich material to work with, to surprise with. Almost half the dancers are American; a large group originates from Mediterranean countries (France, Spain and Italy); and only four dancers have grown up in Germany. (There are no English or Russian dancers in the company.) The working language is English, but German is also used in communication with technical staff in the Opera House.

Itinerary of this Book

In Chapter 2 the theoretical framework of a transnational ballet world will illuminate ethnography on patterns of mobility and the notion of national ballet styles. The ambiguous relationship between cultural capital on the one hand and the marketing and funding of ballet on the other, where dancers are caught in the middle, is also a part of the transnational context. Chapter 3 starts out with a comparative account of how ballet is learned at the national ballet schools of the companies in the study, also considered in relation to issues of transnationality. This is followed by a discussion of the course of a ballet career from audition for a company via breakthroughs to ageing and retiring. In Chapter 4, the culture and everyday life of classical ballet companies are considered. The process of producing ballet performance, mainly from back stage, is the topic of Chapter 5, but audience and critics are also included. The concluding Chapter 6 provides an in-depth account of transnational connectivity in the ballet world, both by mapping how ballet people move around, especially on tours, and how they communicate through media and technology. New forms of technology, like computers and videos, are moreover being used increasingly in contemporary dance productions. This fact points us towards the conclusions of the book, and even further ahead.

Notes

1. This is an instance of Pierre Bourdieu's (1977) notion of body hexis.

2. Roger Hewitt brought to my attention Michel Foucault's (1973) analysis of the painting *The Maids of Honour* (Las Meniñas) by Diego Velázquez. The painting presents Princess Margarita and her entourage in the studio of the painter by accentuating light and space. Like the dancers imagining the audience behind the mirror, the painter in *The Maids of Honour* is looking at the spectators of the painting, observing them, as it were. In the picture the spectators are thus observing themselves being observed by the painter. There is a mirror in the painting that (in contrast with Dutch paintings, where mirrors are used to duplicate a different version of the theme of the painting) does not reflect anything the spectator can see in the painting, but King Philip IV and his wife Mariana, who are outside it. They are the models of the painting the painter is about to paint.

The Maids of Honour is exhibited at the Prado in Madrid. Because of its large size, it has to be viewed through a mirror (Hewitt, personal communication).

3. On the medical problems of eating disorders (anorexia nervosa and bulimia) and their impact on delayed menarches among American and Chinese female ballet dancers at national ballet companies, see Hamilton *et al.* (1988). They report how serious eating disorders are correlated with selectivity, in the sense that American dancers in the less selective American companies were found to suffer more from eating problems (46 per cent versus 11 per cent) than Americans at a company school. The authors argue that dancers who have gone through a severe early selection may in fact have hereditarily slender bodies. The problem of anorexia in the ballet world remains, of course. I did on a few occasions observe coaches taking women dancers to task for being overweight. It also happened that women dancers told me about eating disorders that they implied had been caused by coaches.

4. See Altorki and Fawzi El-Solh (1988) on Arab women studying their own societies.

5. See Wulff (1995a) for a discussion on studies of youth culture and the problem that youth culture scholars are mostly young. When I was doing fieldwork on young teenage girls in South London, I understood that I had forgotten how I saw the world at fourteen years of age. Since my relationship to the girls was not of an enculturating quality I noticed other concerns of theirs than their parents and teachers did.

6. This argument ties into a dialogue between Hastrup and Icelandic anthropologists over her writings on Icelandic culture and history that seems to have started in Hastrup (1985). See also Pálsson (1995) and Hastrup (forthcoming).

7. See for instance Janet Adshead *et al.* (1988) for a formalist approach to dance analysis. Susan Leigh Foster's (1986) *Reading Dancing* applies semiology to the work of four contemporary choreographers in the United States. See also the volume edited by Gay Morris (1996) on formal analysis versus cultural theory in dance studies.

8. See also Kaeppler (1978), Spencer (1985), Ness (1992), Lewis (1992), Grau (1993), Y. Daniel (1995) and van Nieuwkerk (1995).

9. See Sally Ann Ness's (1996) article on the problems of finding accurate methods for the cross-cultural study of dance, especially in Western analyses of non-Western dance.

10. There is a thriving dance scholarship growing out of dance history, sociology, anthropology, ethnology and comparative literature influencing and debating each other's work across as well as within the disciplines. Much of this work emphasizes interdisciplinary lines of thought, such as feminist critique, notions of the body and body politics, dance and movement analysis, as well as French psychoanalytic theory. Kendall (1979), Banes (1987, 1994, 1998), Jowitt (1988), McRobbie (1991), Adair (1992), Thomas (1993, 1995, 1997), Franko (1995), Browning (1995), Savigliano (1995), Goellner and Murphy (1995), Foster (1995, 1996a,b,c), Morris (1996), Guest (1996) and Desmond (1997) draw on some or all of these approaches.

11. Globalization and transnational connections are growing in number and frequency today (Featherstone 1991; Robertson 1992; Hannerz 1992, 1996; Appadurai 1996). This development may be understood in terms of networks, a large number of which consist of transnational extensions of occupational communities and cultures. See Sharon Traweek (1988) on high-energy physicists, Christina Garsten (1994) on Apple Computer employees and Ulf Hannerz's (1996) chapter 'Trouble in the Global Village: The World according to Foreign Correspondents'.

12. The British Royal Ballet and the American Ballet Theatre share their positions as national ballet companies with one (New York City Ballet) and two (Birmingham Royal Ballet and English National Ballet) other companies respectively. The three classical companies in focus here are so-called 'repertory companies', which means that they perform classical ballets like *Swan Lake* and *The Sleeping Beauty*. In addition to the classical repertory they perform modern and contemporary productions, which are often mounted by guest choreographers.

13. Another study to be made is one on Russian and Eastern European ballet companies. An interesting issue to explore would be how they interact with Western companies, especially after the political changes in 1989–91.

14. Marilyn Strathern (1987: 16–17) identifies the problem of 'how one *knows* when one is at home'. She suggests that personal credentials are not enough for this: there has to be a cultural continuity in the eventual writings and accounts by the people about themselves.

15. My informants told me that the Opera House was set on fire by someone who was receiving social security and mistook the building for the offices of the social services.

2

The Transnational Context

In the relationship between culture and place from a macro perspective[1] the transnational ballet world is both homogeneous in work practices and heterogeneous when it comes to national employment laws and funding systems. This chapter will show that the transnational nature of the ballet world does not make national culture or the meaning of place obsolete. Ballet people are constantly negotiating national and transnational cultural processes. Sometimes one kind is more prominent than the other. There may be tensions between them, but also sparks of interchange. Ballet centres are characterized by national ballet styles, for example, which can be seen as one way to profile ballet companies and individual dancers transnationally. Yet it is in the contrast with transnational contexts that the national ballet styles become truly national.

The notion of 'a ballet world' is prevalent among ballet people. It is, however, the American sociologist Howard Becker's (1984) work on *Art Worlds* which has inspired my concept of a *transnational* ballet world.[2] Becker prepares the ground for the idea of a transnational art world, as he states that art worlds may be of different sizes: from small, local and esoteric groups to large, inclusive, international ones. This can obviously be applied to a discussion on ballet worlds as well. Becker criticizes the imagery of the individual artist, with a special talent, producing art entirely on his own. All artists, Becker suggests instead, are part of art worlds populated by other artists as well as by a range of other people, sharing the same conventions and making contributions more or less routinely to the actual production of art works. The latter, it follows, are in fact collective works. In his article 'The Field of Cultural Production, or the Economic World Reversed', Pierre Bourdieu (1993) on the other hand stresses the struggle for individual recognition in what he calls artistic fields. They are social worlds with their own power dynamics, yet subordinated to larger power structures in society. Becker (1984) has a concluding chapter on reputation where he argues that the cooperation behind art works also makes the reputations of artists and works – but it is not rewarded, because of the pervasive idea of art work as produced by individual artists. Although ballet performances are collective work, and dancers are dependent on each other on stage not least because of the risk of injuring each other but also for the making of the performance, there is competition between individual dancers who are striving upwards or who are eager to keep a top position on the one hand and the company as a unit on the other. There are, for example, subtle ways to excel even in a line of corps de ballet women who are supposed to do the same steps in perfect unison, by dancing slightly before the beat or with personal expression, thereby attracting the attention of the audience at the expense of the other women.

The three classical ballet companies in this study were about the same size during the time of my field study: there were eighty dancers at the Royal Swedish Ballet, eighty-eight at the British Royal Ballet and seventy-five at the American Ballet Theatre. This is a common size of classical companies – it is the one needed for performances of traditional productions of the classical ballets; yet the ballet directors harboured visions of expanding their companies further. The New York City Ballet, the Paris Opéra Ballet and the Kirov Ballet are examples of big companies with over one hundred dancers. Contemporary companies are smaller: Ballett Frankfurt accommodates about forty dancers. Most dance troupes that are also of transnational fame are even smaller than that, consisting of approximately twenty dancers.

Classical ballet companies still have a pyramidal appointment hierarchy reflecting the role distribution in classical ballets from the nineteenth century, and thus an outmoded social structure, a relic of a time when there was not much room for personal expression. The vast majority of dancers in classical ballet companies still occupy positions at the bottom as corps de ballet dancers, or artists, as they increasingly tend to be called. A somewhat larger group are appointed as soloists (and first artists as well as first soloists at the British Royal Ballet), and then there are a few principal dancers at the top. There are just a handful of principal character artists at the British Royal Ballet, listed after the principal dancers in programmes. At the Royal Swedish Ballet principal dancers may be honoured by the title Royal Court Dancers (modelled on Royal Court Singers at the Royal Opera House in Stockholm).[3] Contemporary ballet and dance companies have equal ranking, meaning that all dancers are appointed as soloists, although an informal hierarchy tends to crystallize anyhow, since some dancers perform more prominent roles and more often than others. Nowadays most dancers in classical companies aim at least initially at becoming principal dancers: they want to be able to dance leading roles, make more money and be recognized.

Becker (1984) even points to the importance to the art world of people who manufacture and distribute the material equipment of artists – thus he notes that dancers' shoes and costumes, for instance, are absolutely necessary items for ballet dancers. These people are also engaged in intense personal interactions in the ballet world, and even involved with its core understandings and experiences. In the ballet world, some of the support personnel (Becker 1984: 77) around the dancers used to have professional artistic ambitions, like one stage manager who went to ballet school with the dancers and another one who was a piano student. A wig-maker once had different kinds of artistic interests: he wanted to become a scenographer when he first came to the theatre. Some support personnel in the ballet world pursue art as amateurs. There was thus a dresser who played in a jazz band and a secretary who was an amateur actress. Most support personnel in the ballet world, from coaches and choreographers to physiotherapists and ballet directors, are ex-dancers, however, and thus well grounded in ballet culture.

Although the dancers are at the focus of this study, on stage they are often supported by a conductor and an orchestra that, like the dancers, also are visible for the audience. If they did not already know about it, the audience can read in the programme that the performance would not have come about without a choreographer (who made the steps or used established steps in new combinations), one or two coaches or ballet masters (also called répétiteurs) who are in charge of rehearsals, and a dance dramatist (or librettist), who wrote the plot if there is one (unless the choreographer did that). There are also costume, lighting and set designers, electricians, carpenters, property men, and a stage manager (who is in charge of the technical side of performances backstage). The audience may catch a glimpse of stage-hands rushing on and off stage. For a ballet performance is the combined product not only of dancers, choreographers and conductors, who are rewarded in public, but also of those who work more or less invisibly backstage, such as ballet pianists (who accompany daily training and rehearsals)[4] and choreologists (or notators, who write down – notate – new ballets and translate notations at revivals). Physiotherapists, perhaps a psychologist, wig-masters and make-up artists are other backstage people. Video technicians document rehearsals and performances for further rehearsals backstage, while much of the work of company photographers at ballet companies is quite visible, since it appears in newspapers and programmes. Ballet companies are run by ballet directors, who are assisted by a ballet producer, an artistic coordinator, administrators and secretaries. Agents (or impresarios) make transnational arrangements for individual leading dancers, coaches and entire companies. They all work in the transnational ballet world, contributing to dancers' careers (and simultaneously to their own). And this is an important point in this study: *not* only famous dancers and choreographers move around, but in addition those who work backstage and remain unknown to the general public (although they may acquire transnational reputations in their line of work) also travel and relocate to other countries. Many of the less visible people in the transnational ballet world fled to the West from the former Soviet Union or East European countries, just like the star dancers.

Marketing and press departments deal with public relations. This is also where private sponsors and donors come in. The exact composition of all these categories varies to some extent from one company to another. But all companies have audiences, among whom they take note of the critics especially. Ballet companies also have boards. Those ballet companies that work at opera houses share their boards with the opera. Classical ballet companies have their own patrons, royal ballet enthusiasts: the Swedish Princess Christina is an honorary member and patron of the Royal Swedish Ballet, the British Princess Margaret is president of the Royal Ballet in London, and Caroline B. Kennedy is honorary chairwoman of American Ballet Theatre, succeeding her mother, the late Jacqueline Onassis, who was also a trustee of the company for many years.

Ballet as an 'International Language'

Since classical ballet is non-verbal, dancers, coaches, directors and other people in the ballet world talk about ballet as a 'language' with 'vocabulary' and 'syntax'. This language is usually construed as an 'international language'. 'International' implicitly meaning 'Western', even though this aspect is seldom problematized. An exception is, however, the article entitled 'Is Dance an International Language?' by Chris de Marigny (1990: 2), where it is suggested that neither classical ballet nor abstract dance is easily translated between different parts of the world. The international language view is also discussed in a review by dance scholar Alexandra Carter (1993) of the series 'Dancing' that was broadcast by the BBC. Aiming at a trans-national market, this anthropological series dealt to some extent with the forms, but mainly with the functions of dance in a number of cultures.[5] In her review of the series, Carter accepts the focus on dance as a cultural discourse, but objects when classical ballet is portrayed as offering '"universal" truths' (1993: 60) by way of fairy tales. Instead, ballet's relationship to social class and its depiction of the masculine and the feminine should be investigated, she suggests.[6] When ballet is said to be an 'international language' that 'people from other civilisations and other worlds would be able to understand' (1993: 60–1), Carter disagrees. Without denying that the arts often depict universal themes, she points at the cultural meanings of symbols, exemplifying her case with the Christening gifts that the fairies present to Aurora in *The Sleeping Beauty* and the classical ballet mime for a wedding ring. Clearly, not only ballet and contemporary dance, but also ethnic dance, presuppose a certain cultural knowledge.

The fact that classical ballet dancing is non-verbal, thereby transcending boundaries that are in large part defined by language, is of course crucial for guest performances abroad as well as for tours. The audience need not know the language of the dancers to enjoy their dancing. Since the basic ballet steps are the same wherever classical ballet exists (although they are executed slightly differently in the national ballet styles), and are everywhere referred to in French (as with, for example, *pas de deux*, a dance for two people, and *arabesque*, a position with one leg extended behind and usually with one arm in front, and the other behind), this becomes a shared technical language. That is, what dancers and coaches need is to be able to pronounce the French terms; the spelling does not seem to be a widespread concern. There is also a sprinkling of English terms to designate steps that originate from modern and contemporary dance. This homogeneity is one important factor in transnational guesting and visiting. Dancers, choreographers and coaches can work for shorter or longer periods in countries where they do not speak the native language. English is used increasingly, however, in coaching and choreographing.

According to Howard Becker (1984) professional artists tend to share the conventions of their art internationally, and are thus able to cooperate. This is particularly true in ballet. In this highly specialized occupation, there is a transnational consensus on standards, especially on outstanding and terrible ballet. A 'first-class dancer' is 'first-class' everywhere (even if local politics may try to hide it). Ballet people discuss technique and artistry: one dancer is good technically, another artistically; the best ones have both talents, but major character dancers are also regarded as important for the perform-ance as a whole.

A Tradition of Mobility: Establishing Ballet Centres

Ballet sprang out of the growing commercial wealth that gave noble Italian families opportunities to support the arts, which they did as a part of their search for Renaissance refinement and pleasure.[7] They enjoyed a preclassical dance that was a mixture of peasant folk dancing and court processions. The first ballet production, the court ballet, *Ballet Comique de la Reine*, was mounted in the sixteenth century by Italian-born Balthasar de Beaujoyeulx[8] at the court in Paris. Together with many other Italian artists, he was brought to Paris by Catherine de Medici, who financed and encouraged lavish performances in order to educate and entertain the French nobility. About a hundred years later King Louis XIV (who danced ballet himself), initiated a professionalization of ballet by establishing training academies and commercial theatres. In the eighteenth century there were ballet companies in a number of countries all over Europe.

It was in France, however, during the Romantic period,[9] that pointe-dancing and bell-shaped tutus became connected with ballerinas, especially after Swedish-Italian Marie Taglioni's exceptional breakthrough as La Sylphide in the ballet of the same name in 1832. One of her partners was August Bournonville, of Danish-French origin, who went back to Denmark, where he worked as director and choreographer for nearly half a century. The French dancer Marius Petipa also worked that long as a choreographer in St Petersburg, where he created classics like *The Sleeping Beauty* and in 1895 a restaged acclaimed version of *Swan Lake* together with Russian Lev Ivanov, who did most of the choreography for *The Nutcracker*. (The Russian Pjotr Tchaikovsky wrote the music for all three ballets.)

In the early twentieth century, the impresario and producer Sergei Diaghilev formed a company of Russian dancers, the Ballets Russes. It premièred in Paris and went on to give annual seasons there, as well as extensive tours in London and New York among other places. One of the choreographers of the Ballets Russes, the Russian George Balanchine, was encouraged by Lincoln Kirstein, an American art lover from a prosperous business family, to move to New York. Together they founded the School of American Ballet in the mid-1930s and the New York City Ballet in the late 1940s. By then, the other major ballet company in New York, American Ballet Theatre, had been in existence for almost ten years. It had been set up by Lucia Chase, an affluent woman who used to dance, and featured both classics and modern pieces by different choreographers. One of these, Agnes de Mille, mounted one of the first ballets with black dancers. She created the cowboy ballet *Rodeo*, which was to became an early signature piece of the American Ballet Theatre. The Irish dancer Ninette de Valois was also with the Ballets Russes, albeit earlier. In the 1920s she began working towards establishing a national ballet company in England, which eventually was to become the Royal Ballet.

Later another, even more widely known, type of transnational movement in the ballet world occurred when the megastars Rudolf Nureyev in the early 1960s and Mikhail Baryshnikov in the early 1970s defected to the West from the former Soviet Union. So did Natalia Makarova, an outstanding ballerina who was to become acclaimed as a choreographer, and many others.

Patterns of Transnational Mobility

One spring during my field study, there was a crisis at the Royal Opera House in Stockholm. *Swan Lake*, the ballet of ballets and a reliable box-office puller, was scheduled – but there were no dancers who could dance the leading roles. One was on maternity leave, another was injured – in fact so were two and even three, it turned out when the ballet director started asking down the ranks. As the performance day came closer, it became clear that foreign guests would have to be invited, if Prince Siegfried were ever to meet the Swan Queen. With the help of an Italian agent, an American woman principal from New York and a Hungarian male principal dancer working in London were flown in. They had never danced together before, and had only five days to rehearse (the woman struggling with jet lag). But they had danced *Swan Lake* many times, and seen the ballet and heard the music on innumerable occasions. For even if there are different productions of this classic, they do not diverge all that much. Thus a professional classical dancer can go anywhere in the world, learn the local production of *Swan Lake* at short notice, and perform it – with great success.[10]

For centuries the pattern of transnational mobility in the ballet world was formed by touring as well as by dancers and ballet masters who moved to other countries and settled there. They were either attracted to early ballet centres (especially Paris) by artistic mentors and financial patrons, or they built them, as Marius Petipa did when he went to St Petersburg as one among a number of famous dancers and choreographers from Italy and France who were invited there (Cass 1993).

Sponsorship and audiences were also arranged, and still are, through the establishment of ballet societies and friendship circles: the Camargo Society was founded in 1930 in London by the ballet writers Arnold Haskell and Philip Richardson, and the Ballet Society was set up by Lincoln Kirstein and George Balanchine in 1946 in New York. Also Sergei Diaghilev was dependent on ballet lovers among the upper classes, that is in the European financial aristocracy, to keep the Ballets Russes going (Koegler 1987).

The dispersion of the Ballets Russes's dancers after the death of Diaghilev in the late 1920s proved crucial for the establishment of ballet worldwide. Russian Anna Pavlova kept an especially intensive touring schedule for many years, going to Scandinavia, South America, Australia, Japan and Cuba.[11] Later the Royal Ballet in London had a global impact on ballet by touring and guesting in Britain's former colonies of South Africa, Hong Kong, Australia and New Zealand. Dancers from these countries also came to train with the Royal Ballet in London. Countries as distant as Israel and China both owe their ballet traditions to Russian teachers who started building ballet schools and companies there (Koegler 1987).

Ballet people tour, in fact, more than ever, and they still move to other countries. In addition to this mobility from one place to another, there is now a new kind of mobility in the transnational ballet world: from a foreign base, dancers, choreographers, ballet masters, and conductors may go back and forth between two and three countries over the course of many years because they have long-standing agreements with more than one company. They are often famous and have a following (which may even follow them abroad to a certain extent); but not necessarily so. Transnational mobility is, again, not exclusive to the stars: in the ballet world unknown people travel as well.

Another more recent type of transnational mobility in the ballet world are the quick long-distance trips that ballet directors and producers especially sometimes take in order to prepare tours or watch productions they consider taking on. Because of the busy schedule of ballet companies, directors may have to squeeze in visits to many different countries in a short time. One of the directors at the British Royal Ballet only had one week for three countries in two continents to finalize arrangements for the upcoming 'South Korea–Japan–USA tour', for example. And at the American Ballet Theatre, as things got really hectic, the director travelled to Australia, arriving just in time for a performance, spent the night, and then flew back to the United States the next morning.

Transnational experience and exposure are regarded as desirable for dancers' development and reputation. It is believed that new colleagues, choreographers and audiences, especially in ballet centres, further dancers' careers. One way to get transnational exposure for young dancers is to take part in international ballet competitions. Festivals and galas (fund-raising, or celebrating a successful director and/or choreographer, or commemorating a prominent choreographer and/or a dancer) tend to be for dancers and companies that are more established, with transnational reputations, often representing different countries. In the summers, many young dancers go abroad to train with renowned coaches, often to New York, where they have studios. During the time of my field study, dancers could 'buy class' for about $10 per day in New York.

Every ballet production is a result of the cooperation of people from different countries. These people do not necessarily meet; but it is common-place that choreographers, composers and designers should come to premières and revivals of the pieces they have worked on. A mixture of nationalities is furthermore nowadays to be found not only in contemporary companies but also in most classical companies. Apart from dancers who are 'half-native' and some who are immigrants in the second generation, quite a few are foreigners. About 20 per cent of the dancers in the three classical companies I deal with here were born and bred abroad. The Royal Swedish Ballet is not as Swedish as its name implies, since its dancers also come from North America, Western and Eastern Europe, and other Nordic countries, mostly Finland. American Ballet Theatre has a number of Russian and Latin American dancers, and a few Japanese, Chinese and European dancers. The effort to form a 'national' dancer, such as an 'English dancer' at the British Royal Ballet, seems to be contradicted by a predominance of foreign principals who together with the other dancers originate from mainland Europe, especially southern Europe, and also from Australia, South Africa, Latin America, Japan, China and Kazakhstan. Some have trained at the Royal Ballet School; but not all of them.

National Ballet Styles

There are quite elaborate ideas of national ballet styles in the transnational ballet world.[12] In a remarkably similar way, it is being recognized from centres as well as peripheries in which country a dancer has been trained. This may of course differ from the dancer's nationality. The point is, however, that many ballet people still regard ballet styles as reflections of 'national personalities' or of 'nations'. Both individual dancers and ballet companies are being launched transnationally as representing a particular national style. Yet younger dancers are increasingly learning not only to change ballet style, but also to switch back and forth between different ones, as well as between old national styles and new choreographic styles like the one developed by William Forsythe. Such flexibility is often required by visiting contemporary choreographers who are commissioned to mount new ballets on classical companies.

The idea of national ballet styles can be traced back to the major ballet schools' providing different types of training that have been acclaimed transnationally: the French, the Russian, the British, the Danish and the American schools – the traditional ballet centres, in other words. There used to be an Italian ballet centre in Milan in the nineteenth century that was crucial for establishing classical ballet technique. But the Italian style is not construed as a national ballet style today, and neither is Italy entirely united as a nation. The Italian style is thus not used as a feature of nationalism like the other ballet styles.

Dancers, coaches and choreographers generally hold the view that dancers from the English school dance 'magnificently, but slightly reserved', Russians 'move in a big way, they are very dramatic (in order to fill their big stages)'. The French are regarded as 'chic, technically perfect with clear lines', Danish dancers as 'cute'; and Americans dance 'fast, with good technique, even athletic'. These characterizations are sometimes used as negative distinctions, as when dancers with the Royal Swedish Ballet state that they should really not be dancing George Balanchine's *Theme and Variations*, since 'we don't dance like that', i.e. speedily with accentuated footwork. There is no Swedish school: the Swedish dancers are trained in a mixture of Russian and English styles, with some American influence. And it is this mixture that dancers in Stockholm, London, New York and Frankfurt all come back to: dance styles are becoming increasingly mixed nowadays.

At the American Ballet Theatre in New York there was an additional tendency to attribute 'different' styles to different companies in New York; New York City Ballet being characterized by technical virtuosity and speed and American Ballet Theatre by theatricality. But there was again, at the same time, a consistent emphasis on the present 'mixing', 'crossover' and 'hotch potch of bits and pieces' in dance and ballet styles. Yet as one of the prominent ballerinas at American Ballet Theatre also told me: 'a good dancer can do any style'.

It can, however, take a very long time to learn a certain choreographic style properly. When William Forsythe's productions are danced by companies other than his own, they tend to do it with great success, but not always as articulately as his own dancers. Forsythe's own dancers have (in most cases) been practising his steps and concepts for years, some for more than a decade, whereas other dancers usually only have about a month to learn them. And this shows in their respective performances.

At the classical companies it was quite common for dancers to move between rehearsals of classical and of modern choreographic styles during the same day. One day at American Ballet Theatre, for instance, I saw dancers go from a rehearsal of Twyla Tharp's contemporary ballet *How Near Heaven* that was about to world première to a rehearsal for a revival of the classical *La Bayadère*. Talking about ballet styles in the dancers' lounge between rehearsals, some of the women dancers said that they sometimes change even classical styles when they move between different studios and coaches. (Frequent and sudden changes between national as well as choreographic styles may, however, be harmful to the body, and increase the threat of injuries, since different muscles are used for different styles.)

Critics also contribute to the debate about national ballet styles. *The New York Times*' chief critic Anna Kisselgoff (1983) has argued against the linkage between styles and national personalities, saying that they are in large part stereotypes. Instead she emphasizes the importance of certain individuals, mostly choreographers, in the formation of ballet styles, which can then acquire certain national features. Such creativity often seems to have been released by a stay abroad, or a move to another country, like that of the Russian George Balanchine working in New York with New York City Ballet. Kisselgoff, too, held the view that it was probably the fast pulse or 'urban energy' in New York, as she told me in an interview, that influenced Balanchine to train his dancers in speed. (This they could do, he discovered, if they did not put their heels down.) If Balanchine had stayed in England, where he worked for a while, Kisselgoff thinks that, since he was 'aiming at the essence of dance, not story-telling which they require in England, he probably could not have been going on doing abstract ballets', which he became famous for in the United States. Thereby she also hints that audience taste may vary nationally.[13]

'The Balanchine dancer',[14] critics and dancers agree, is a tall, slim girl with long legs who moves fast, originally trained by Balanchine. When this style travels to Europe, in the form of American dancers who move to European companies, guest or tour in Europe, it is perceived as an 'American' style. An American woman dancer who danced the Swan Queen in Stockholm as a guest, a principal dancer with the American Ballet Theatre, identified herself as a 'Balanchine ballerina', thereby excusing or rather explaining why she was dancing faster than her partner in one of the rehearsals in Stockholm. Almost a year later, when I met her at the American Ballet Theatre in New York, she admitted that she had in fact only been coached by Balanchine once, when he had come to the American Ballet Theatre for one day to have a look at the rehearsals of one of his ballets. The dancer had been overwhelmed, she told me, when she had heard Balanchine say about her: 'She looks like one of our girls!'

The legendary New York critic Edwin Denby (1986: 466–7) says in his essay 'In the Abstract' (which he wrote in 1959 in a ballet programme) that dancers from the Bolshoi Ballet would not be able to keep up with the fast Balanchine rhythm. In line with this view, which I encountered again many times among dancers and coaches, it would be impossible to teach Scandinavian dancers the speed of American dancers, for example. The presence of a Swedish principal dancer with the American Ballet Theatre contradicts this idea, however; trained in Stockholm, he was recruited at eighteen to the American Ballet Theatre, where he became an athletic and speedy dancer. Denby (ibid.) concedes that there are individual exceptions. He also offers the intriguing proposition that there is a correlation between the phrasing, how national companies mark the beat of the music when they dance (behind, across, on top of the beat), and the rhythm of their respective languages. In Paris they dance 'staccato, chattery, and charming', in Moscow 'legato, singsong, and soulful', in Copenhagen the 'dancer "swallows" part of a classic step now and then'. Despite their different languages, Denby discerns a similarity between the Royal Danes and the Royal British in a 'discreetly majestic' look. And he compares the 'distinct and steady action' of the dancers at the New York City Ballet with 'driving a car'.

Clearly, Denby's conceptions of how the French language, Russian, Danish and British English sound are filtered through his own American English, and also seem to be coupled with Western notions about national characters. He does not mention that all dancers in one company do not hear the music in the same way. There are not only different kinds of musicality among dancers – some are even said by their colleagues and coaches to lack musicality.[15]

Not only is the style of dancing discussed by ballet people and critics in terms of nationality; so is artistry. This becomes especially evident when companies go on tours abroad. When the Royal Swedish Ballet played *Don Quixote* in London, for instance, *The Times*'s critic Nadine Meisner (1995) was quite astonished to see that these Swedes, 'Spanish Swedes' as she called them, danced 'as though they were the most Spanish of Spaniards, all zest and passion and proudly arching backs'. Otherwise, it is common to present at least one ballet featuring national themes on foreign tours, as a way to profile companies transnationally. On its tour to Japan, the Royal Swedish Ballet thus danced the modern ballet *Miss Julie* created by Birgit Cullberg in 1950 from August Strindberg's play.[16]

The Contemporary Connection: Conflict and Crossover

In the early twentieth century a major shift took place in the ballet world, dividing it into classical ballet and modern dance. It was prefigured by the Russian dancers and choreographers Michel Fokine and Vaslav Nijinsky, who broke with the traditional lines and language of ballet. Yet a more thorough change occurred in the United States, and spread to Germany, coinciding with the modernist movement in the arts. The point of departure for modern dance was a repudiation of ballet as constraining and conformist. Like their forerunner, Isadora Duncan, many of the first modern dancers were independent women: Martha Graham and Mary Wigman were among these strong-willed individualists who created their own choreographic styles on their companies. Their dancing was expressive and barefooted, with large swinging motions, occasionally using verbal utterances (which did not prevent transnational guesting and touring, since they happened infrequently in the performances). There was also a notion that modern dance movements

44

were 'primitive' in the sense that they were more 'natural' than those in classical ballet. By the mid-century a new development in modern dance came about through linking it to novel mergings of art forms, including for instance the participation of the audience in dance performances. Merce Cunningham and composer John Cage showed dance set to silence as well as to loud flashes of music and shrieks out of tune with the dancing. In the 1970s the Judson Dance Theater was termed (in fact termed itself, cf. Banes 1987) postmodern for having dancers and choreographers doing performances together with musicians, poets and painters (Cass 1993). Recent forms of modern dance are called contemporary dance, and are subdivided by dance critics and writers into categories like postmodern, minimalist and physical theatre, although few choreographers like to be pinned down under those headings. The relationship between ballet and modern dance used to be characterized by more of a mutual ideological conflict than today. Increasingly, there is crossover – often transnationally – both in the form of dancers and choreographers who move back and forth between the two kinds of companies, and when it comes to steps and styles. Both matters are included in this study.

Although William Forsythe and his contemporary ballet company Ballett Frankfurt operate at the intersection of neoclassical and contemporary traditions, they prefer to situate themselves in contemporary ballet. Dance scholar Heidi Gilpin (1993: 105) has written about Forsythe's choreography in terms of his attention to 'the specific residual effects of failure in movement explorations' and a 'postballetic movement style that at times looks like punk on pointe'. Relating to Rudolf van Laban's movement system, Labanotation (cf. Chapter 6), where all human movement is anchored in the body's centre and takes places within the scope of a cube (the 'kinesphere'), Forsythe makes steps that move out of the cube. He plays with movements that do not flow from the body's centre, but investigates different centres and other dimensions for his choreography.

An open form that generates new possibilities is central in Forsythe's choreography, sets and light design, as well as in Thom Willems's music. The open form also structures the work process, as is evident in Forsythe's interest in improvisation and in having choreography and music fuse or collide by way of chance (cf. Chapter 6) in performance. Forsythe does not always separate rehearsal from performance: not only does he continue to make changes after premières, but also during performances. Then Forsythe and Willems are to be found in the audience with headsets and microphones 'conducting' the performance through communicating with dancers, technicians and musicians about steps, sets and sound.

Forsythe uses words, voices and silence as music. His texts are poetic, mathematical combinations, clever plays with words, double entendres, that unexpectedly turn into nonsensical structures and back again. An original thinker, Forsythe looks for inspiration in academic discourse, architecture, fashion, film, new technology, video installations and popular culture. Combining fragments of memory and fantasy into collages of dance, he does not tell stories but explores and creates emotions that become existential and entertaining themes. Forsythe likes to be elusive both in relation to dance writers and his audience. He despises artistic and intellectual representations of his work, arguing that they are inaccurate. Still, Forsythe has made an acclaimed dance video *Solo* and he has been one of the forerunners when it comes to using new technology in performances. ALIE/*NA(C)TION*, which world premièred in 1992, was an early technological production where the dancers danced to film clips in the wings. In *Eidos: Telos* the dancers were inspired to improvise sections from an alphabet, the initial letters of words and expressions like 'spatial reorientation', that change colour and shape with the rhythm of the music, and were displayed on monitors in the wings.

Artists between Cultural Capital and Commerce

In her study on IRCAM (Institut de Recherche et de Coordination Acoustique/ Musique), the institute for research and production of computer music in Paris, Georgina Born (1995) points at the growing interest in 'high culture' and its reproduction as a topic of social and cultural studies. Born (1995: 7) argues for the ethnographic method as unusually apt for capturing 'the workings of dominant western institutions and their cultural systems . . . to uncover the gaps between external claims and internal realities'.

The 'high culture' of the classical ballet world is a far more complicated matter than it tends to appear from the outside. Because of historical and contemporary connections to European court milieux and high strata in Western society such as the *haute bourgeoisie*, ballet is perceived as 'high culture', even as an élite pastime. The social class of the audience is assumed to include the ballet dancers. This is a misunderstanding. There are exceptions, especially among leading dancers, but most of the corps de ballet dancers in the classical companies in this study – who constitute the vast majority here – are from the upper working class to the middle middle class. Importantly, cultural capital does not define back stage as it does front stage: many ballet dancers do not possess much cultural capital,[17] they just provide it for the audience. (The disposition that cultural capital entails concerns consumption of the arts, not production of them like professional dancing.) Neither are ballet dancers particularly comfortable with marketing or fund-raising. Identifying themselves as artists, they find themselves caught in the tension between cultural capital and the market. Celebrated on stage by balletomanes, ballet fans, theatre-goers and royals, many dancers' hidden injuries of class (cf. Sennett and Cobb 1973) are never fully healed. They surface occasionally in the everyday life backstage, as when a dancer complained to me that he found the audience 'limited' because 'many think ballet is difficult. And they've decided that it has to be posh here . . .'.

There is an interesting tradition in the ballet world of educating ballet students, and even more young professional dancers, not only in ballet and ballet culture, but in taste and manners, a rapid course in cultural capital. Senior ballet people see to it that young dancers get some familiarity with 'high culture' by taking them to plays and art galleries. The dancers thereby acquire an ability to appreciate and discuss visual art. This happens in patron–client relationships between a coach and a dancer, or a choreographer and a dancer, for example.

Pierre Bourdieu (1993) elaborates on his concern with social structure in 'Outline of a Sociological Theory of Art Perception', by pointing at how preferences among consumers for certain clusters in the field of culture corresponds with levels of education. One such cluster is thus painting, music or literature. Painting is linked to the ballet world through this kind of education of younger dancers. There is also a striking number of dancers who do painting as a hobby – to the extent they have time for a hobby. They thereby turn this pattern of consumption into production, albeit not on a professional level.

On special occasions, dancers are instructed by coaches and directors how to behave and dress. This usually happens at company meetings or by way of notes on noticeboards before a visit backstage by private donors or representatives of corporate sponsors, but also when television crews are coming to film, or when the company has been invited to receptions and dinners in connection with premières or tours. These functions are often regarded as necessary but not really enjoyable, and are talked about in terms of 'acting'. The illusion on stage can be said to be extended to these promotions parties. Those few dancers who have cultural capital through their upbringing, often well-known principal dancers, are invaluable assets in these situations. They are asked to represent the company with their fame and habit of making formal conversation. They know how to behave confidently without being pushy at embassies and banquets in first-class hotels. Their cultural capital is often enhanced by what one might term a *hip capital* that they have built up through cultivating network links with famous people in media and show-business culture, where they also appear themselves, sometimes by invitation, in order to embellish an opening at an art gallery or a film première. An aura of hipness is also suggested by one's lifestyle outside the theatre, including dress, vocabulary and holidays.

Although dancers are aware of each other's class, there is a notion in the ballet world that 'dancers are classless' that seems to have grown out of their work situation. Dancers work in practice clothes and stage costume, which are a kind of equalizer (especially practice clothes); but so is the bodily closeness and the fact that language is not used all that much. All this makes ordinary class distinctions less visible. Class cannot be detected in how dancers move or dance. Different class positions are moreover often bridged on one level through bonds that are created between dancers, especially partners who have shared the exposure and vulnerability on stage.

Dancers, primarily famous principals, ballet directors and choreographers, meet people from the upper classes, aristocracies and royals, not least in connection with marketing, fund-raising and tours. Such professional links can become personal and develop into friendships.[18] Taken together, there is thus a vast spectrum of social class in the ballet world.

It is not always the case, but there is a tendency for corps de ballet dancers who are from upper-middle-class or upper-class homes to stop dancing if they realize that they will not be promoted to soloists and thus not become principal dancers. Although dancers, like other artists, enjoy a certain social respect for having an 'interesting' job, it is really only the famous dancers who are credited with a wider social prestige. This is reflected in the fact that they have relatively high salaries, in contrast with most dancers, the corps de ballet dancers, whose pay is rather low. Many dancers have, in fact, some difficulties making ends meet.[19] Only a few dancers of world fame have very high salaries.[20]

Funding Ballet

European ballet funding is based on public subsidy, and thus differs from the American model, which is built on philanthropic and corporate support (cf. Ostrower 1995). The Royal Swedish Ballet and Ballett Frankfurt are both predominantly state-subsidized, whereas the British Royal Ballet relies to a greater extent on private and corporate sponsorship, and the American Ballet Theatre does so almost entirely. Embedded in the Swedish welfare system, the Royal Swedish Ballet is the most 'secure' company when it comes to social benefits. Swedish dancers can get a contract after three years in the corps de ballet, a contract that lasts until retirement in their early forties, when they have to find another job. According to Swedish law, they cannot be dismissed before that. Some, although not many, admit that they stop making efforts to improve themselves as dancers, which usually means working on ballet technique by taking class six days a week, doing workout regularly to become even fitter and stronger, and planning their diet. When dancers refrain from taking class regularly and show signs of losing technique, it is commented on by colleagues, coaches and ballet directors. Incidentally, this happens at the British Royal Ballet, the American Ballet Theatre and Ballett Frankfurt, as well, where contracts are renewed once a year. This cannot be taken for granted, however. Some time after I had left the field, one of the male principals of a transnational reputation in one of the classical companies was fired on account of 'bad behaviour'. He had three warnings and then he was fired, one of the other dancers told me over the telephone. The fired principal, who is highly sensitive and temperamental, had a long-standing conflict with a coach, he used to tell me. The coach kept insulting him, saying that he could not dance, which hurt him deeply. Their conflict had grown worse during rehearsals for a revival of a classic piece, until it reached a point when the principal lost his contract 'with immediate effect'. He later joined another company as a principal dancer.

In Stockholm, the system with permanent contracts is regarded by many dancers as a nuisance that has to be accepted, since it means that they all enjoy some security if they get injured or pregnant and have to stop dancing for a while.

During the 1994–5 season, eight of the forty-eight women at the Royal Swedish Ballet became pregnant, some of the pregnancies being unplanned. This is, however, an unusually high number in a ballet company, not least in the light of the knowledge that very few women dancers are able to recover their fitness completely after having had a child, especially if they are over thirty years old. One of the women at the Royal Swedish Ballet who became pregnant was a principal dancer, and since another one already was on maternity leave and a third one was injured, the ballet director was left with only two women principals. Corps de ballet dancers and soloists were thus given opportunities that they would normally not have had at that phase in their career, and perhaps never at all. The situation became further complicated by the fact that a woman dancer who was on leave had a male partner who was not fitted in body type and temperament to dance with any of the other women in the company. He thus had to wait for his partner to come back before he could get his career going again. Meanwhile, a new team had to be created.

In Sweden new parents can share the paid twelve months of parental leave between the two of them. Since four of the eight female dancers who bore children at the Royal Swedish Ballet were married to or were living together with male dancers in the company, the ballet management had to deal not only with one woman after another taking maternity leave, but subsequently with one man after another taking paternity leave.

At the Royal Swedish Ballet, dancers furthermore have a legal right to be on unpaid leave for altogether three years to study or to take up another job. The union and a jury of dancers' representatives have a say about appointments – although each side tends to emphasize the other's power. There are unions at the British Royal Ballet, the American Ballet Theatre and Ballett Frankfurt, as well. All unions engage in debates over working hours, especially when guest choreographers come and demand longer working hours than what is stated in the dancers' contracts. This has happened in Stockholm, London and New York. The unions can influence salaries, which for instance may be called for on tours because of the longer working hours, or when something out of the ordinary takes place, as when the British Royal Ballet was being filmed performing *The Sleeping Beauty* for broadcast by the BBC. The American Ballet Theatre had to struggle with periods of lay-off when the dancers were paid through unemployment benefits.

Marketing Ballet

The relationships between ballet and the market are considered to be uneasy in the ballet world for a number of reasons. First of all, there is a belief that the market wants to buy other 'commodities' than the ballet world is prepared to sell. It is the general anxiety among artists at having to adjust to the market in order to make it. From the dancers' point of view the commodity in this transaction ought to consist of an excellent performance, while for 'the buyers', i.e. the audience, the cultural milieux of gilded opera foyers with thick carpets and the opportunity to rub shoulders with famous people in the intermissions may be what matters.

Sociologist Joseph Bensman (1983: 27) states that 'the familiar devils of economics' have always been around in the performing arts. Bensman points at how the church, the aristocracy, the dynastic and the national states all supported the performing arts as means to further their own religious, political and national agendas. In the twentieth century, even the welfare state's contributions to the performing arts are in line with its political intentions. Writing about the process of the autonomization of the artist in the article 'The Market of Symbolic Goods', Pierre Bourdieu (1993) argues that with the establishment of an art market, artists were freed of the dependency on patrons; which, however, was replaced by a yielding to commercial demands.

In Haskell and Teichgraeber's (1995) comprehensive edited volume *The Culture of the Market*, forms of 'high culture' such as art and literature are depicted as relating to the market by way of ambivalence and conflict. In spite of the widespread deprecation of ballet in the market-place among the dancers, I often heard classical dancers (not the Frankfurt dancers) complain that the marketing of their company was inefficient. The dancers had all kinds of suggestions to enhance the accessibility of the company and make it more known to a wider audience, from broadcasting sequences of upcoming performances on television, to selling tickets at low prices to tourists at hotels, and performing and lecturing (so-called 'lecture-demonstrations') in schools. Some of this had in fact been done by the companies. The marketing departments tended to refer to lack of money and personnel when they were confronted with ideas they did not work with at the moment. At the American Ballet Theatre, the marketing department described its marketing as 'aggressive'. This did not only entail large, illustrated newspaper articles and advertisements, posters in town, and features in breakfast shows or culture programmes on television and radio, especially before premières and tours and at the start of a new season, but also gimmicks like having famous dancers dance on a canvas and then selling it as a painting. Once when the company was on tour in Chicago, some of the dancers were filmed for local television as they were dancing the swans from *Swan Lake* in front of real swans at the Zoo. Much of the marketing of the American Ballet Theatre was undertaken with the competing ballet company, the New York City Ballet, in mind. This competition reaches its peak every spring when the American Ballet Theatre performs at the Metropolitan Opera House ('the Met Season') for eight weeks, across the plaza from New York City Ballet's State Theater at Lincoln Center.

As a part of schemes to attract new audiences to classical ballet, dancers from the American Ballet Theatre have performed on a cruise, the British Royal Ballet in a shopping mall in an inner-city area of London, and the Royal Swedish Ballet in a department store in Stockholm.

When French star dancer Sylvie Guillem does her famous trick of lifting her leg very high in advertisements for Rolex watches in national and international magazines and newspapers that say that it looks like 'six o'clock', she promotes herself, not her company. There may be a tension between the marketing of individual dancers on the one hand and the whole company on the other. Marketing by the company goes with casting, but some successful dancers become quite skilled at marketing themselves. This contributes at the same time to making ballet more known in general. Those dancers who are in transnational demand for guest performances, or even want to be available for openings in other companies, get agents that look for opportunities for them. It is common for famous dancers to establish their own relationships with the media by giving out free tickets and invitations to dress rehearsals, receptions, dinners, and even weddings and other social functions outside the immediate realm of the theatre.

Otherwise, it is the staff in marketing departments that are in charge of the company's public relations, national and transnational. There are usually at least one press officer and one or two people who work with marketing. They arrange press conferences, write and send out press releases and advertisements both to national media and international dance magazines, and contact journalists when they need an advance feature article or a promotion article on a certain dancer that the ballet management wants to launch. Marketing departments see to it that videos of the company, and postcards, t-shirts, cups, bags, umbrellas, jewellery and so on displaying the name of the company (and recent tours) are sold at box offices and at stalls in the foyer during intermissions. In London and New York, where there is still a cult of star dancers,[21] signed pointe-shoes (worn by famous dancers and then signed by them), are also for sale.[22] Videos of the company and of individual dancers are sent to other companies abroad as a way of promoting them for visits and tours.

In Stockholm the marketing department at the Royal Swedish Ballet is striving to widen the audience classwise. This stems from conscious efforts towards cultural democratization (cf. DiMaggio and Useem 1983), in this case generally inspired by the radical ideology of the 1960s and more specifically by a resolution of the Swedish Parliament in 1974 requiring that the Royal Opera House in Stockholm (that is the Royal Swedish Opera Company and the Royal Swedish Ballet) 'make culture accessible for all citizens irrespective of age, home locality, income or social position'. It was also pointed out that 'commercial considerations were not to control what was being offered' (Sandström 1993: 2).

According to Bourdieu's (1993) discussion in 'The Market of Symbolic Goods', the marketing department at the Royal Swedish Ballet, but also that at the American Ballet Theatre, are thus aiming at marketing ballet out of its field of restricted production to the field of large-scale production. Applying his concept of consecration (distinctive legitimization), Bourdieu (1993: 120–5) separates the two of them: the field of restricted production is recognized by the cultural élite, and hence more prestigious than the field of large-scale production that gives in to the demands of the market. This does not mean that the field of restricted production is independent of a market: its market is just a different, smaller one. At Ballett Frankfurt, where William Forsythe attracts a young avant-garde or alternative following, the contemporary ballets are also a kind of restricted productions, albeit of another type and taste than classical ballets.

At Covent Garden in London, there are a few special performances each season with inexpensive tickets. Some are matinées for school classes, which happen all over the ballet world now and then. Other performances are 'low price performances for low income groups only', it says in the information booklet. This may be an honest attempt at drawing new audiences to ballet at Covent Garden; but the question remains whether it is all that efficient. Does not this designation in fact increase the intimidation of the people who cannot afford regular performances, when they come to the palace-like Covent Garden? Performances for 'low-income citizens' seem more like a concession to the idea of cultural democratization than a feasible way to broaden the class background of the regular audience at Covent Garden. The inexpensive performances are, however, rather a consequence of the rigid British class system than a conscious strategy by the management at Covent Garden to cement the notion of élitism there.

In New York there is an elaborate informal ticket economy. The Theater Development Fund and other agencies sell tickets at lower prices than the box offices, and outside the New York State Theater at Lincoln Center ballet tickets are sold from person to person during the day of a performance and before it starts.[23]

The system with private and corporate sponsors and donors is most extensive in New York and London, where there are hundreds of them. It is far less developed in Frankfurt, and least important in Stockholm. Yet tours, guest performances, programmes, certain ballet productions and scholarships for dancers to train and work abroad are made possible through sponsoring by business corporations that make and sell all kinds of commodities, from cigarettes and matches to automobiles, cosmetics and designer fashion. Pharmaceutical appliances and breweries have also taken an interest in tax-deductible ballet sponsoring. In return for their support, the corporations get free tickets, free usage of boxes in the opera houses, and access to dress rehearsals and receptions where dancers are present. The names of private and corporate sponsors are to be found in long lists and advertisements in the programmes of the productions, and the names of the corporations and private donors who have donated the largest sums of money are displayed on brass plates in the foyers of the opera houses.

Although private donors who give substantial sums of money to a company are treated with much respect in the ballet world, representatives of sponsoring corporations may not fare equally well. It is, again, the artists' unease with economics that surfaces. This is illustrated by the following piece of elevator ethnography from backstage:

The elevator was crammed with still sleepy dancers, dressed in layers of more or less rugged dance wear on their way to morning class. As the elevator stopped at a floor above the one we were heading for, the doors opened and we saw three formally dressed ladies in their fifties. They gazed uncomfortably at the crowded elevator, realizing that there was no room for them.

One of the male dancers then said with a provocative tone of voice: 'Good morning, girls! Welcome to the ballet!' The doors closed in front of the slightly confused ladies. In the elevator, the dancers were shrieking with laughter. Stimulated by the exhilarated reaction, the male dancer continued: 'They haven't been called girls for a very long time. They are our sponsors. I've been licking both here and there!'

This had clearly had been successful, since I had overheard the ladies saying to each other the evening before that they had found the dancers really nice, in particular this male dancer. To address these middle-aged ladies with the term 'girls' was a way of symbolically reducing the power of the market. The comment (which could be interpreted as sexist and ageist) also referred to the infantilizing custom of calling women dancers, especially corps de ballet dancers, 'girls' (and the men consequently 'boys') that still lingers on in the classical ballet world.

Marketing is important for ballet, since it provides opportunities for dancing as well as recognition. And this is understood by the ballet world. Yet there is still a mistrust of ballet in the market-place. This unease was most obvious in Sweden, where many dance commentators and practitioners, in line with the national system of state subsidies, expressed an ideological resistance against marketing ballet. It surfaced occasionally in Germany at the contemporary avant-garde company Ballett Frankfurt, but even more rarely at the national classical companies in Britain and the United States. At the same time as dancers would like to widen the class backgrounds of their audiences, they are hesitant about moving into an artistic field of large-scale production (Bourdieu 1993), where commercial considerations control repertory, appointments and casting. Ballet companies may be reluctant to be associated with business corporations that are suspected of polluting the environment, making unhealthy products or exploiting their employees. The crucial dilemma for ballet companies, however, is that they are dependent on philanthropic and corporate sponsoring for their existence. This is also true of the state-subsidized companies. They just do not get sufficient funding from their states or municipalities. Yet there are ways of managing the market for ballet companies, coping with it, and even using it, and without succumbing to it. There is a certain degree of acting when a ballet management promotes its company, and when dancers are behaving well with sponsors and journalists. There are dancers who were not equipped with cultural capital from their homes when they came to the ballet world, but who acquire some with time. Dancers know how to perform promotion, or they will be taught how to do it; but the point is that they do not really enjoy doing it. In fact, they tend to prefer to be dancing in the studio or on stage.

Notes

1. Cf. Appadurai (1988), Gupta and Ferguson (1992) and Hannerz (1992, 1996).

2. For other applications of Becker's (1984) concept of art worlds, see Ericson (1988) on painters in the Stockholm art world, Finnegan (1989) on local musicians in an English town, and Lagercrantz (1995) on actors in the Stockholm theatre world.

3. At the Paris Opéra Ballet the top dancers are awarded the title *étoile*.

4. It is regarded as desirable in the ballet world to use pianists who play the music, and not tapes, especially for studio rehearsals, since a piece of taped music sounds the same every time, whereas a pianist cannot but play slightly different versions of the same piece of music. If dancers rehearse to a tape there is a risk that they adjust their dancing to the taped version, from which the live orchestra in performance will differ.

5. In an early statement of the anthropology of dance, Joann Kealiinohomoku (1983 [1970]) endorses the view that ballet is a form of ethnic dance, since it reflects Western cultural traditions. As interesting as this idea seems, it does not make up for the fact that Western cultural traditions are quite fragmented by subcultures, class, gender, and ethnic and national identities that are closer to folk dance or popular dance than to classical ballet. After all, taken together few Westerners have been in contact with or care about classical ballet.

6. Hanna (1988) and Novack (1993) analyse class and gender in ballet, whereas Sherlock (1993) deals with class and gender in contemporary dance. Burt (1995) discusses gender in ballet and dance, in particular masculinity. Foster (1996c) is a gendered reading of ballet history.

7. Except for a few indicated references, this section is based on Cass (1993).

8. The conventional spelling of the name of this choreographer is Balthasar de Beaujoyeulx. Cass (1993) spells his last name Beaujoyeux.

9. One aspect of Romanticism in the arts that has an anthropological twist was a fascination with exotic themes and characters that occasionally appeared in the ballets. The Austrian Fanny Elssler danced the *cachucha*, a Spanish character variation, in Paris. In the early twentieth century the Russian Michel Fokine, one of the choreographers of the Ballets Russes, created *Sheherazade* around a harem woman who betrays her sheik with a slave. And back in St Petersburg in the late nineteenth century, *La Bayadère*, by Marius Petipa world premièred. *The Nutcracker*, which was also created during this period, includes Spanish, Arabian and Chinese sections (Cass 1993).

10. This obviously does not apply to contemporary productions of *Swan Lake*, even though they contain choreographic, narrative and musical references to the classical production. The Swedish choreographer Mats Ek created his version of *Swan Lake* for the Cullberg Ballet, and more recently, in 1995, Matthew Bourne presented his interpretation danced by Adventures in Motion Pictures in London. Incidentally, both productions feature male (barefoot) swans.

11. The very first time ballet was performed in Cuba was, however, when Fanny Elssler danced there in the mid-nineteenth century. Almost a century later, a ballet

class was formed, training a number of dancers who won recognition at international competitions. With the revolution in 1959, ballet has gained an even larger audience (Koegler 1987).

12. Discussing the musical construction of place, Martin Stokes (1994) connects national musical styles with ideological control over conservatories, archives and the media in modernizing states. Within such systems music and dance are being used as political resistance. Classical ballet is seldom associated with political resistance, although the court ballets from the late sixteenth century and early seventeenth century contained political references (Olsson 1993). When Antony Tudor was ballet director of the Royal Swedish Ballet, he created *Echoing of Trumpets* in 1963 for the company. It is an anti-war drama about a Czech village that is destroyed by the Nazis (Skeaping and Ståhle 1979). *Echoing of Trumpets* seems to show how things turned out after the warning of early Nazism in Germany that the choreographer Kurt Joos delivered in 1932 through his famous piece *The Green Table* (Cass 1993). See also Wulff (1998) on politicized dance in Israel.

13. See Guilbault (1983 quoted in Born 1995) on the rise of abstract expressionism in postwar national American painting as a part of the modernist movement. This painting style coincided in fact with Balanchine's abstract ballet style.

14. Taking the idea of the male gaze in feminist film theory as a point of departure, Ann Daly (1987) pictures 'the Balanchine woman' as in the centre yet subordinated by the male (heterosexual) gaze. For a critique of this argument see for instance Jordan and Thomas (1994). Foster (1996c), Thomas (1996) and Manning (1997) develop gaze theory in dance further. See Arlene Croce's (1977) 'Balanchine's Girls: The Making of a Style' for a review essay on the American ballet style.

15. How then can the corps de ballet, at least sometimes, form straight lines? When they are not dancing, the corps de ballet are dissolved into a multitude of body shapes, heights, and individual movement patterns. In the ballet world, straight lines in ballet are credited to schooling and skilled coaches who have trained this mass of unlike people with varying musical talents to listen to the particular score for a ballet similarly enough to make them move 'like one body'.

16. See Näslund (1995) on how this ballet had an international breakthrough at its première with American Ballet Theatre at the old Metropolitan Opera House in New York in 1958.

17. This concept was coined by Pierre Bourdieu and Jean-Claude Passeron (1977: 30), meaning 'the cultural goods transmitted by the different family PAs (pedagogical actions), whose value qua cultural capital varies with the distance between the cultural arbitrary imposed by the dominant PA and the cultural arbitrary inculcated by the family PA within the different groups or classes'. In *Distinction*, Bourdieu (1984) develops the concept, identifying cultural capital as a form of knowledge, a code or a consumption competence that is applied consciously and unconsciously in relation to culture and the arts.

18. On a desk at the office of the Royal Ballet in London, I saw a card with a quotation from Queen Victoria that illuminates one aspect of the scope of social class in the ballet world:

'Beware of artists
they mix with
all classes
of society
and are therefore
dangerous.'

19. According to Leach (1997) short-term contracts, often for one production only, force many dancers to live on unemployment benefits periodically or even take up jobs outside the dance world occasionally. On the whole, the longer working hours per week, the physical strain and the relatively few financially productive years of dancers are not remunerated in salary or pension.

20. The salaries differed between the companies, reflecting national union laws and salary politics. The Swedish corps de ballet dancers thus had higher salaries than their colleagues abroad, whereas the Swedish principals had lower salaries compared to other principals, let alone stars of world fame. Some companies moreover paid their dancers twelve months per year, whereas other companies paid just for the weeks of the seasons, which could be about half the year in some cases. Those dancers who could, took up other jobs or offers during such periods of lay-offs or holidays. In 1993–6 corps de ballet dancers earned from $400 to $1,048 per week and soloists from $1,125 to $1,200 per month, and the salaries of principals ranged from $1,500 per month to $2,560 per week. Famous principals could also be paid sums like $30,000 for a couple of guest performances with another company. Dancers who got offers from other companies were moreover able to raise their salaries on the assumption that they would stay with their own company. Their salaries were yet far away from 'the six-digit incomes' in $US that Hanna (1988: 143) mentions as a result of the postwar dance boom, culminating with Mikhail Baryshnikov and Rudolf Nureyev making astronomical sums of money. When Rudolf Nureyev died, the New York estate of his immense fortune was sold at Christie's at $7,945,910 (Gladstone 1995: 21).

21. Mostly because of the constant risk of injuries, recorded messages with up-dated information about the casting of leading roles are provided at Covent Garden. This is a service to the audience, in particular balletomanes, who often go to performances in order to watch a particular dancer.

22. In an essay on balletomania, dance historian Walter Sorell (1981) brings up an anecdote about a Russian balletomane who paid 200 roubles for a pair of Marie Taglioni's ballet shoes in 1842. They were then cooked and served at a gala dinner honouring Taglioni, who was leaving for France.

23. During my field study, regular prices for ballet tickets at the Royal Opera House in Stockholm ranged from $1.50 to $21, at Covent Garden in London from $3.20 to $96, at the Metropolitan Opera House in New York from $18 to $110, and at the opera house in Frankfurt-am-Main from $18 to $93. It should be pointed out that the inexpensive seats usually entailed a restricted distanced view of the stage, or standing. There were also various discounts for children, students, pensioners,

and members of ballet societies, as well as seasonal subscriptions and stand-by tickets at half price one hour before performances. Discounts did not usually include premières and performances featuring famous guest dancers; however, such special performances were in fact often more expensive than other performances. At galas the prices rose to hundreds of dollars.

Work as Vocation

A ballet career starts with an audition at a company and runs via débuts and breakthroughs to ageing and finally early retirement. In this chapter, the course of transnational ballet careers is traced. Coaching and choreographing relationships, including creativity blocks when the rehearsal process seems to go nowhere, are also acknowledged, as is the occurrence of dancers' agency in rehearsal and performance. A point is made about the prevalence of camaraderie despite the fact that the ballet world is structured by competition. One aspect of this is constant and frequent *peer-coaching*, dancers helping each other to remember steps and solve technical problems about spacing and timing on stage.

It takes a long time to acquire the skills that are needed during the short career, about twenty years, of a professional ballet dancer. Ballet is usually learnt from about the age of ten, and in contrast to most of their contemporaries outside the ballet world, ballet students are already beginning a vocational training as children.[1] The fact that ballet is non-verbal raises the question of how it actually is learnt, not least since most teachers and coaches are too old to demonstrate the steps. The social nature of learning ballet is thus explored analytically.

Learning Ballet and Decorum

Skills can be said to be learnt through mimesis or paraphrase, that is a servile striving to duplicate the model versus a more innovative imitation (cf. Edelman 1997: 170).[2] Leaving the classical debate as to whether total mimesis is possible aside, I would even question whether it is desired in the arts. To dance 'like Nureyev' or 'like Fonteyn' is considered to be very good, but not good enough, since a certain originality is also required. And of course, no one dances *exactly* like Nureyev or Fonteyn: that is the other point here. On top of national and choreographic styles, every dancer dances in a unique way.

Since ballet is learnt little by little during such a long period of time, almost ten years, learning through mimesis or paraphrase can be detected with girls as well as boys, but does not really become an issue until ballet students are accepted into a ballet company as young adults. For this is when some originality on the part of soloists will be rewarded, as long as the tradition the young dancers were trained in comes across. There is also a truth in the idea that in order to experiment – to develop into an acclaimed dancer with a personal style – one has to master some basic skills that are internalized more by way of duplication than of creation. Master–apprentice relationships have been abolished in many lines of work, in favour of what are construed as postions of equality between teacher and student, despite the fact that there is a structural hierarchy built into the teaching situation: the teacher knows more than the student. (This does not legitimize bullying, which was a common cause of complaint among ballet students about some of their teachers.)

Master–apprentice relationships are still accepted and even favoured in the arts (cf. Gardner 1993; John-Steiner 1985). In the ballet world, it is considered an important part of a dancer's reputation to have been trained by a distinguished teacher or coach – especially when this particular training is obvious in his or her dancing.

Jean Lave and Etienne Wenger (1995) have analysed how learning happens. Their account is not intended as a programme for teaching, but rather as an explanation of learning as a social activity with agency. Stating that 'learning is a process that takes place in a participation framework, not in an individual mind' (1995: 15), they stress the social nature of learning. It occurs in a community of practitioners where the learner is peripheral at first, but slowly moves towards the centre. Ballet students thus learn ballet by watching ballet performances and by taking part in them dancing children's roles. They also watch ballet video, read ballet and dance magazines, and even more importantly, talk to adult dancers that they not seldom are related to or know personally through family networks. Lave and Wenger (1995) bring up stories and community lore in learning as one way of talking about a practice, whereas talking within a practice involves exchanging information about immediate goings-on.

Lave and Wenger argue against the notion that verbal explanation precedes demonstration. There is an obvious gap between the verbal description of a combination of steps and the steps' being executed – something gets lost on the way. Yet in class, while the teacher is instructing the ballet students verbally and bodily and giving them 'corrections', as it is called when a step does not look the way it is supposed to look – it is often a student's friend who sorts out the mistakes for him or her, or else they figure out a step together. This is the beginning of peer-coaching and a camaraderie that structures a lot of ballet culture. Lave and Wenger seem to have thought along these lines when they discuss apprenticeships and claim that 'apprentices learn mostly in relation with other apprentices' (1995: 93).

The crucial aim of education, according to Larry Gross (1973), is to acquire symbolic competence. He goes on to state that this is accomplished in large part through direct experience, which connects to Lave's and Wenger's (1995) discussion about the social character of learning. Gross identifies different kinds of modes of symbolic behaviour (primary, derived and technical, of which dance is a derived mode) that cannot be satisfactory translated into other modes; an elaborate physical gesture or a Bach fugue thus cannot really be verbalized.

A common way to try to bridge the gap between dancing and the verbalization of dancing is the use of onomatopoeic words in ballet teaching and coaching. English-speaking teachers often say 'Eeeeeeee . . .' when the music starts, in order to get the dancers into the rhythm. 'Dadada!', 'scubidoo!' or 'diggedi-do!' I have heard for counting the beat. When dancers do *arabesques*, for example, it is hard to stay in the position, but since it is regarded as desirable to stay as long as possible, the teacher may encourage dancers who 'stand in *arabesque*' (as the expression is) to 'stay, stay, stay!' Another frequent verbal formulation about an *arabesque* is the call: 'You grow and grow in the *arabesque*! You grow indefinitely!' This refers to the visual experience of an *arabesque*: a good *arabesque* looks as if the lines from the hands and the foot that are in the air continue beyond the actual limbs.

In teaching, but also in coaching, there is a widespread use of metaphors, more or less idiosyncratic. 'Straighten your back!' may thus be achieved by 'Be like a pencil!' or 'As if your head is drawn upwards by an invisible string!' A dancer can find the balance in a jump through the instruction 'Go up! Be an elevator!' The injunctions 'Use the floor!' or 'Push the floor!' may be a way for the dancer to find the right speed for a jump or a turn. Terms like 'inside leg', 'outside leg', 'back leg', 'front arm' and 'supporting leg' signify where the legs and the arms are supposed to be in relation to the rest of the body or the step, and where the centre of gravity in the body should be in order to achieve this.

What is more, in comparison with other educational situations, there is a unique and complicating feature of teaching and coaching ballet: because of age, a ballet teacher, a coach, or a choreographer is (in most cases) unable to demonstrate the steps the way he or she would like them to look. The teacher or choreographer has a mental picture, a memory if they are basic ballet steps, of what they are supposed to look like – but is unable to execute them in that way. Nor can he or she, again, verbalize them completely. Ballet is thus learnt to a great extent through being in the ballet world, through watching others dance and processing this information together with other ballet students.

As ballet students gradually learn the about two hundred steps of classical ballet, they are simultaneously socialized into ballet culture, not least into a decorum that calls for a certain politeness involving, for example, frequent thanking and apologizing. This is a heritage from the time when ballet was thriving at European courts; but it may also be seen as a way to make things run more smoothly in a setting where people work very close to each other. This decorum has probably persisted in the everyday life in the ballet world out of sheer necessity: dancers are often skin-to-skin when they dance. Backstage facilities, from dressing-rooms and green rooms to cafeterias are (with some exceptions) surprisingly crowded places, not only in old European opera houses, but also in many newer theatres in Europe and in the United States. The graceful posture of a ballet dancer, with a straight back, lends itself to polite interactions entailing a control of body and movement that comes automatically to a dancer, at least in more or less formal situations.

Not only do teachers and coaches teach ballet students decorum as well as ballet; older students teach younger, and older professional dancers feel responsible for younger dancers in this respect. One of the older women soloists kept telling me about incidents when she was taken to task as a young dancer by the older women dancers for putting her make-up on in the wrong way or using the wrong kinds of ribbons on her pointe shoes in performance.

National Ballet Schools and Transnationality

Dancers often told me that they had been put in a local ballet school as young children 'because I was such a lively kid, moving around all the time'. It was usually their mothers who saw to this and later, often encouraged by the teacher, arranged for their daughters to audition for a national ballet school, that is, to prepare for ballet as a career. The ballet mother is indeed a notion arousing mixed feelings in the ballet world. On the one hand, many dancers who have made it to the top know that they would not have been able to do this without their mothers, who drove them long distances to ballet schools, supported them emotionally and financially, and 'sewed their pointe shoes' (i.e. attached ribbons and in Sweden a small, round crocheted piece to the front of the pointe shoe). When the careers of the dancers finally get going, many of these mothers learn how to handle press relations. Ballet mothers are sometimes said to be frustrated dancers, and/or it is said that they have taken up this obsession with the careers of their daughters because they cannot find anything else to do in life.[3]

Boys often start dancing because their sister is dancing, and they might as well come along – then it turns out that the boy is the more talented. A number of dancers have told me that they demanded to take ballet lessons as small children after having seen a ballet performance or a ballet on television. It is also quite common that physical education teachers discover a dancing talent, and encourage the student to audition at a national ballet school. There are local ballet schools that are informal pre-professional ballet schools. They are considered 'the best ballet schools', and are connected to the national ballet schools through networks of families, friends and colleagues. Ballet masters sometimes teach in both places, for example.

Although the Swedish Ballet School, the Royal Ballet School and the School of American Ballet all declare that their main purpose is to train ballet students for their respective companies, there is only room for one or two new dancers each year. So the vast majority of ballet students when they have finished ballet school, go to other companies (and also to show business) often abroad.

The Swedish Ballet School in Stockholm is located in a spacious, well-lit building across the stretch of water opposite the Royal Opera House where the Royal Swedish Ballet is housed. Most of the dancers who are currently with the Royal Swedish Ballet trained at the Swedish Ballet School.

When King Gustavus III established the Royal Swedish Ballet in 1773, he also founded the Royal Ballet School, which was reorganized into the Swedish Ballet School in 1981. The school then moved from the Royal Opera House to the present building and was integrated into the Swedish school system. There is an interest at the Swedish Ballet School in leaving traditional authoritarian ballet pedagogy behind to try out new methods for healthier training, both mentally and physically.

The Swedish Ballet School accepts students from the age of ten. They can stay for six years, but they are assessed once a year, and some are recommended to quit 'since they may have developed physically in such a way that they may harm their bodies if they continue to practise'. This is in fact the most productive explanation I heard in the ballet world, much more useful for a young ballet student who loves to dance than to be told that he or she 'is not good enough', which is the conventional way of getting rid of ballet students. At the Swedish Ballet School there is a new audition for the next three years of senior high school and a choice of a classical or a modern programme. The director of the school told me that they look for 'inner fire and a feel for dance, movement and musicality' when students audition. In order to get funding from the municipality the school has to fill every class with thirty students, whether there are thirty students that they consider suitable for dancing or not. Of 231 students, about one-third are boys. There is a small number of non-white students.

I watched a girls' class on my visit to the Swedish Ballet School. Fifteen older teenage girls (eighteen-years-old) were doing barre exercises, all except one wearing their hair held together in a bun at the back of the head. Only one of them was wearing a navy-coloured leotard; the others were all in black leotards, skin-coloured tights and white ballet shoes. But since they were wearing all kinds of legwarmers, trousers and sweaters over their leotards, especially at the beginning of the class before they got warm, the leotards did still did not give a particularly uniform impression. The teacher was warm and encouraging. She gave corrections in a positive tone of voice. The girls worked very hard.

The Royal Ballet School in London is divided into the Lower School, located in White Lodge in Richmond Park, for children between eleven and sixteen years of age, and the Upper School, for students of the ages of sixteen and over, sharing studios with the Royal Ballet at Barons Court. In 1955, the royal hunting lodge, White Lodge, originating from 1727, was acquired as a boarding school for the younger students.

In 1995 there were altogether 237 ballet students at the Royal Ballet School. The majority, 161, were girls. Few were non-white. In a brochure giving information about the Royal Ballet School (undated: p.39) it says: 'Graduates from the Upper School enter many ballet companies in Britain and Europe but the main purpose of the School – the reason for its existence – is to provide dancers for the two Royal Ballet Companies. With very few exceptions, the soloists and Corps de Ballet of The Royal Ballet and Birmingham Royal Ballet (formerly Sadler's Wells Royal Ballet) are ex-students from the Royal Ballet School. Students from European Community countries may graduate from the School into the Companies, as may students with outstanding talent from non-EC countries.'

This can be seen as one transnational feature; another is guest teachers from foreign international ballet companies who come and teach class. There are also exchange programmes of students with the Paris Opéra School, the Royal Danish Ballet School and the Beijing Dance Academy. The 'Search for Talent Programme' looks for new students not only in the United Kingdom but 'throughout the world', according to the aims of the Royal Ballet School that are presented in the *Annual Report* (1992–3: 1). Another aim of the Royal Ballet School is said to be to 'Maintain its standing as a world-class centre of excellence'.

In all this there is a transnational awareness of the rest of the ballet world (except of the United States) and with a self-identification of itself as constituting a ballet centre.

I heard many stories from dancers and coaches about the Royal Ballet School long before I visited it, or ventured into classes at Barons Court.

Without my having asked about it, dancers told me about boarding-school pranks, such as a group of boys stealing beer from a locked cupboard and getting drunk. Since the students were not allowed to leave the premises without permission, it was exciting to try to get out, and then run to a nearby off-licence to buy cigarettes. But also young women dancers remembered that 'we had such fun!' smoking on the roof in the middle of the night and 'baking' on the roof in the spring sun instead of studying for O-levels.

There was a definite consensus that those few who were fortunate enough to have been the favourites of the teachers were doing fine, while others had often been deeply hurt by the traditional ballet pedagogy, with its characteristic elements of humiliation. 'They break them down in order to build the kind of dancer they want here', a coach at the Royal Ballet Company told me.

One of the dancers, a woman soloist, talked about the colours of the 'ballet uniforms', as they are called in Britain (where many schoolchildren still wear school uniform, cf. Wulff 1988). The girls at White Lodge thus wear leotards (pink for the youngest, then light blue, dark blue, cerise, and black) and the boys (black) tights and (white) t-shirts. All students in one year wear the same colour, but different years have different colours. Incidentally, this colour system is on the whole transnational.

Many of the social and pedagogical hardships of White Lodge can be attributed to British boarding-school culture in general, rather than to this place in particular.

One steaming hot May day I was approaching White Lodge in the minibus that runs from the rehearsal studios of the Royal Ballet and the Upper School at Barons Court. As we rode through the serene Richmond Park we passed a group of deer lying in the shade under a big tree. The road narrowed down into a small winding track leading up to the white manor house, flanked by its two wings.

In the entrance hall, just inside the entrance door, there was a life-size bronze statue of Margot Fonteyn in a tutu. One of the teachers showed me that one of 'Fonteyn's fingers was all shiny, because the students 'touch it for luck' in order to acquire some of her dancing powers. The statue used to stand in the corner, but had been moved, in order to keep it out of the students' reach. But they continued to touch it when they passed it.

There was an atmosphere of the great château inside White Lodge, with very high ceilings and huge old oil paintings. A Ballet Museum displaying photographs, newspaper clippings, books, pointe shoes and a bronze head of Rudolf Nureyev manifested the glorious heritage of the Royal Ballet.

I was taken to watch second-year girls do class in the Ashton studio. Nineteen eleven-year-olds, with their hair in a bun, dressed in light blue leotards, pink tights and pink ballet shoes, were taught by a severe woman, accompanied by piano music. The teacher sometimes went out among the girls and pushed and pulled legs and arms to make them look as she wanted them to. As she pulled an arm, she tried to get the girl to look at herself in the mirror. The teacher was nagging: 'You don't want to, you want to . . .', and shouted 'Good!' now and then, addressing one girl after another. Corrections were followed by encouragement – not always for the same girl, however. The class was finished with a *révérence*, a curtsy to an imagined audience, practising thanking for the applause in a curtain call. For now the girls applauded the teacher.

Later I watched a boys' class. They were also eleven years old and dressed in white t-shirts, black tights, white socks, and white ballet shoes. Their hair was cut short. The Russian teacher, a man, was sitting on a high stool, blustering. He kept up a negative tone all along, picking on one boy after another. One boy turned away, blushing. 'If you want to stay here, you have to learn to hold your arm like this!', he threatened another boy.

Once a year there is an assessment of the students' dancing, and some are 'assessed out' because they have not developed in line with the ideal of an English classical dancer.

The School of American Ballet in New York was set up in 1934 by Lincoln Kirstein and George Balanchine 'for the purpose of establishing an American school for classical ballet . . . The second but no less immediate goal was the establishment of a permanent ballet company that would employ the school's young professionals to dance in a new and growing repertory' (Lassalle and Burgess 1995: 5). In the information brochure about the School of American Ballet it says further: 'Balanchine extended the classical vocabulary forged in 19th century Russia by Marius Petipa and developed a new classicism with a deeply American character which became internationally recognized for its superior speed, clarity and musicality' (ibid.). Further on the school positions itself in the transnational ballet world by stating: 'As one of the foremost conservatories of classical dance in the world, SAB produces dancers for virtually all of the leading ballet companies in the United States, as well as elsewhere.'

There are, I was told by the executive director, about 350 students at the School of American Ballet, and among these approximately 265 are girls. There is a more prominent element of non-white students at the School of American Ballet than at the Royal Ballet School or the Swedish Ballet School; but the main impression is still that of white students, despite the multi-culturality of American society.

The School of American Ballet is housed high up in one of the skyscrapers in Lincoln Center, next door to the Metropolitan Opera House and across the plaza from the New York State Theater. I passed by a receptionist and a guard on the ground floor and took the lift to the fifth floor, where the studios are located. There was another reception area and wide, well-lit corridors with framed pictures of Balanchine and ballet history events; I noted as I walked along lines of boys in black tights and white t-shirts sitting on the floor with their backs to the wall. This building is quite new; it was built in 1991. It was basking in light, which was revelatory. The atmosphere was spotless, almost antiseptic.

I watched a class of seventeen-year-old girls, all dressed in black leotards, skin-coloured tights and pink pointe shoes. The teacher, a famous ex-Balanchine ballerina, conducted the class softly to Chopin waltzes that the pianist played. These girls were already disciplined. They were struggling, every one of them, in their still unripe steps.

Later, one of the girls took me to her dorm, even higher up in the building. We passed two receptions, a guard and a gate. There was a magnificent view of the Upper West Side of Manhattan from the small room that the girl was sharing with another girl. My informant told me that they hardly ever went out – only to watch the company perform at the New York State Theater. The walls in the room were filled with ballet pictures, newspaper cuttings of idols like Mikhail Baryshnikov, and photographs of the girls from a Bolshoi summer camp and when they had been performing Balanchine's *Serenade*. There was an ascetic living-room next door where all the girls who were living on this floor watch ballet video.

When I left the quiet, ordered building, I was struck by the contrast of the bursting ethnic mixture just outside in the street.

The School of American Ballet and the Royal Ballet School still cultivate their respective ballet styles, Balanchine and the English style. At the Swedish Ballet School, the students are mostly taught the Russian style, the Vaganova. And some of the American students went to the Bolshoi summer camp. Russian styles also influenced the teaching at the Royal Ballet School, however, not least through Russian teachers there. To this transnational feature is added the fact that, just like professional dancers, ballet students go abroad in the summers to practise with famous teachers.

Both at the Royal Swedish Ballet and at the American Ballet Theatre new corps de ballet dancers told me that they had been horrified at 'the lack of order' when they first came to the company straight from the school. It was the 'bad manners and disorderly dressing in class' that had shocked them the most. On other occasions established dancers spoke about the lack of respect among the ballet students who take part in performances: 'we were taught respect as children; now they use the elevator, we were not allowed to do that', 'now they go through steps on stage – we had to do it in the studio'. Older dancers came back to the fact that they thought that young dancers did not show the same kind of respect to them as they did to older dancers when they were young.

Company Class: The Necessary Routine

When dancers inform people outside the ballet world that they are dancers, they still meet the questions 'But what is your real job?' or 'What do you do during the day?' The career of ballet dancers relies on the daily work in the studio, where dancers spend most of their time 'taking class' every morning and in rehearsal in the afternoon. I encountered an awareness, among both ballet managements and dancers in all four companies, that taking class regularly is both crucial and hard for a dancer. There is a saying in the older generation in the ballet world about the necessity of practising and especially taking class every day for a dancer:

> 'If you miss class once
> you will notice.
> If you miss class twice
> your colleagues (or teacher) will notice.
> If you miss class three times
> the audience will notice.'

There are various means of control meant to help dancers do their daily training, such as having them tick off their names on a list (or having a secretary do it) and punishments such as written warnings if the dancers fail to show up often enough (less than four days a week) and even the risk of getting fired. Still, there are dancers who enjoy taking class, who like the secure routine of it: some talk about it in terms of a 'cleansing'. Retired dancers do not always miss the stage; they may just as well miss taking daily class. I also detected a derogatory idiom, sometimes expressed through jokes, among dancers about colleagues who did not take class as often as they should. Since men and women partly need different training in classical ballet, with men practising strength and stamina for jumps and lifting and women balance for *pirouettes*, for example, separate classes for male and female dancers are still often arranged at classical companies. The dancers tend to go to the teachers they prefer, whether it is a men's or a women's class. This means that one class may become very crowded, and the ballet management then has to ask dancers to stick to the class of their sex unless they are principal dancers. Principals get their own classes in some companies, and are usually allowed to go to any class they want to. Some principal women told me that they preferred to take class with the men, 'since they are less envious'. There is very little competition between the sexes in ballet.

Different teachers, moreover, teach class in different ways, even in the same company; and some teachers change their teaching every week or so. Although most companies have their own teachers, it is also customary that visiting coaches who are appointed to set a ballet should teach class, though famous choreographers who are invited to create a new ballet for the company are not. Ballet directors may take classes as a way to check on how the dancers are doing, or to nurture some of them; and in emergencies, when scheduled teachers are ill.

Here follows an ethnographic case of a 'girls' school' taught by a Russian ballet mistress at the Royal Swedish Ballet. It illustrates the issues of trans-nationality, gender as girlish femininity, discipline and politeness:[4]

The dancers came strolling to the studio carrying bags, handbags, water bottles and pointe shoes. Still sleepy, there was nonetheless an air of determination about most of them, but it was also as if they went on tracks to do this monotonous exercise that they have done almost every day since they were about ten years old. Dressed in dance wear, old leotards or t-shirts[5] and tights under woollen sweaters and plastic trousers, they started warming up at their place by the barre.

In the ballet world, t-shirt, sweatshirts and pants displaying company names are a part of building a sense of community as well as promoting the company. These items are also for public sale at ticket offices and in ballet bookshops. In connection with tours, special t-shirts are made referring to the tour, at first as promotion; but afterwards they become souvenirs that the dancers keep to remember a hard but often happy time. Displaying a t-shirt from a company abroad in class or rehearsal is usually a way to show that the dancer has been with them for shorter or longer periods of time or has friends there. T-shirts with non-company dance motifs, like one saying 'Dance or Die. New York City', were also worn in class and rehearsals. The general implication of t-shirts is that they express cultural meaning: dancers in particular, who are usually so careful with their appearance (not least because they are being judged all the time), do chose what they wear in class and rehearsals according to notions of belonging and identification, sometimes as a critical or ironic commentary.

The ballet mistress, an ex-Bolshoi dancer, arrived and started the class immediately. Her instructions were in a mixture of English, German, Swedish and of course French, for the ballet terms. As she went through the next exercise some of the dancers 'marked it' a little with their hands. Each exercise took between half a minute and one minute, gradually using more muscles. She counted in English: 'One, two! One, two!' The pianist, a Japanese man, also listened in order to know what kind of tempo she needed.

Like many ballet studios, this one was a bit run down, and the acoustics were not very good. The piano music echoed rather harshly between the walls. Two of these were displaying posters of past and present productions (*Swan Lake* and Maurice Béjart's *Rites of Spring*, one of the major successes of the company), and announcements of tours in Paris and Moscow. On a third wall were some old black-and-white framed photographs of acclaimed Swedish dancers. The fourth wall was covered with the mirror, reflecting everyone and everything in the studio all the time.

The dancers were already absorbed in their steps. As the class progressed and they got warmer and started to sweat, they peeled off the warm clothing, putting the garments in a pile under the barre. The ballet mistress thanked them after every set of movements. She kept to a rather fast tempo. As she went up and down the rows of women, she pulled a leg here, and bent an arm there in order to get them to look as she would like them to. She asked one of the women to repeat a movement, while the others were waiting and watching. Pleased, the ballet mistress complimented her: 'Good!'

After about half an hour the ballet mistress asked the women to put the barres away, i.e. the movable ones that had been standing in the middle of the studio, to make room for floor exercises. The women changed to pointe shoes for the *adagios*, slow series of steps, and *pirouettes* in the centre of the studio. And then the dancers lined up in one corner and jumped on a diagonal, one after the other, across the floor.

The class finished after about one hour and fifteen minutes with the *révérence*. The dancers applauded the ballet mistress to thank her, as is customary in the ballet world. Sometimes the teacher applauds the dancers, pointing her or his hands towards the dancers, as a way to thank them for the applause and their work. This polite back and forth clapping reflects the clapping after a performance: first the audience claps, and then the conductor and/or the designers, and the choreographer, or other prominent people like composers or ballet directors, who come on stage are applauded, and thank the audience for the applause. The conductor claps the orchestra, and the choreographer the dancers.

Rehearsal: 'Fill the Music!'

When preliminary casting lists have been posted on the notice-board, the rehearsals start: the corps de ballet learning their variations of steps in one studio, at first without music, and later accompanied by piano music; while the leading dancers learn solos and *pas de deux* for the same acts in a different studio. As the rehearsal progresses, bits of the narrative (if there is a narrative) of the ballet or the kind of feelings that the steps are meant to express are explained verbally by the coach. Some choreographers and coaches go through the story with the dancers, before they begin learning the steps. Copies of summaries of the stories – whether folktales, classical or literary – are sometimes posted on the notice-boards for the dancers to read. Since leading roles are more elaborately portrayed, those dancers who dance leading roles get more narrative coaching as well as dance coaching than individual corps de ballet dancers. After a few weeks, leading dancers and corps de ballet dancers are all put together for a 'full call' in one studio. This is followed by one or more 'stage calls', with some sets, lighting and costumes. A 'full call' on stage was also termed 'tech rehearsal', especially before premières of new productions and for visiting companies in some theatres and opera houses. The instruments and equipment producing the electronic avant-garde music at Ballett Frankfurt usually went through a 'sound check' before performances. At the general rehearsal, 'the general', or 'dress rehearsal', the production is almost complete, with orchestra and conductor also present. There may even be an invited audience of retired dancers, donors, balletomanes, critics and others from the national or transnational ballet élite. A significant difference between general rehearsal and performance is that a general rehearsal may be interrupted by a dancer or the coach if something goes wrong, whereas a performance continues no matter what, except in cases of severe injury (see Chapter 5).

Supporting roles, such as peasants in *Giselle* and courtiers in *The Sleeping Beauty*, found in the background of mass scenes in classical ballets, are not rehearsed in detail. The dancers are just told when they have to move and within what space. They tend to 'act' with their friends on stage, sometimes making up stories in advance, sometimes surprising each other. Some dancers converse according to the plot of the ballet, inventing lines; others talk about different, perhaps personal, matters. This often varies from one evening to the next. 'Extras' are retired corps de ballet dancers or people from other lines of work who come in to perform even more peripheral roles, holding a candlestick or mingling at the back of mass scenes. They do not dance at all.

Rehearsal periods tend to be a process of initial expectation followed by monotony, with elements of chaos and creativity blocks that sooner or later develop into progress, whether it is a new production that is being made up as the choreographers and the dancers go along, or a revival of an old production.

Coaches and Choreographers: 'Speak to Me!'

Coaches, or répétiteurs as the older generation say, are ballet masters or ballet mistresses who rehearse, one could say teach, ballet productions. Since they used to be dancers and have danced the classical ballets themselves, they can make use of their 'muscular memory' of the steps. Prominent ex-dancers do enjoy a lot of respect in the ballet world, both as ballet directors and coaches, which ties in with the distinction between doing ballet and watching ballet (see Chapter 2) and the importance of inside experience in the ballet world. Their experience is held in high regard and cultivated, transferred to younger generations. There is even a custom of bringing in retired dancers (even from abroad) to teach particular roles that were created for them by the choreographer. In big rehearsals there is often more than one coach in the studio, and perhaps a choreologist as well. Unless the pecking order between them has been settled, the dancers may witness a power struggle between the coaches.

It is considered highly prestigious for a dancer to have a 'role created on her (or him)' by a choreographer. Repertory companies like the classical companies usually have one or two resident choreographers, 'house chore-ographers'; but they also invite guest choreographers. Choreographers create, or 'mount' as the term is, new ballets. That is, they make the steps and the concept of the production or the story, if there is one. Choreographers choose the music or commission a composer to write it. If a choreographer does not design the lighting, the set and the costumes, he or she makes the decisions about them.

The relationship between a dancer and his or her coach and the chore-ographer is obviously vital for the outcome of the performance. William Forsythe describes it in terms of 'a pact' between him and his dancers. Mutual trust, respect and an ability to spark each other through continual exchange are the cornerstones in this delicate communication. These relationships often resemble love relationships, and can last over the course of many years, even when the people involved are based in different countries. During the phase of creativity blocks before premières conflicts do occur, however, even in close coaching relationships. These, too, are typically solved.

The intensity of the coach–dancer relationship and the time devoted to it also mean that there is a shortage of coaches; one coach is unable to build close working relationships with more than a few dancers. And even if principal dancers are supposed to get 'private coaching' for leading roles as well as for *pas de deux* sections in major ballets, rapport does not always spring up between coach and dancer. A prominent dancer has influence over the ballet management, and may demand to be given a new coach. If the coach on the other hand is established as a coach and used to be a distinguished dancer, he or she may have the dancer 'taken out of roles' – even, in extreme cases, fired.

There is a notion that 'everyone is important in big ballets', i.e. the corps de ballet and even 'extras' (or 'artists' as they are called at Covent Garden). This is true, at least as far as general impression goes; but not the whole truth, since dancers who perform leading roles and solos clearly get more attention from the audience. Not only do they usually dance during longer stretches of time on stage than the corps de ballet, they are also in focus when something dramatic happens in the narrative (and thus in the choreography and the music as well).

When dancers learn corps work, they are taught that even though they are supposed to 'look alike', dancers in the back row are also visible from the audience. This, dancers in the back row do not seem to believe; nor do dancers in the front row usually understand how exposed they in fact are.

Agency in the Studio and on Stage

There is a notion, even in the ballet world, that classical dancers are oppressed: that they only do what they are told to do. Although I often heard dancers (predominantly corps de ballet dancers) complain over lack of information about the story of ballets and about decision-making in general, I did observe expressions of dancers' agency in the studio and on stage. In rehearsals I saw dancers refuse to do variations of steps that hurt their bodies, or that they just did not like, suggesting changes that were incorporated in the ballet. This occurred in classical as well as in contemporary work. It also happened that dancers argued for changes in the classical ballets that would accentuate a step that they were especially good at, or avoid one that they did not do so well.

At a rehearsal of a new ballet that Ashley Page was mounting for the British Royal Ballet he asked a man and woman to do a *pas de deux* where the woman turned around with one leg raised in the man's arms. It did not work: they lost their balance. They tried again. The woman was in pain. 'No, I can't do it!' she said resolutely; and so they moved on.

It also happened that dancers changed the choreography in performance without telling the coach or the choreographer beforehand. This was one reason why coaches told me that they felt 'like a nervous wreck' when they were watching performances from the audience, since 'on stage you're in control'. Another reason was that 'you know where there may be a leak': there were times when dancers on stage could have used some assistance, but were out of reach for them. At one point, in an intermission of a classical ballet, I observed a coach ordering changes in the wings just minutes before an entrance of a line of corps de ballet women. When she had left, they agreed to do just as they had been doing already, and ignore the changes. Overhearing a conversation between two dancers, a female soloist and a male principal, I noted that the woman was complaining that she had to 'do bits I don't want anyone to see!' The man then answered irritatedly: 'So change them! I do!'

Once before a première at the British Royal Ballet, a male principal went into a fit over a costume he did not like. The trousers were too big, and the jacket was uncomfortable. The designer who was present in the studio was extremely upset over this reaction to his new accomplishment, and left the room with hurt feelings, screaming that he did not want to discuss any changes. The day after, the dancer performed dressed in his private trousers. The jacket had been changed so that it fitted him even when he moved.

Ballet Careers

The decision to become a professional dancer is often made after a ballet revelation, an extraordinary experience of ballet art. It is also common that a teacher has been pivotal for a dancer in pursuing a ballet career. So have ballet mothers, orchestrating (usually) a daughter's progress from the background. A ballet career starts with an audition, which usually means that the dancer takes class with a company, and may then be accepted as a corps de ballet dancer, if it is a classical company. Alternatively a ballet student who has been a 'paid student' or an apprentice and taken part in productions now and then may be offered a contract with the company. A number of 'débuts' from the first time a dancer performs in the corps de ballet to the first time a dancer performs a particular leading role, all make up different rites-de-passage into a ballet career.

Born in San Rafael, California, to a father who delivered milk and a mother who was interested in music, an acclaimed American ballerina who became a first-class dancer remembered how she started dancing:

> I would be standing on my father's feet and dancing. We always had music in our house. I must have been five when I saw Nureyev and Fonteyn dance a section from *Le Corsaire* in Ed Sullivan's show on television. Then I wanted to be a ballet dancer. I learnt tap dancing and acrobatics. Later I saw Toni Lander dance in *La Sylphide*. I begged and begged to dance. My parents sent me to a YMCA summer class. The teacher said I was bored, because I caught the combinations so fast. I was bored. She recommended me to a professional school where I went for six years. I applied for a scholarship, since my parents didn't have a lot of money.

She went on to win scholarships that took her through the School of American Ballet. The American Ballet Theatre had a summer programme that she took part in. She was offered a scholarship to stay. On her own in New York, all she did was dance: 'I didn't see anything of New York at the time. I was very, very shy.' One of her teachers at the school of the American Ballet Theatre suggested that she should audition for the company. At sixteen she was accepted as an apprentice with the American Ballet Theatre, and the year after as a corps de ballet dancer. John Neumeier picked her to be in one of his ballets. She went on tours with the company. At the age of twenty-one, she was appointed soloist, and Mikhail Baryshnikov cast her for one of the flower girls in *Don Quixote*. A few years later she made her début as Kitri, partnered by the English dancer Anthony Dowell, in the same ballet at the Metropolitan Opera House. It established her reputation as a an excellent ballerina. Some years later she was appointed principal dancer. One day she got a telephone call from Anthony Dowell, who had made it to Ballet director of the British Royal Ballet. He asked if she could come and dance with his company for a year. At first she was not sure: 'I was so complacent living with my mother, but I realized that it would be good to see if I could function away from this.' She took a leave of absence and danced both classical and contemporary productions with the British Royal Ballet in London. After two years, she hurt her foot, and went back to New York. When she had recovered, she continued dancing leading roles with the American Ballet Theatre until she celebrated her twentieth anniversary with the company in a special performance in her honour at the Metropolitan Opera House. She danced for a couple of years after that with the American Ballet Theatre, but eventually retired in order to live with her English husband and teach at a regional company in England.

A Swedish male corps de ballet dancer told me a quite different story of his ballet career, which had come about by chance. This dancer did not talk about breakthroughs or promotions, and his transnational experience was restricted to tours with the company and foreign coaches, choreographers and companies that had visited Stockholm. Growing up in a working class family he wanted to:

do some kind of gymnastics and there was a local dance class where we lived outside Stockholm. I wanted to do something to develop my agility. I became interested in theatre and opera. My teacher knew someone in the House who arranged so I could visit backstage. It happened to coincide with auditions for the Ballet School. I auditioned and was accepted. After ballet school I got a job in the corps of the Royal Swedish Ballet. It's fun when things are going well, but I've never been interested in success or career, I've had other priorities: outdoor life and my family. It is important to be appreciated, though, to get to dance in as many different pieces as possible, to do exciting choreography like the ones by

Kylián, Cullberg, Robbins, Tetley. Then you know that you are keeping up your level. I've had some invitations 'from the outside [of the House]', but I'm completely happy now, being a dancer here. Summers are holy, I spend them with my family and do other things.

The Making of a Classical Dancer

In her book *Off Balance: The Real World of Ballet*, journalist Suzanne Gordon (1983) focuses on the hardships of ballet: rigorous training, rivalry, sacrificing ballet mothers, injuries, anorexia and the lack of social benefits for American dancers in the early 1980s. Gordon describes the extraordinary event of a strike for better pay at the American Ballet Theatre. The Royal Swedish Ballet is used for comparative purposes to illustrate union protection, workplace democracy, and job security.

Dancers who would like to leave the ballet world early may have trouble finding another job because of their specialized training and socialization, which have occupied them so fully since they were very young. This is one point that Ronald Federico (1968) made in his doctoral sociology thesis 'Ballet as an Occupation'. This social analysis of the working conditions of 145 dancers in twelve major ballet companies in the United States in the late 1960s is informed by Federico's own experience as a dancer. Federico applies Howard Becker's (1963) idea of career contingencies, which takes into account social structure as well as individual changes, incitements and wishes in recognizing different career outcomes. Federico investigated motivation for pursuing a career as a ballet dancer and saw that performing was very appreciated, but also 'physical pleasure, challenge and self-fulfillment, schedule flexibility, travel, and opportunities to meet interesting people' (1968: 58, 64). The politics and disorganization of the company, low social position, poor pay and social insecurity were drawbacks that the dancers mentioned. Yet there were significant rewards in a ballet career, when the dedication paid off.

Discussing the making of a professional dancer, Federico argues that reaching a certain level of competence is important, even though the exact level may appear ambiguous at times. He adds that the opportunity to perform on stage is important for dancers' self-identification as professionals. In my study, I came across notions about professionalism as cover-up and self-control, according to which 'being professional' as a dancer relied on a certain level of routine that had been built up over the course of many years of training and performing as well as spending almost all one's time in the ballet world. It was thus considered 'professional' to make dancing on stage look as if one were enjoying it on a day when in fact one did not, to rehearse even though one could hardly stand up because of jet-lag or pain from injuries, or to perform well with a partner one had just had a major row with.

Politics and Personal Chemistry

Because of the risk of politics, it is considered bad form among dancers to spend too much time at the office talking to the directors. I often heard dancers criticize each other for being disloyal in this respect, yet conceding that 'since others do it, I have to do it, too'. Ballet managements are aware that some dancers try to ingratiate themselves with them in order to get to dance more and more prominent roles, or just to keep a privileged position where they are cast for leading roles as a matter of course. When dancers who are launched by the management approach directors in order to improve their situation even further, the directors do not always think about it in terms of politics, by contrast with what happens in the case of dancers that the management do not think very highly of.

When casting lists have been posted, or new promotions announced, disappointed dancers come in tears to the office and ask for 'a second chance'. This custom has probably come about and lived on because it often works to complain about having been 'taken out', not having been cast for a role one has been learning or not having been cast for roles that one regards as prominent enough. But when dancers get their way against the wishes of the management, they do not have its support, which makes it harder for them the very moment they are about to go on stage. To 'be taken out' could, but does not necessarily, signify the beginning of the end of a dancing career. Since the importance of casting lists is recognized by the ballet management, it sometimes notified dancers through letters or private talks in advance about major changes in casting that concern them.

Dancers who realized that they were in favour with the ballet management and on their way upwards in their careers sometimes ventured into the director's office and calmly proposed that they should do Juliet in *Romeo and Juliet* or Odette/Odile in *Swan Lake*. They did not have to fall apart to get their way. It also happened, however, that dancers went into the office and asked not to have to do roles that they had been cast for, because they did not feel ready for them. They might have been afraid that they were not fit enough, or that they had the wrong kind of body or dancing style for a particular role.

It is not good for a dancing career to get a reputation for being fussy about injuries or illnesses, especially when it risks jeopardizing performances. It might, however, also be a revenge weapon in the resistance against the ballet management by dancers who know that their best time as dancers is over and who are not particularly liked by the management, nor by other dancers.

Views of the Management from Below

Especially in the beginning of their careers, dancers often spend a lot of time on their own and with their friends, trying to figure out what the directors prefer concerning dancing style. Since I had access to different levels in the social structure in the companies, I was able to note that the dancers did not always get it right. The directors sometimes cast their second choice for a leading role when the dancer they really wanted was injured, for example. Such information does not always trickle down to the lower levels in the company hierarchy. In some cases, directors kept leading dancers because they 'had an audience', not because they liked their dancing particularly. Some dancers were moreover assumed by their colleagues to be more appreciated by the directors, than they in fact were; other dancers were in a better position than they realized. There were potential favourites that would blossom within a season or two. The expression 'the flavour of the month', which often came up in dressing-room conversations about casting, suggested not only that directors had their favourites, but also the transitory nature of favouritism in the ballet world, where things change quickly.

A distinguished career as a dancer is the highest symbolic capital in the ballet world, even after retirement. It is therefore almost exclusively ex-principal dancers who are appointed as ballet directors. An international ballet company in a ballet centre tends to be headed by a famous ex-principal who used to dance with the company. Lesser-known companies, in the peripheries, usually also have ex-principals as directors, but not as famous. They may even be directed by an ex-principal from another company. There is a tendency to appoint local dancers with transnational experience as directors of regional companies in ballet peripheries.

There are emerging dicussions in the ballet world over the logic in these customs. The fact that someone was an outstanding dancer obviously does not necessarily make him or her a very good director, nor even a good coach. It is being recognized more and more that dancing, directing and coaching are different talents that may coincide in the same person, but do not do so as a matter of course.

Career and Camaraderie

Despite the fact that the ballet world is structured by constant ranking and competition, there is actually a pronounced camaraderie. It grows out of the particular intensity and closeness of the ballet world, especially the bodily nature of dancing (cf. Chapter 4 on ballet body-work). The camaraderie takes the forms of peer-coaching in rehearsals and performances, verbal assistance on stage (especially when a young dancer is performing a role for the first time), and good luck wishes and presents before premières and débuts, but also support in the dressing-rooms when things have not gone so well professionally or personally. It was usually older dancers who comforted younger, relatively inexperienced ones after a disappointing casting or a difficult rehearsal, offering advice on how to handle certain coaches. Another way to help each other was to watch a première or a début from the audience and initiate applause and cheering.

To camaraderie belonged the habit of complimenting one another on an unusually beautiful variation of steps or a very well danced performance, in the wings, in the dressing-room, the day after or the next time one met. It was sometimes regarded as a manifestation of formal decorum, however, rather than an honest expression of admiration.

To offer to replace someone who was unable to perform because of an injury that was getting worse or some other illness at short notice was yet another form of camaraderie. This may further one's own career a bit, since one is gaining points with the management, unless it is corps work that does not really provide an opportunity to shine.

Peer-coaching about remembering steps or spacing and timing on stage could take place in panic in the corridor or in the wings just minutes before performance or an entrance, but was usually enacted on an ordinary day in the background of a rehearsal or in the dressing-room. Younger dancers asked older colleagues especially if they had performed the roles before. Dancers who were good at remembering steps usually shared their knowledge freely. Some dancers who also had a compassionate personality became 'kernel' friends (Wulff 1995b) of the company, guiding young dancers and encouraging established dancers when they experienced setbacks in their careers. Kernel friends may be men or women, but there were only a few of them at a time in each company. They functioned as a glue that kept the company together, and seemed to feel free to take on this role too because they realized that they had passed the peaks in their own careers. Kernel dancers tended to be asked all the time about steps, and they offered explanations to dancers who they believed were in need of them (which occasionally was not appreciated). Corps de ballet dancers who were doing the same combinations of steps in lines on stage also helped each other, as well as soloists in different casts, and even a partner who remembered how an earlier partner had done it.

Principal dancers of the same sex who were in competition most of the time might temporarily join forces for a special cause. They were then allies, but not friends. Most alliances changed over time, usually in response to casting, sometimes back and forth. Since such changes may be difficult to keep track of for others, I noted down a lot of dated speculations and beliefs about friendship clusters and cliques.

Competition and 'Healthy Competition'

There is a traditional notion outside the ballet world that the ballet world is very competitive, especially among female dancers. Ballet historians such as Joan Cass (1993) mention the legendary rivalries in the ballet world, like those in Paris between Marie Camargo and Marie Sallé in the eighteenth century, and between Marie Taglioni and Fanny Elssler about a century later.

Many times I heard dancers assess the careers of colleagues they considered more successful than themselves. More often than not they tried to explain away their success by discrediting them. Typical comments were thus: 'She's very good artistically, but not so good technically', 'He's just a technician', 'The director is in love with her' or 'Her parents give money to the company.'

It was mostly top dancers who seemed to be concerned about competition, aware of it, and the victims of harassments resulting from it. But also new corps de ballet dancers and soloists who aimed upwards dealt with it, were forced to face it, or were actually stimulated to keep improving themselves by it. Perhaps as a reflection of a kind of competitive strain in American society at large, the expressions 'healthy competition' or 'good competition' were common at the American Ballet Theatre, but not so at the other companies. Only on a few occasions was competition described as useful in Stockholm and London.

Competition surfaced in company class, where a large part of the company was present. Dancers then aimed at classical ballet excellence by outnumbering a rival in number of *pirouettes*, lifting their legs higher, or standing the longest in balance – all skills regarded as prestigious in ballet. It was a way to get the teacher's attention, and the respect and admiration of one's colleagues. Otherwise competition came up in rehearsals of preliminary casts when selection for final casting was still in progress. When final casting lists were posted, and once a year when promotions were announced, the fortunate ones often had to deal with one or two evil comments, inevitably from 'the company bitch'. In exceptional cases, they were harassed through anonymous letters and handwritten comments on the casting lists. There was most competition between dancers who were 'on the same level', which usually meant not only that they were the same age and had similar body size, but also that they had been classmates, even friends, since ballet school.

With time, a special connection was simultaneously built up between dancers of the same body type and age who had danced the same role in different casts over the course of many years.

In all companies in the study, dancers told me emphatically that in 'our company people stick together, but abroad they put glass in each other's shoes!'. The old saying 'to put crushed glass (or nails) in each other's shoes' turned out to be very difficult to verify when I came to companies in other countries. The metaphor was used frequently, however, to signify competition or the threat of competition, especially between women. The closest I got to substantial evidence was stories about the custom of 'taking out the elastic in someone's skirt' and 'ripping up a rival's costume' in the dressing-room just before she was needed on stage. One dancer assured me that she had seen a ripped up costume in a dressing-room in Paris when she was dancing there. The costume belonged to a girl who had just been promoted.

Watching performances from the wings, I did witness a few attempts by dancers to destroy steps for a rival on stage (cf. Chapter 5 on watching from the wings). In a performance of the second act of *Swan Lake*, for instance, a woman, who had recently been promoted to soloist and was regarded as a favourite of the management, danced past a corps de ballet woman who was not doing as well careerwise. The corps dancer then tried to disturb her rival by way of wit: 'Hello, darling!' The soloist, who must have heard the comment, did not seem to notice. When she came back, the corps dancer tried again: 'Password!' It did not affect the soloist's dancing.

By contrast with most other occupations, there is again very little competition between the sexes in the ballet world – since most roles in classical ballet are danced by either men or women. There may be competition between male and female leading dancers in the same company who are not regular partners, or between dancers from different companies who do guest performances together now and then.

Competition did not only occur among dancers (and coaches), but also between choreographers when they created new pieces for the same mixed programmes. And there was competition among leading dancers over good coaches and rehearsal time, i.e. what to rehearse the most. When it came to rehearsal time, dancers competed with each other, but also visiting choreographers competed over studio and stage rehearsals, if there was more than one going on at the time. The scheduling reflected the current local power structure of the company and in the office.

There were, however, some instances during my study when the competition degenerated into harassment. At one point an acclaimed ballerina returned to the stage after having been on maternity leave. Her comeback was prepared by advance feature articles in daily papers and magazines.

One such article was posted on the notice-board in the theatre with the words 'thinks' and 'our greatest ballerina', which appeared in different contexts, underlined in red so as to make one sentence of them. After her comeback performance, she got anonymous letters urging her to stop dancing.

Partnering, Rapport and Teams

A dancing career is much enhanced if a dancer has someone to be teamed up with. Partners need to match each other in size according to the idiom of classical ballet: the man should be taller, generally bigger, than the woman, even when she is on pointe. They also have to go together in movement quality: some dancers move in a big way, others in a small way, for instance, which also affects how tall they seem to be on stage. Partnering is a question of technique and rapport that is influenced by the hierarchy in the company. Male corps de ballet dancers told me about the anxieties of dancing short variations with female soloists, let alone principals. They also commented when a leading principal woman 'treated me like an equal; not everyone does that'. Some women principals thought it affected their career badly to have to dance with someone who had a lower position than they had themselves.

Partners on stage were not necessarily friends outside the theatre. Even backstage, on a daily basis in class, corridors and canteens, some partners seemed to be totally incompatible as people; but when they started dancing together they released hidden qualities in each other, thereby reaching into new artistic zones together. One male principal explained to me that he forced his partner to look him in the eyes; another said successful partnering had to do with 'experience'. Despite the fact that male dancers are supposed to act protectively of their women partners in classical ballet, if the woman is older and more experienced as a dancer it may well be she just as much as the man who makes 'a secure partner'. Either of them, not necessarily the man, may take the responsibility for their joint performances. It is still customary to launch a man and a woman as a team; not two men, as could very well be the case in contemporary companies that feature duets of men, almost as often as of a man and a woman.

Success: The Shock of Breaking Through

Unexpected opportunities frequently arose, pushing dancers forward in their careers. Many major breakthroughs have happened when one dancer is unable to dance a role because of an injury, and another has been asked to do it at a short notice. Yet success always seems to come as a surprise even at a planned début. A male principal with the Royal Swedish Ballet recollected

Looking in the mirror. Choreographer William Forsythe and dancer Maurice Causey. © Agnès Noltenius.

Ballett Frankfurt in a stage call of 'Sleepers Guts'. © Agnès Noltenius.

Sewing pointe shoes. Belinda Hatley of the British Royal Ballet.
© Helena Wulff.

'Swan Lake', Royal Swedish Ballet, Hans Nilsson and Anneli Alhanko. © Mats Bäcker.

Hans Nilsson and Anna Valer in 'Swan Lake'. © Mats Bäcker.

Anders Nordström in 'Peer Gynt' by John Neumeier. © Mats Bäcker.

Royal Swedish Ballet in 'Dancing on the Front Porch of Heaven' by Ulysses Dove. © Enar Merkel Rydberg.

Jan-Erik Wikström and Marie Lindqvist in 'The Tempest' by Glen Tetley. © Enar Merkel Rydberg.

Marie Lindqvist and Anders Nordström in 'Mozartina' by Björn Holmgren
© Enar Merkel Rydberg.

Marie Lindqvist in 'Swan Lake'. © Enar Merkel Rydberg.

Zoltàn Solymosi and Susan Jaffe rehearsing 'Swan Lake'.
© Enar Merkel Rydberg.

After performance. Johanna Björnson with her dresser. © Helena Wulff.

his début at the age of nineteen as the Bronze Idol in *La Bayadère*. When he had finished his solo, the audience screamed so loud that 'It was like a wall – I was pulled backwards by the sound!'

Another male principal, a Swede who was a leading dancer with the American Ballet Theatre for many years, also had his breakthrough as the Bronze Idol, but at the Metropolitan Opera House in New York. There were posters of him all over the city advertising this Met season. His mother told me that his younger teenage brother, who is deaf, came to a performance. He was seated next to a man dressed in white spats. The younger brother thought he was a gangster. When the applause and the cheering broke out, and the audience rose in his brother's honour, he managed to tell the man in white spats that the dancer was his brother. In the excitement, the man then lifted him up above the screaming crowd!

Yet an unexpected opportunity that resulted in a breakthrough took place when a male corps de ballet dancer had asked the director if he could learn the Jester in *Swan Lake*. She said no. But the dancer persisted: he went into the studio where the dancer who was cast for the role was learning it, and learnt it discreetly in the background. Two days before the première, the cast dancer fell ill, and so did his understudy. The ballet management tried to get a Swedish dancer who was dancing with the English National Ballet in London and who had done the role to great acclaim, but he was unable to come. In panic and late at night, the ballet director then called the dancer whom she had denied to learn the role, and implored him to do it at the première. He said no: 'It would be suicide, I don't know it that well.' The director called again, even later, and then the dancer changed his mind. The next morning – the day before the première – he rehearsed from 8 o'clock in the morning all day on stage with a video of the steps and tapes of the music. When the première had started, he was still rehearsing in a studio. Then he went down on stage and performed the Jester. The success was immediate and overwhelming. 'And the ballet management', he told me with a smile, meaningly, 'was so grateful . . .'.

As in all careers, success in a dancing career has to be confirmed over and over again. Yet there are dancers who reach a certain level of reputation, even stardom, that tends to linger on even when they are in fact declining as dancers.[6] Writing about stage actors, Gilman (1982) points out that when an actor has been recognized as a star actor by the audience, it will not take to anyone else. The audience has made an investment that it prefers to cultivate.

In the ballet world there is a kind of safety net for the very best dancers: they are protected by the ballet management, who continue to cast them for roles they are in fact too stiff to dance; and by press and marketing departments, balletomanes, the audience, critics, and even by fellow dancers who used to be in competition with them. When dancers realize that their toughest rival has irrevocably lost technique because of an injury or a pregnancy or simply through ordinary ageing, they too, defend her or him, since they know that their own position will improve.

Ageing and Retiring

Ballet companies can be said to harbour three age groupings. They are usually single-sex, and most clearly distinguishable on tours. The age groupings are linked to the three stages in a ballet dancer's career. The young ones are between about the ages of twenty and twenty-five, and still have all their options open, although some of them are identified as having more 'potential' than others by the ballet management. Then there are dancers around the age of thirty, when they usually experience their first substantial decline in form. For the women, this may occur after a pregnancy. But there is still hope for a second peak, which will inevitably go down when dancers reach their late thirties. And therefore dancers who are in their mid-thirties to around forty also tend to stick together.

Just as tensions of various kinds, both conflicts and romantic attractions, that occur because of the physical closeness in the ballet world, are sometimes handled by way of jokes, so is the ageing process. In one case, it was moreover put together with the meaning of gender and performed as a practical joke: when an attractive woman dancer turned forty on a tour, she was awakened by fifteen corps de ballet men dressed in nothing but their suspensories. The boys sang to her, and each one of them hugged her, the woman told me afterwards, when we talked about the hardships of getting old for dancers and women in general.

Ballet dancing is a short career – it only lasts for about twenty years. Early retirement is lurking around the corner. The category 'retired dancer' is moreover very wide in terms of age. It stretches from people in their early forties to those who are in their eighties or even nineties. This becomes especially obvious at the annual spring party of the Royal Swedish Ballet, when retired dancers are invited. By contrast with most other occupations and professions, seniority is not a capital in ballet. Usually the dancers themselves notice that they are getting old. Before anyone else can see it, they feel it: dancing becomes harder, and declines in form will not be recovered. Many dancers try to avoid facing this 'fact of life' as long as it is possible, making efforts to improve their condition, and protesting loudly when they are 'taken out of roles' they used to do, or not cast for roles they consider prominent enough. At thirty a dancer is said to be growing old, although the truth of this does in fact vary. Sooner or later ageing dancers inevitably start losing form. Their artistry may not suffer, however. Many dancers who have a talent for artistry become much more expressive and interesting as dancers when they get older, although they appear most to their advantage in contemporary work. Ageing leading dancers take part in sections in galas because they are brief and thus not too demanding, or they perform 'walking roles' like kings and queens in the classical ballets. Such roles are not really appreciated by dancers who used to do leading roles or solos, however.

Since dancers retire in their early forties (or even earlier),[7] they can be said to have two careers, although there is often a continuity between the first one, the dancing career, and the second one. Most non-dancers working at the four ballet companies in this study were ex-dancers, but there was not room for all the ex-dancers from the companies there, nor anywhere else in the ballet world. Some ex-dancers stay on in the theatre teaching class or coaching rehearsals, or work with the administration (usually in lower positions), stage properties and video archives, which also includes documenting rehearsals and performances. Ex-dancers also take up jobs as stage managers or retrain as choreologists, physiotherapists or company photographers. Not many make it as choreographers. Some set up private ballet schools for students outside the theatre. The majority of ex-dancers have to look for outside work.

Founded in 1993, the International Organization for the Transition of Professional Dancers (IOTPD) is working towards establishing pension schemes and second careers for dancers. Employment laws and social security differ among the seventeen countries that are represented in the IOTPD, and few are adapted to the special needs of a dancer's short, intense, often international career. There are now transition centres in Britain, Canada, the United States and the Netherlands to provide educational and career counselling, as well as economic, legal and psychological advice, study grants and loans to start businesses. The core idea in this organized transition is to transfer the special skills of dancers, such as discipline, flexibility and engaging presence, to new fields (Leach 1997).[8] This is, nevertheless, still an area in the making: far too many dancers never find a job they like, let alone a job at all. Many ex-dancers are left at a loss.

Age and ageing are treated with a lot of caution and veiling in the ballet world. There is for instance a custom of leaving out the year of birth in presentations of dancers' biographies in programmes, which is very unusual in other professional contexts. It is common that dancers who are still in their best years block out the thought of retirement, which is easy, since life as a dancer is very intense. There is not much time to plan ahead, so that as they approach their late thirties, some dancers start to panic. Few enjoy the prospect of retiring, even if they realize that their bodies will perhaps be worn out by then.

It is not only hard on the body to be a dancer, it is also in fact very tiring physically to work as a coach or teacher as one gets older. The fixation with what one's body looks like and how it changes over the years is a feature of ballet culture. As if experiencing the deterioration of one's dancing capacity were not enough, ex-dancers who teach or coach dancers are constantly reminded of their own ageing. For decades their own bodies are growing older, whereas the people they work with, the dancers of different generations that come and go, remain the same age.

A senior dancer who is asked to start teaching class and coaching rehearsals may be appointed 'ballet master' or 'ballet mistress' by the ballet director. Formal training for this occupation, which again tends to be referred to as 'coach' or 'répétiteur', is beginning to be set up at some dance colleges and a few companies, but is still in the process of being established. Many coaches are freelance and spend a couple of weeks or one month each with a number of companies every year. Some have agents who arrange work for them; others go ahead through personal and professional networks.

Ex-dancers who remain in the ballet world continue to figure in the hierarchy, but not entirely on the base of their new positions, which can be both lower and higher than the position they used to have when they were still dancing. Retired dancers who have a new job in the ballet world are often treated by others (and treat others) according to the position and amount of fame they once had as dancers. Successful principal dancers who were coached by an ex-dancer who was reputed to have been a good, but not an excellent dancer, sometimes wondered, they told me, whether their coach had enough knowledge to teach them what they needed to know.

At one point I made the following observation, which also illustrates the problem of getting old for dancers, as well as camaraderie among dancers and the hierarchy in ballet companies: a woman soloist around thirty years of age was comforted by an older principal woman, one of the leading dancers and stars of the company. The soloist had been rehearsing with an ex-dancer of transnational fame, now in her fifties, who worked as a choreographer with the company but was known for being impossible to please, 'since no one looks or moves like she used to' (again, every dancer moves individually). In accordance with traditional ballet culture, the choreographer pushed the women dancers until they fell apart in the studio. It was obvious that the soloist had had a hard rehearsal. She looked quite depressed and exhausted. 'How did it go?' the older dancer asked, 'Was she screaming at you?' The soloist made an affirmative face. The older dancer then went on:

'She told me "you used to be able to dance!"' With an ironic laugh the older dancer added: 'Well, with all respect . . .'.

Notes

1. Richard Schechner (1995: 257) mentions that traditional genres like ballet and noh are taught from a young age. He compares them to initiation rites, where the mind and body of the performers are put back into a tabula rasa. When the training is completed, the performers have become an integral part of the traditions so deeply that they will always be different from other people.

2. Studying how Swedish shunters learn their trade, Birgitta Edelman (1997) suggests that women tend to learn shunting more by way of mimesis, whereas men usually go about it through paraphrase. This is also how she explains the fact that women do better than men at the beginning of the training, but sooner or later quit the job without having made it to boss level.

3. See also Gordon (1983) on the impact of ballet mothers on their daughters' dancing careers. Solway (1994) reports on a ballet mother who had great ambitions for her son Edward Stierle, especially when he was dancing with the Joffrey Ballet. His mother then took to sending positive reviews of Stierle to other dancers in the company. Edward Stierle, who was an acclaimed dancer, died tragically in his early twenties of AIDS.

4. There is a growing linguistic interest in politeness: see for instance Brown and Levinson (1987).

5. Lingering on the cultural significance of t-shirts that display texts and pictures, it is interesting to see that Garsten (1994) relates how transnational Apple employees wore t-shirts to signal both community and difference. This fits into Clifford's (1997: 43–4) suggestion in 'Traveling Cultures' that t-shirts formulate 'fixation and movement, of dwelling and traveling, of local and global'. Along transnational connections, more or less planned, t-shirts may tentatively be used as 'a way of localizing global symbols, for the purposes of action'.

6. See Gamson (1994) for a sociology of culture analysis of entertainment celebrities in the United States, focusing on the connections between texts, producers and audiences. Gilman (1982) places the notion of celebrity between fame and notoriety, identifying celebrity as arbitary fame that 'need not be earned and that's in excess or defiance of reason' (1982: 108).

7. Leach (1997: 43) reports that 'the trend seen by transition centers in Canada, the Netherlands, the UK and the US is that average retirement age has declined dramatically since the 1970's'. There is even a 'drop in retirement ages over the last decade, from mid-thirties to early-thirties or even mid-twenties' (1997: 64). Leach does not provide a definite explanation for this trend, but suggests that growing career demands and unemployment as well as courses of study may be pivotal in cutting a short career even shorter. Among the four companies in this study, it was

primarily at the American Ballet Theatre that dancers, especially corps de ballet dancers, were retiring earlier than they used to.

8. Leach (1997) mentions that the Career Transitions For Dancers in the United States have moved dancers into dance therapy, social work, desk-top publishing, public relations, architecture, and so on.

4

Classical Ballet Culture

Backstage, classical ballet culture differs from contemporary ballet and dance culture in the emphasis on tradition and hierarchy. This chapter explains that in the light of modern ideas of personal expression and laws on democracy in the workplace, traditional deference and discipline are increasingly being questioned at the three classical companies in this study, but not necessarily changed all that much. One way of coping with the necessary perseverance (and the competition) takes the form of euphoric relaxation: 'horsing around' in dressing-rooms and rest areas, the occasional exhilarating party, fits of temper, and hidden and open resistance, both verbal and kinesthetic. Notions of the body, time and gender are central and interconnected in classical ballet culture, yet different in significant ways from how they are constructed outside the theatre in the larger society.

The Company as Family, the Theatre as Home

Because of the intense schedule of ballet companies, dancers spend almost all their time in the theatre, where they develop a loyalty to their company, a feeling of belonging together (cf. A.P. Cohen 1982). Dancers are fond of the theatres where they are based, and when they go on tours they bring their belonging with them – in fact it is even more pronounced. For those dancers who have grown up together in ballet school, this process started many years ago. The belonging is activated on stage, where dancers depend on each other and are united in a vulnerable exposure. Dancers who share apartments and go on holiday in small friendship clusters spend literally all time together.

Another consequence of the long working hours in the theatre is the many multiplex network links: the prevalence of spouses, lovers, friends, fiancé(e)s who also work with ballet or opera (in the studio, on stage and backstage) is high, and thus also the number of ex-lovers and ex-spouses who are still around at work. There are so-called 'ballet families' with up to generations of dancers.

Spouses and girl- and boyfriends who work in the House are often preferred by dancers because of the intensity of a dancing career and the odd working hours. There is a notion that a dancer's life is hard to understand for someone from the outside. Yet many dancers do marry people or acquire partners who have never had anything to do with ballet, opera or theatre professionally. A spouse or a partner who is interested in music may, however, be accepted as *of a similar kind* to ballet people.

Nicknaming Dancers, Ballets and Variations of Steps

Belonging to a ballet company is also expressed through the custom of nicknaming dancers, coaches and directors, as is social identity *vis-à-vis* the local system of social relationships (cf. Mewett 1982).[1] Nicknames were to be found at all levels in the company hierarchy, referring to young and older dancers, the unknown as well as the famous. Dancers with identical first names were thus often separated by the use of a familiar form or some other local elaboration of their names, or simply by their family names, and established familiar forms of first names tended to be used especially for dancers who were popular in the company. 'Bella' at the Royal Swedish Ballet was christened Isabella, but was considered to be beautiful as well. The Japanese dancer Tetsuya Kumakawa at the British Royal Ballet was called 'Teddy' backstage, since his Japanese first name was difficult to pronounce in English. The Dutch dancer Sjoerd Vreugdenhil was known as 'Shorty' at the English-speaking Ballett Frankfurt, not only because Sjoerd sounds similar to 'short' and his family name was very hard to memorize for non-Dutch speakers, but also as a good-humoured comment on the fact that he was unusually tall. Although these forms were used by both coaches and dancers, coaches also had their own nicknames among the dancers, not always positive ones, of which they were not always aware.

Yet the nicknaming of ballets and variations of steps is even more important in a cultural analysis of a ballet company. They are obviously unique to the ballet world, and they, too, are of social significance in displaying belonging, hierarchy and, occasionally, hidden resistance. Nicknames of variations of steps also functioned as a way to learn and remember different sections in the ballets, as well as the order of them. Invented by dancers, coaches or choreographers, nicknames of ballets and variations of steps were used by the company or just a few dancers who were dancing a particular section, but were often around for just one production. Some nicknames travel transnationally – mostly those of classical ballets. Nicknames were used as abbreviations for long names of ballets that had to be mentioned innumerable times, sometimes out of extra affection as signalling the large amount of work that had been put into a production or a variation, and a long, not always easy, rehearsal period. *The Sleeping Beauty* was identified as 'Beauty' in London, and also by critics and other dance writers. I heard *Don Quixote* referred to as 'Don Q' in Stockholm, London, New York and Frankfurt. *Romeo and Juliet* was 'Romeo' in all four places. In Stockholm, the dancers moreover called *Don Quixote* 'Donkan', and sometimes *La Bayadère* 'Bayan', both Swedicized forms. In London, *Swan Lake* tended to be 'Lac', which was short for the French name *Le Lac des Cygnes*.

Variations were sometimes nicknamed after what the choreography can be said, with a certain irony, to look like or the music to sound like. When the Royal Swedish Ballet danced George Balanchine's *Theme and Variations*, one of the variations was nicknamed 'the car wash'. It consists of four women dancers in blue tutus. One of them is kneeling while the other three are turning so close to her that she gets the blue, stiff tutus in her face – like the blue brushes in a car wash sweeping over a car. In *Theme*, as the ballet tends to be called, there is also a step called *ciseaux* where the legs of the dancers open in the air like a pair of scissors, which is the literal meaning of the term. The step was thus referred to as 'the scissors' at the American Ballet Theatre. Other French ballet terms were also translated into English (or Swedish), either because they were difficult to pronounce for non-French speakers, or they sounded similar to an English word that might as well do, or because they illustrated an especially figurative step or position. *Le poisson* thus became 'the fish' in English: a woman dancer is leaning forward over the thigh of a male dancer with her legs stretched behind them both. The man is keeping her in place by holding his outstretched arm against one of her legs.

At the American Ballet Theatre in a rehearsal of the act 'The Kingdom of the Shades' in *La Bayadère*, one of the coaches asked a woman principal to 'do "On Wisconsin!"' This is a series of *soussus*, when the woman dances on pointe on the diagonal of the stage, by opening and closing one leg with every step, to a fast, catching rhythm. To my question the coach explained 'we have called it that since school'; but he did not know the origin of the term. He thought that the music was an old folk-song.

During a rehearsal of *Swan Lake* I discovered that some of the corps de ballet men were talking about 'the Colorado spruce'. It was in the Mazurka, they told me later, that they thought that, when they were in costume, and with the steps, they looked as if they were forming a Christmas tree. A principal man, who had never heard of this, was however eager to tell me about the song 'Oh, please let me kill myself!' that goes with Tchaikovsky's score – and the plot – in the last act of *Swan Lake*.

It was also at the American Ballet Theatre that a couple of corps de ballet women talked about a very slow and long turn on pointe as 'a floater'. It was supposed to look gentle and effortless. In a new ballet that was being created during my field study, there was a section that some of the dancers called 'birding' to illustrate the idea that they were running in a circle 'keeping their places, unlike in ballet, where you change places', they informed me.

One particularly inventive coach at the British Royal Ballet had his own names for many variations 'because I get so tired of counting' or to illustrate what they looked or sounded like. In *Dances Concertantes*, choreographed by Kenneth MacMillan, this coach called some long, light steps 'moonsteps', because they looked as if the dancers were walking on the moon. And once when Princess Diana was watching a performance of *Swan Lake*, one section went really badly. The dancers were supposed to dance in couples in a circle and then move on to a new partner, but it all ended up in a mess, with some dancers finding themselves on their own and men with another man. After that, the coach termed this section 'Princess Di'.

Ballet Discipline

Although the traditional ballet discipline was still there, old-fashioned as it may be, there were signs of dispute about it, especially in Stockholm, reflecting the more radical notions of political democracy in Sweden. I also detected an admiration among the older dancers for younger dancers' insistence on leaving rehearsals early in the afternoon in order to pick up their children at day-care centres. There were more formal rules of order at the British Royal Ballet than at any of the other companies. It was thus not permitted to wear watches (since they may injure other dancers) in class or rehearsal, nor to wear short trousers revealing bare legs. There was also a rule against eating sweets because of the risk of choking when a dancer moves around.

Dancers may still get warnings for bad behaviour. In one company the dancers were requested to sign in an hour and a half before performance. If their names were not present fifteen minutes before performance they were called by the stage manager over the Tannoy system. Sometimes dancers were in the theatre, but had forgotten to sign in. If they forgot, or failed to sign in, they got three warnings, which were posted on the notice-board. If it happened a fourth time, they had to pay a fine of $US 25.

It is regarded as very bad form not to turn up to a rehearsal without any explanation. This is not least a practical consideration, since the rehearsal may have to be changed or even cancelled if one dancer has failed to appear. Dancers depend on each other in this respect.

Proper Behaviour and Sanctuary Spaces

The decorum in the ballet world is especially worked out for the spaces around and in or on the studio and the stage: these are particularly sanctuary spaces. There are 'old theatre rules', saying, for instance, that one does not bring open drinks to the wings or on stage, nor does one go on stage dressed in outdoor clothes (all this obviously refers to non-performance time), or leave the theatre with stage make-up still on. Other crucial rules are not to disturb rehearsals, preferably to wait until a combination of steps is finished before entering a studio, and never to start talking to or distracting a dancer, a coach or a pianist unless there is an emergency of some kind. A visitor, whether it is a fellow dancer who is watching the rehearsal or a friend of the coach, walks discreetly along the walls in a studio, and never across the floor while the rehearsal is in progress.

When dancers make a mistake in rehearsal, especially leading dancers who are learning a *pas de deux*, they may upset the rhythm, and the variation has to be interrupted. Then it is customary to apologize, to say 'It was my fault.' (Afterwards, out of reach of the coach, the dancers may have a fight about it, however, accusing each other of making mistakes.) To interrupt a rehearsal is also a way to figure out what went wrong, why it did not work. Many times, moreover, I watched corps de ballet dancers missing a step in class or in rehearsal, and looking very embarrassed. They did not usually interrupt the variation, but might receive a correction from the coach when it was finished. When the rehearsal is over, the coach thanks the dancers, and if he or she has thanked the pianist, the dancers do so, too. Then they thank the coach and each other. On returning to the wings after a *pas de deux* on stage, partners thank each other.

Although dancers complained in all companies that 'people don't always say hello' on a daily basis, probably because they have already seen each other across the studio in morning class, there is again a tradition of polite greeting in the ballet world, echoing courtly manners from centuries back, entailing a bow with a straight back, legs together. This is also performed when ballet people meet each other in the foyer in intermissions or at receptions and on other more formal occasions. Then the bowing is mischievously exaggerated, as a way of communicating community.

Dressing-rooms: 'The Safe Space'

In the crowded, hectic world backstage there is a lack of privacy. During the course of an ordinary working day, dancers are rarely on their own, let alone on a performance day or on tours. The dressing-rooms are, however, considered 'the safe space', because here dancers can withdraw into intimate conversations out of sight of coaches and ballet managements and get comfort from colleagues, and some rest (on a mattress on the floor or on a couch). They cannot count on being on their own for very long, however. Sometimes they try to get a nap in rest areas and green rooms instead, often with a towel covering their eyes; but these are usually even noisier places. At the Royal Swedish Ballet, for instance, four principals share a dressing-room, as do eight soloists and corps de ballet dancers. On tours, up to sixteen dancers may have to share a dressing-room. Very few theatres provide even the stars with private dressing-rooms. The standard of the dressing-rooms I saw varied very much, from simple changing-rooms, smelling of old sweat furnished with wooden benches and a locker for each dancer, to spacious, well-lit dressing-rooms for leading dancers only.

There is a kind of mystique surrounding the dressing-rooms. This is where a great deal of the social learning takes place, and the transformation into roles before performance. Since it is 'a safe space' this is also where masks fall off and where a certain amount of giggling and exhilarated behaviour occurs. The atmosphere is often warm and friendly, even intimate, and tends to include everyone present. Although there is an effort to support each other in the dressing-room, mean comments and jokes are made about other dancers who are not present. One evening before performance the girls, in various states of nakedness, make-up and costume, were roaring with laughter over a woman dancer in the company who had slipped on bird's dung and sprained her ankle. The woman was not very popular, because she was unreliable when it came to performing. She had a history of withdrawing at the last minute, even during performance. The story about the woman went up and down the rows of tables in the dressing-rooms: 'She can dance on pointe, right – and then she loses her balance in the middle of bird's dung!'

Women's dressing-rooms are usually much more adorned than those of the men. There is an air of girlish femininity in the making in women's dressing-rooms. A typical women's dressing-room for corps de ballet and soloists at the Royal Opera House in Stockholm had eight places in two rows, each facing a mirror framed by big strong bulbs. There were pastel-coloured cotton wool, 'private' make-up, stage make-up, including false eyelashes and 'pancake' (a creamy skin-coloured stage make-up), powder, eau de toilette, hair spray, tampons, sweets, biscuits, painkillers, soft drinks, fruit, cigarettes and brushes on the tables. Here and there soft animals were climbing up the mirrors next to pictures of husbands, children, pets and holidays, as well as postcards from New York and the Mediterranean. From the wall, newspaper clippings were calling: 'Dance – a nice way to lose weight!' and 'Dance your ass off!' A Garfinkel poster said: 'I might as well exercise, I'm in a bad mood anyway!' A couch and a table in the corner told of relaxing moments. There was also a coffee machine on a shelf. Behind the door a washbasin was tucked away, and on the inside of the door there was a big head shot of Mikhail Baryshnikov.

Resistance: Hidden and Open

In a sense resistance can be a kind of agency – at least open resistance. A few times, I witnessed shouting matches between dancers and coaches where the dancers were in control. But on the whole, there was more hidden resistance than open in the companies. It was a youth-cultural resistance against adult institutional power, an outlet for conflicting generational (not class) interests, from below.[2] It could be dancers who thought that they deserved to be launched more actively by the management or who disliked a coach who put their careers more or less at risk by engaging in open or hidden resistance.

One morning in a women's class, the teacher, a famous ex-ballerina, was late. The dancers and the pianist were waiting for her. This is very unusual, and regarded as bad form, diverging from both discipline and decorum. Then the teacher arrived, in a strikingly good mood and with a new red hair colour; still in her coat, she urged the dancers to start without her. When she went out to hang up her coat, one of the dancers giggled and said to me in a low voice: 'Why did she do that to her hair?' The teacher came back and started going through the exercises. She talked to the dancer who did not like her hair colour, who nodded politely. When the teacher turned her back to the dancer, she made a face. Since there were mirrors on three walls in the studio, this was a risky undertaking.

The Royal Opera House in Stockholm was going to be renovated. As a part of the preparations the dancers found a big sheet of paper, mostly blank, on the notice-board in their corridor, with a handwritten text at the top saying: 'The stage is going to be renovated for the year 2000. Believe it or not! The technical director would like to know what the company thinks needs to be improved?' A few days later there were some anonymous suggestions written in different sizes and handwritings with a number of pens in varying colours:

> 'The temperature.
> The lighting (blinded from the side).
> Carpet in the wings.
> Mirror in the wings.
> Make all doors around the stage tight so we get rid of the draught.

Footlights back.
Special ballet floor for performances and rehearsals.'

The fact that it is difficult to dance on a rake, even if one is used to it, came up when someone added:

'Slightly less rake, perhaps?'

Which was answered by:

'Flat floor out of question, then the whole auditorium has to be rebuilt.'

Someone else persisted:

'Flat, bloody flat.'

Whereupon a jocular tone turning provocative was introduced:

'More female stage workers! (Attractive! Preferably!)
Minibar, please!!
Pornographic video'.

An opportunity to take part in the decision-making at the Opera degenerated into a prank of hidden resistance, perhaps because the dancers were not used to any substantial influence. Occasionally, I witnessed coaches taking part in hidden resistance together with dancers. During a tedious rehearsal, a coach and a dancer (who was temporarily injured but was watching in order to learn the steps) were sitting next to me, watching. The coach had a notebook, so they started writing messages to each other in it in order to liven things up a bit. They chuckled, and the dancer showed me what they had written. As I joined in their suppressed giggles I tried to memorize as much as possible of their exchange. What follows here is a slightly censored version. The coach had started by asking the dancer about an upcoming tour:

'Will you do *Manon* on the 6-7?'
'No, I'm lifting . . .'

He was referring to the rehearsal we were watching and the monotony of learning the special kind of lifts that characterized this ballet. Now the coach was showing his irritation with the ballet:

'What is this shit?'

The dancer was amused to hear this from his coach:

'You know the choreography!'

He was alluding to the numerous and long rehearsals during the past weeks of the ballet. They all certainly knew the choreography, in other words.

'Ba, ba, ba'

This onomatopoeic expression was typically used by the choreographer when he was marking the beat.

'Bored, 6 hours of rehearsal on Friday without music and he will say "ba, ba, ba".'

They were giggling happily.

In one of the companies, a male soloist who used to be very promising had been cast for a minor role in *The Sleeping Beauty* that he did not want to do. In a rehearsal, he was bored. He also had a mint in his mouth. The coach asked the dancer to take the mint out. He refused. Then the coach said that if he did not take the mint out, he would have to leave the room: 'Don't you want to be in here?' The dancer did not, so he left the room, or rather was sent out, running down the stairs. The rehearsal continued in a subdued mood, and in the break I went with the dancers to the canteen, where the dancer who had been sent out was lingering. 'He knows he can't break me!' the dancer told me. A friend of his suggested that the coach had been treating the dancer badly for a while 'since he has been dancing really well recently. He does that then, tries to break you down.' The next day, I met the dancer on the way to a rehearsal of the same variation as on the day before. 'I've brought three mints' he said mischievously, showing them to me, 'just in case.' His open resistance had moved into hidden resistance.

Joking: Verbal and Kinaesthetic

Most joking I came across in the ballet world was verbal, but there was an unusually high quantity of kinaesthetic joking, taking the form of *interaction reference*, i.e. a communication by way of steps between dancers when they met in corridors, lifts, and studios, as well as outside the theatre in the street, in restaurants and in their homes. It was a way of greeting colleagues, saying goodbye and commenting ironically or jokingly on a monotonous or funny rehearsal, a rival dancer, an unpopular coach or just one of the classical variations in general. Both kinaesthetic and verbal jokes and ridicule also took the form of good-humoured banter, and can be distributed among themes of sex, gender, career, toilet stories and breaking the sense of (ethereal ballet) style, which were all to a certain extent intertwined.

As Karin Norman (1994) has pointed out about working-class women in a small town in Sweden, irony, especially in the form of obscene jokes, does not only symbolize social reality; irony and obscene jokes also create reality. People who engage in joking alter their relationships to the phenomenon that they are joking about. By laughing together at something that is problematic socially, it becomes easier to handle, even if it does not change in itself, but just the joking people's relationships to it. It is moreover probably the ambivalent nature of jokes that makes people dare to get close to sensitive areas.

One category of jokes in the ballet world, as at every place of work, targeted the management, including coaches and choreographers, and colleagues who were more successful than oneself. Making fun of them was a way to reduce their influence and accomplishments symbolically backstage, even though it did not have an impact on how their colleagues were viewed from front stage.

Sometimes jokes sounded worse than they were in fact meant to be: they were not malicious, and would never be addressed directly to the object of ridicule. In one of the companies, there was a young, very promising dancer who was exceptionally good at balance. This obviously disturbed the older women principals a bit, especially those who were less good at turning and balancing. I thus overheard comments and jokes about this dancer such as: 'She was standing in *arabesque*, for like half an hour. Having a cup of coffee!' (which obviously is absolutely impossible physically).

Information, News, Rumours

Politics is another feature of places of work, especially at levels in careers where people are striving upwards. Such politics often have to do with managing information. It was, again, common for dancers to complain of not getting enough information about current events and future planning. They were not aware that the ballet management did not necessarily know more than they did about certain issues, at least not at a particular point in time, since information is always changing, on the move. A great deal of the affairs of a ballet company moreover circle around on-going negotiations (about repertory and tours and the like), and this probably makes it difficult to keep a large number of people informed simultaneously. Although company meetings were important occasions for providing news and opportunities for voting, different versions of pieces of news often leaked out beforehand from principal dancers or coaches who confided both in the management and the dancers. Furthermore, dancers projected their wishes and fears about their careers as well as speculations about each other during recurrent conversations, which affected how some information was phrased.

Managing information was thus one way of engaging in politics in a ballet company. Through personal chemistry and networking some dancers got access to classified information from the ballet management, and learned that keeping quiet about important matters was a source of influence, as was presenting an event differently depending on to whom one was speaking and in what context the conversation took place. There was a lot of misinformation around, partly because false information was planted, and partly because information was often distorted in transmission. Jokes and speculations may be interpreted as actual facts, for instance, and then live on as such.

The most significant kinds of news and rumours in a ballet company concern promotions to posts as soloists and principal dancers (since that may mean that other dancers who were close to being promoted never will get another chance), casting, new appointments and, of course, romance. I was quite astonished to learn the speed with which some really sensational information travelled. This can be attributed to the architecture and routines backstage. If a piece of information was being told in a dressing-room with four or eight women dancers when they arrived in the morning, they then went to class, where they spread it up and down the barre to the other women, and in the afternoon they would have rehearsals together with the men, who then would learn about the latest scandal or tragedy. In about three hours, everyone in the company knew.

In the information flow in a ballet company one crucial topic was rumours about dancers who had been warned by the management that they 'might have to leave the company' or in Sweden that a young dancer who had spent three years with the Royal Swedish Ballet 'might not get a contract'. Such rumours usually turned out to be wrong, perhaps because the warnings often did lead to dancers' making an effort to improve their dancing (which in fact may have been the reason for warning them). It also happened that a dancer who had been 'asked to leave' got his or her contract back because another dancer was unexpectedly leaving.

Time: Living for the Moment

At the same time as ballet dancers take part in a culture of great and celebrated time depth, one of the core understandings of the ballet world is that time is precious. Dancers are young people and their careers are short. The risk of getting injured and losing form are also constantly there.

Time in the ballet world can preferably be linked to the theoretical interest in time as socially and culturally constructed. Eviatar Zerubavel (1981) notes that relatively arbitrary conventions structure social time and how social groups that share diverging schemes that separate them from other people are united by this. Dancers often work when other people are free, in the evenings and on Saturdays, and on national holidays. Time also matters in the actual dancing. A dancer should not be 'late', that is after the beat, nor 'early', and partners and the corps de ballet should aim at being 'together', doing the same steps simultaneously (see also the section on proxemic unity below).

The occurrence of AIDS adds to the sense that time is short. In all four companies in this study there had been a few cases of AIDS: dancers, a coach and/or a choreographer had died. Some dancers who were HIV-positive had left the company, and others were believed by fellow dancers to have left because they had HIV. There were many worries and much talk about AIDS and who might have been infected, not least because of the long incubation period and the fact that someone who is infected may live for many years without knowing about it. The knowledge that some people who have the diagnosis do not want to go public with this information also led to speculations and rumours, which spread transnationally, especially when they concerned prominent ballet people who were inspirational coaches or choreographers, let alone employers. During everyday work in the ballet world, company class and rehearsals, it moreover happened quite often that dancers grazed areas of skin, on their knees for example, and some blood appeared. On a few times I noticed a tension in the studio, as when a dancer whose boyfriend had died of AIDS started bleeding from a small wound in his hand during a rehearsal. The coach then shouted: 'Are you bleeding?', as a warning to the other dancers it seemed, and the rehearsal continued. The dancer was not in fact infected with the HIV virus.

Also anorexia and other eating disorders as well as the use of various kinds of drugs make time short in the ballet world. Dancers know that their time is soon running out, and this is why they not only rehearse, but also perform when they are ill or injured. Everyday life in the ballet world is characterized by a completely absorbing present where dancers have to concentrate on the here and now. Dancers are required to develop an absolute presence of mind, especially on stage. Parallel to this absorbing presence there is a lot of waiting in the everyday life of a ballet company: for one's turn to dance during big rehearsals and performances, especially for the corps de ballet. (See also Chapter 5 on waiting in the wings during performances.)

Yet the momentous presence in the ballet world contains *changes*. This is both important and typical; casting lists and daily schedules, 'the calls', change so often that the dancers have to look at them several times every day in order to be on time for the right rehearsal. Dancers have to be on time once an hour or every other hour, since this is the usual length of rehearsals.

To dancers' preparation for changes belongs a readiness to replace a colleague who gets injured at a short notice. Sometimes the dancer has 'learnt the role', but not performed it yet; sometimes he or she has danced it before. It may also happen that a late rehearsal is the only option if a performance is to come off at all. During very important performances, such as premières with royals and critics in the audience, when a leading dancer is on stage in spite of an injury there may even be an understudy in costume ready in the wings.

There is a certain transnational variation in the cultural construction of time in the ballet world, in line with the general pace of the society of each national ballet company. In the United States, time was construed as very short: there was a widespread urge to do one's best now, or there may never be another chance. When injuries occurred on stage, it happened more often than in the other countries that another dancer who was watching stepped in to save the performance. From this comparative perspective, dancers in Sweden constructed a longer time perspective. The attitude that 'I can rehearse this variation tomorrow' or 'I can dance this role next season' was more common in Sweden than in England or the United States. There was room for more second chances in Sweden, especially during the season when eight women dancers become pregnant.

Ballet Body Work

Graeme Salaman (1974) has noted that members of occupational communities tend to internalize a particular value system. In the instance of ballet dancers, their extreme body consciousness would seem to be the most clear-cut example. In this way the study of ballet culture relates to the escalating interests, in several disciplines, in the body as a site of culture (Blacking 1977; B.S. Turner 1984; Featherstone *et al.* 1991) and embodiment (Csordas 1994a).[3] Loïc Wacquant (1995b: 65) points to a paradox in recent sociological studies on the body: they contain very few 'living bodies of flesh and blood' that show different ways that social worlds form bodies and distribute them over the social structure. In Wacquant's colourful ethnographic study of boxers in Chicago, he analyses how boxers use their bodies as a form of capital, a bodily capital.

According to the argument in Michel Foucault's (1979) influential work *Discipline and Punish*, the power of discipline creates docile, political bodies that become more capable but also subordinated. For decades, dancers spend almost all their time disciplining their bodies into the steps of classical ballet. Dancers internalize the dance, they 'become' the dance – their work – far more than is the case in other occupations, since the ballet dancer's body is his or her instrument.[4] Dancers use their body all the time when they work, and they work almost all the time, from daily class in the morning through rehearsals in the afternoon and often performances in the evening, until late at night. Dancers also use their bodies *differently* than other people when they do not dance. They are extremely skilled at non-verbal communication, which sometimes leads to misunderstandings when dancers interact with non-dancers. Dancers 'write' elaborate non-verbal intertextual 'texts' that only other dancers (or ballet people) can 'read'.

There are extensive notions in the ballet world with respect to body types and movement talents. The ballet body types can be divided into categories according to kinds of roles in classical ballets. One classical body type is thus the *soubrette*, a small woman who moves fast, while the *danseur noble* is a handsome male dancer who dances elegantly, the generic prince. There is the 'lyrical' dancer, who is the traditional ballerina type with stage personality and a pretty face, and the *demi-charactères*, or the 'character dancers' as they tend to be called nowadays, are often male dancers with a pronounced acting talent who are cast in roles like the Jester in *Swan Lake*. Dancers who do not fit very well into any of these body types, or perhaps only get to do corps work or one or two solos as character dancers, may however blossom in contemporary companies, where their special body types and stage personalities can be used. I learnt of dancers who had been held down in classical companies developing rapidly when they came to contemporary companies. Unfortunately, I also noticed many dancers in the classical companies who had individual talents that were unable to grow because they were cast to do corps work all the time: there are not all that many solo sections in classical ballets.

Linked to the ideas around classical body types in the ballet world is the categorization on the basis of what are regarded as crucial skills in classical ballet. It is important to be good at turning and jumping, so dancers are identified as 'a turner', 'a jumper' or 'a pirouetter', although most dancers turn or 'pirouette' better on either the right or the left leg. Dancers who are not very good at such steps are characterized as 'not a turner', 'not a pirouetter' or 'not a jumper'. The characteristic steps of the women dancers in *Swan Lake* imitating the delicate shy movements of swans (especially flapping their arms like wings) are not supposed to be used in other ballets, unless as a reference in contemporary ballet. When women dancers consciously or unconsciously move like the *Swan Lake* steps, especially during a period of time when they are performing *Swan Lake*, it is called 'swanlaking'. Male dancers who express too much emotion and temper as the Prince in *Swan Lake* may be criticized for 'donquixoting'.

Dancers are totally dependent on their bodies, and on staying in shape at all times. By contrast with athletes, for example, who build up a basic fitness that they improve before competitions, dancers who are on their way upwards in their careers or who are anxious to keep an acquired position constantly have to strive to get better. Taking the old saying 'you are only as good as your last performance' seriously, they dance on and on.

Mind and Body, Culture and Nature

Judging by René Descartes's classic separation of body and mind, in which the mind is of a higher order than the body, dancers do not fare very well. Dancers express themselves through their bodies, sometimes in subtle ways that require practice (and perhaps a special sensibility) to be understood. Out of this comes the notion that dancers are stupid, which on the whole is at odds with my experience of them.[5] It is obvious that some dancers are more talented than others in using words; the best ones may become choreographers. It is important to remember that dancers do not get as much practice in speaking as people who go to school longer. But verbal talent is obviously not the sole kind of talent.

When new choreography is created in the studio, or when dancers are learning new roles, it is common for them to form a mental picture of what the steps should look like, but then it takes a while before 'the body understands', as they say, before they can execute the steps. There is usually a time-lag built into the process, even if again some dancers absorb the steps faster than others. Some coaches may try a different tempo, or move the dancer to another part of the studio to see if that helps him or her to do the steps. When it comes to revivals of productions the dancers have danced before, perhaps a year earlier, it often happens that 'the head remembers, but not the body' so 'I must hear the music to remember these steps.' The fact that dancers internalize the dance, that the steps are inscribed in their bodies and are activated by the music, I observed many times when dancers waited in the wings for their entrances and another dancer was on stage doing a role that the dancer in the wings was doing in a different cast. He or she was then unable to stand still, but 'marked' the steps with the music while the dancer on stage did the same steps there. Once in a dressing-room before performance, one of my informants, a woman corps de ballet dancer, was getting ready for her entrance. We followed the performance through the music from the Tannoy system, and when a section started that the dancer had just learnt, she started 'marking' the steps while sitting on her chair, saying 'I can feel it!' (This obviously does not work when dancers dance to silence in parts of or throughout contemporary pieces. Then they rely on a separate structure of counting.) Dancers can remember steps for years, saving them in their 'muscular memory' – up to five years, I noticed, but not for much longer. After twenty years steps are forgotten, unless a dancer works as a coach and has been teaching the steps to young dancers since then.

One of the central ideas in the ballet world is the division between having a 'good body', a 'natural talent' as it is called, which designates softness of the limbs and musicality on one hand, and 'not having the right mentality' on the other. The dancers who combine these characteristics are regarded as a bit lazy, which can cause envy, since they do not have to work as hard as most of the others have to. A dancer with a 'natural talent' but who is said 'not to have the right mentality' does not, however, reach the top. The opposite also occurs: there are dancers who do not in fact have the physical talent that is regarded as necessary to become leading dancers, but who, with enormous willpower and carefully calculated schemes for diet, fitness and active thinking about how to do steps, still reach very close to the top. This 'thinking dancer',[6] as it is put, solves technical problems about steps and spacing, and makes an effort to remember combinations of steps. An important part of figuring out how to do steps is to prevent and avoid injury. These dancers also try to visualize how steps may go wrong on stage, and then practise ways of 'rescuing' them in the studio. 'Thinking dancers' have learnt quite comprehensively from books, tapes and courses on mental training about how diet and training practices influence hormones, stamina and body shape. They usually practise more than their colleagues, before and after ordinary working days in workouts in the theatres and elsewhere in town. There are not so many of them, only a few in each company, but they have all surprised coaches and colleagues. In the long run, they acquire 'work victories' (the Swedish expression is *arbetssegrar*). Connected to the contrast between 'thinking dancers' and those with 'natural talents' or 'good bodies' is the internal distinction between 'workhorses', who work very hard and can make surprising progress, and 'racehorses', who do not have to work so hard, yet find themselves on top, above the 'workhorses'.

Classical ballet is easily identified as a cultural artefact, even 'unnatural', as it so happens the dancers themselves exclaim. When modern dance developed in the early twentieth century, it was again often hailed as 'natural', and even 'primitive' (Cass 1993: 226) and 'healthy' (Kendall 1979: 17–31), by contrast with classical ballet.[7] This does not mean, however, that contemporary dancers in the 1990s are less prone to injuries than classical dancers. Judging from my observations and interviews with the Royal Swedish Ballet, the Royal Ballet in London, the American Ballet Theatre, the Joffrey Ballet in New York and Ballett Frankfurt in Frankfurt-am-Main, as well as interviews with company physiotherapists, there was no significant difference when it came to rates of injuries in classical and contemporary companies.[8]

Culture of Injury and Pain

The threat of suffering setbacks in one's career because of injuries, or even worse, of having to stop dancing prematurely, is constantly there. This happens often enough to be regarded as a trauma by dancers. Most injuries occur in rehearsals, some in daily class; but it also happens that dancers are injured on stage in performance. Injuries are never glorified, they are too painful and potentially too serious (occasionally disabling) for that. Yet there is a prestige hierarchy, where injuries that happen on stage are on top. There is a kind of similarity with wounds that soldiers get in war, or icehockey players in national league matches, which hints at a certain heroism.[9] But then dancers, like anyone else, may be injured outside work. So a woman dancer who was unable to dance for a few weeks was especially frustrated, she told me, because she had hurt her arm when she slipped on the floor in her bathroom – 'it didn't even happen at work!' A male dancer who broke his ankle when he fell down in a ditch one dark night on holiday, told me about the incident with the same unhappy tone of voice.

With the expansion of studies on the body and embodiment, the social and cultural meanings of pain have been scrutinized. Extensive discussions on embodied pain and suffering are thus provided by Loïc Wacquant (1995a) on boxers and Palmer (1996) on cyclists. Both authors note that the physical torment that is one facet of these skills makes boxing and competitive cycling appear inhuman and incomprehensible from the outside. The analogy with ballet dancing is obvious. On an everyday basis, the body is talked about in the ballet world mostly in terms of pain from injuries.[10] The conventional interactive greeting 'Hello, how are you?' is strikingly often answered with 'Not very well, I'm afraid. My foot hurts' or even 'My whole body is aching.' The latter is explained by company physiotherapists as 'psychological', especially when casting lists have come up, or before premières.

Psychologists Tajet-Foxell and Rose (1995: 34) report higher pain and pain tolerance in ballet dancers than in a control group. The difference is explained by ballet dancers' physical training and fitness, but psychological factors are also included: dancers are so used to the sensation of pain from physical activity that they even recognize that they have some control over it. This, Tajet-Foxell and Rose conclude, may in fact be part of the reason why the dancers had higher pain-tolerance thresholds and yet still experienced the pain more strongly than the control subjects did. Dancers are more versatile in dealing with pain. In a physical therapy study on musculoskeletal pain and work conditions of one hundred and twenty-eight classical ballet dancers in Sweden, Ramel and Moritz (1994: 11) found that the vast majority, one hundred and twenty-one, had been injured for some period of time during the previous year, mostly in the lower back, feet, ankles and neck. The authors did not see any significant difference between men and women when it came to injuries. This may seem surprising, since men and women do not do exactly the same steps in classical ballet. The fact that men often lift the women, and are required to jump higher and with more elaboration than women, while the women stay longer in balance, not to mention dancing on pointe, would suggest that injuries would differ. This was at least what a physiotherapist who worked with one of the companies in my study pointed out to me: men have more back injuries than women, who are usually injured in their knees and feet. During my observations of the Royal Swedish Ballet, the British Royal Ballet, the American Ballet Theatre and Ballett Frankfurt, stress fractures and sprained ankles, as well as spurs in ankles and muscle-ruptures, were common.

Explaining the social construction of pain among pianists by the political economy of the concert market, Alford and Szanto (1996) describe the view that pain is necessary in order to acquire a virtuoso technique. This pain is, however, often denied. There is a rule in the ballet world against casting or promoting dancers who are injured. In order to be cast in leading roles, or at least important roles, it thus happens that dancers who are injured hide their injuries and rehearse, or even perform, on painkillers, anaesthetic creams or injections. The injuries can then get worse, and the dancer is thereby jeopardizing performances. An injury, moreover, not only harms the injured dancer's career, but also potentially that of his or her partner, who may then not have anyone to dance with for a while. So on top of the physical pain, injured dancers often experience not only a psychological frustration over not being able to dance for a period of time, but also guilt over affecting others adversely. It is the camaraderie and sense of community in the company that then comes to the surface. The fact that one injured dancer has to be replaced by someone else may furthermore lead to chains of replacements in a particular production. I both observed and heard about a number of cases of relatively unnoticed corps de ballet dancers who unexpectedly got a chance to do a solo (by a guest choreographer), but then were injured and never got to perform it.

Although some dancers get through a dancing career with few minor injuries, almost all dancers get injured – and have pain. To endure pain is regarded as necessary in a dancer's career, even though it is clear that the pain tolerance thresholds vary individually and contextually. Many dancers experience pleasure in pushing themselves until they get pain – as long as it improves their form and they look fine in the mirror. But when the pain becomes unbearable, it is not fun any more. I saw a number of injuries happen, and a couple of dancers sent to hospital; but I never witnessed an emergency that called for the First Aid equipment that is available in studios and backstage. At Covent Garden in London and at the Kennedy Center in Washington, DC there were even First Aid rooms set up for dancers, stage-hands and other personnel who work in the risky setting backstage.

But if pain is a part of the everyday life of dancers, there is also the *pleasure* of being able to move and control one's body beyond ordinary motor activities, and at times reach into a state of flow (Csikszentmihalyi 1990). This may happen in daily training and rehearsal, but most significantly in performance. Loïc Wacquant (1995a: 507) makes a case for 'the sensual rewards' of boxing, even comparing the preparations before a bout, the heightened excitement and finally the climax of a bout to an orgasm. Moments of flow – when dancers feel completely in control of their bodies, and experience power as a consequence – are the rewards, and one important reason, for struggling with seemingly endless hardships: practising almost every day for decades, coping with pain, and in most cases remaining unknown.

Proxemics and Proxemic Unity

'We were like one body' is a common description of exceptional rapport between partners, a man and a woman, two men, the corps de ballet or even occasionally the entire company in big scenes. This can be related to Edward T. Hall's (1959, 1966)[11] ideas on proxemics, especially the four distance zones of intimate, personal, social and public relations, further divided into close and far phases and shaped by people's relationships and feelings towards each other. Since this proxemic pattern is generated from middle-class Americans, Hall is eager to point out that it is not valid for all cultures. He also says that work relationships tend to occur within the close social distance. Proxemics in a ballet company are, however, different from those at other places of work. Drawing on Hall, Swedish dance scholar

Cecilia Olsson (1993: 114) has coined the concept proxemic unity (*proxemisk enhet*) to signify the zone of closeness, or artistic rapport that springs up between dancers on stage 'as if they were one person'. When dancers work together and create proxemic unity, it is thus similar to an intimate distance zone, rather than close social distance. Yet in performance dancers work within the far phase of the public distance because of the audience.

At the American Ballet Theatre, I heard the expression 'we were like one body' about the corps de ballet (the French *corps*, incidentally, means 'body') innumerable times about one performance on a tour of the act 'The Kingdom of the Shades' (from *La Bayadère*) – called 'Shades' or 'the white act' for short. Staged by Natalia Makarova for the American Ballet Theatre in 1974, it became a tremendous success (Barnes 1977). Arlene Croce (1977) wrote a rave review entitled 'Makarova's Miracle' in *The New Yorker*. Twenty years after the première, the company had not danced 'Shades' for a while. Now it was coached by a woman who was in the corps de ballet in 1974. And at the première of the tour, with a younger generation of dancers, something extraordinary happened: the corps was completely together. 'When the corps brought down the House in Orange County' was remembered as a historical performance when the corps de ballet got the loudest and the longest applause – not the soloists, as is usually the case. Not surprisingly, it was corps de ballet women who told me about their unexpected accomplishment. In the end they were so tired of standing in *arabesque* while the audience screamed for about ten minutes that they shouted 'Stop it! Stop it!' out of exhilarated exhaustion. Their unprecedented success was reflected in the reviews that subsequently were posted in the dressing-rooms.

If proxemic unity is one aspect of the plethora of proxemic relationships and zones on stage and back-stage, dancers' body consciousness and awareness of other bodies, especially in motion, relate to further issues of proxemics and kinesthetics. Dancers are, for example, strikingly skilled at communicating without looking at each other, which is something they learn in dancing but carry over to how they move and behave when they are not dancing. Dancers often scan what is going on beside them without turning their heads, which is a kinaesthetic knowledge derived from ballet. Two dancers may be deeply involved in conversation without looking at each other: one of them lying on the floor under the barre stretching, and the other one standing on the other side of the barre bending backwards in the opposite direction. A part of this, which also originates from the form and space of dance, is that dancers are skilled at communicating with their backs, calling attention to their presence, or relating to someone.

There is also a sensibility to the presence of many other bodies in dancers' body consciousness, and to how they move in relation to one's own move-ments. This knowledge is clearly derived from dancing together with many dancers in the studio and on stage. It is applied in dressing-rooms and canteens, when dancers carry on conversations across the room, often over the row of mirrors that separates dressing-room tables from each other. They do not see each other, yet they are aware of each other's presence and communicate with each other. It becomes a kind of ping-pong conversation because of the distance that separates the speakers.

Another example of dancers' movements when they are not dancing occurred in the kitchen of a dancer in the middle of a boisterous party. As people were standing talking in groups, a corps de ballet man did a set of somersaults as a matter of course. No one commented on it, or seemed to think that it was remarkable in any way; it was just his way of showing happiness. The other dancers knew that he sometimes did things like that; they were also much more used to these kinds of movements than many other people outside the ballet world.

Dancers' extreme sense of movements makes them excellent at imitating, and also ridiculing, other people's characteristic postures and walking styles. It does not have to be somebody who is threatening socially or careerwise in the theatre, nor somebody they know. It can be a colleague or a coach, but it may just as well be the American Nancy Kerrigan's skating style that dancers exaggerate in a break between rehearsals. My point is that dancers are very skilled at picking up movement qualities and patterns that they happen to come across. Dancers also perceive much of everyday life around them in terms of ballet culture and ballet steps, both in the theatre and outside it. An ex-dancer turned coach imitated what her jealous ex-husband looked like when she came home late, by lifting her arms backwards and taking on a grim facial expression: 'just like Rothbart' (the wicked magician in *Swan Lake*), she said. Or there was the coach who said one day that 'this morning my dog woke up stretching her paws just like Pavlova (in the *Dying Swan*)'. On a walk with a dancer, we saw some ducks tentatively going back and forth before they crossed a road, and the dancer remarked to me 'Look, they are rehearsing!' And spotting swans swimming on a lake, a coach immediately associated the scene with his favourite dancer and how he used to coach her for Odette/Odile in *Swan Lake*.

Gender: Close Colleagues

Despite the designation 'gender studies', which seems to indicate an equal attention to how men and women are constructed socially and culturally, often in relation to each other, studies on gender have focused on women. This has also been the case in studies on dance and gender. There has been, however, a recent small shift towards paying attention to men in Ramsay Burt's (1995) *The Male Dancer*, dealing with representations of masculinity in dance, and Mark Franko's (1995) *Dancing Modernism/Performing Politics*, accentuating male issues in modern and postmodern performances. The steps and stories of classical ballet, featuring fragile women and strong men in traditional gender roles, have otherwise been obvious topics for feminist critique[12] in terms of subordination and domination contextualized in a patriarchal order in wider Western society. This has recently been challenged by Sally Banes (1998) who argues that women have in fact been represented in more complex ways in ballet and dance, including women's agency.

Contrary to a general belief outside the ballet world, especially among non-ballet-goers, that ballet is essentially a female skill, the majority of women dancers over men in the classical companies was in fact rather small.[13] Federico (1974) argues that the gender percentage of classical companies produces more equal relationships in the ballet world than in the patriarchal order outside it. Most directors of ballet companies are, however, men. If they are gay, they occupy a marginal social position in society at large, subordinated in relation to heterosexual men. Gay directors and other prominent ballet people still have to keep their personal partnerships in the background, and may ask a woman friend to accompany them to receptions at embassies and sponsoring and promotion dinners with royals and donors. Or how else does one respond to invitations that are addressed to 'Ballet director and wife'? The hypocrisy of the people who arrange these functions becomes especially blatant when they are not only aware of the long-term partners of gay ballet people, but even know them personally. Male homosexuality is not accepted enough in the ballet world, nor outside it, for gay couples to be invited to public events. There is also, still, a habit of concealing homosexuality, at least initially, in the ballet world. After all, the older generation in the ballet world came of age when homosexuality was still unlawful in Britain and in some parts of the United States. A number of them were public figures, which meant that they had to be extra careful. Once, at a party, a ballet person of the older generation entertained a group of younger ballet people (including the ethnographer) by telling stories from the ballet world of the 1950s: 'In those days we were taught "sleep with anyone you want to! Sleep with an elephant if you want to – but don't bring the elephant to the theatre!"'

The element of gay men in the ballet world leads to layers of alliances and antagonisms, and male bisexuality produces a kind of *mobile gender*, with some men having both female and male lovers, or living with another man for twenty years and then with a woman for twenty years. The knowledge that a man who lives with a woman 'used to be gay', or 'was gay for a while ten years ago', or that a man who lives with another man 'used to have girlfriends' adds to this sense of mobile gender, which can be analysed as one aspect of closeness between genders and hence colleagues, blurring the gender boundary.

In the productions of the classical ballets in France during Romanticism, when many of the ballets that still are danced came about, it was the man who supported the woman, lifted her, and held her when she was pirouetting. The choreography made the woman dancer the star. But before Marie Taglioni's successful pointe-dancing, August Bournonville studied ballet in Paris for Auguste Vestris. He was exceptionally skilled technically, and when Bournonville went back to Copenhagen and founded the Danish ballet style, he remembered this male dancer and thus gave a more prominent position to the male dancer in his ballets than was the case in the French style. Also the Ballets Russes emphasized the male dancer, largely thanks to the exceptional Vaslav Nijinsky (Cass 1993). Much later, Rudolf Nureyev's electrifying stage personality coupled with his virtuoso technique marked the beginning of yet a further new era for the male dancer – 'Prince's Lib', as the renowned British critic Clement Crisp (1995: 22) has called it with his typical disarming wit. 'This hunger he had to perform, he had such nerves, *all* the time' a colleague of Nureyev told me. Nureyev also revived the choreography in old ballets to suit his magnificent dancing, thereby accentuating the male dancers.

Yet many male classical dancers, especially principals, still complained that their job only consists of holding and lifting the ballerina or 'rescuing' her when she forgets steps or makes mistakes. This dilemma becomes easier to handle through jokes. The men say that they feel like 'lifting-cranes', at least in some roles. One dancer liked to yell 'Porter, track 2!' Another one said that he was thinking about writing his memoirs, which he would entitle *My Life Under a Tutu*.

Dancers' habit of being close to one another physically, especially when they dance, leads to a lot of touching, kissing and fondling that would be regarded as strange, even offensive, in many other settings. Terms of endearment are often also coupled with this, especially by someone in a higher position, such as a coach or a choreographer addressing a dancer of a lower status about how to do steps, protectively and pedagogically, and at times patronizingly, building confidence. It can also be a senior pianist talking to a young dancer, or a famous conductor working with a coach. The use of 'darling', 'honey', 'love', 'dear' and so forth usually indicates a liking, even an affection, but of varying kinds and duration. Much closeness that occurs in the studio falls off outside it. (In the beginning of my field study I took it for granted that dancers who were clinging to each other, sitting on each other's laps during a break, resting with their heads on another dancer's lap, fondling each other, were lovers; but it turned out that some of them were just dancing partners and friends.)

When a woman dancer is menstruating, she talks about it openly and about the worries of pain and leakages during performance. Because of the physical closeness in the ballet world, there are many layers of closeness between women and men; between two partners, as well as between a coach and a dancer. The men in these teams are often aware of and learn to handle the women's menstrual cycles; mood swings as well as increases in weight. Some of the men are married to or live together with the women they dance with, and they tend to be particularly sympathetic and supporting when their wives or partners are menstruating, even to the point that it becomes a joke among other men in the company. It is common knowledge in the ballet world that when a woman's period is about to start or has just started she is unable to use her full capacity as a dancer, whether in rehearsal or perform-ance. In the old days at the Bolshoi, I was told by a coach who used to dance in former Soviet Union, they did not schedule performances for ballerinas when they were menstruating. All this awareness and talk about menstruation sometimes makes the men produce jokes like 'I feel tired today. I have my period', or claim that they cannot dance 'because I have period pains', or even that 'I've had my period for twenty years!', signifying the length of time this dancer had been dancing with women partners and other women dancers who were menstruating.

On the tour to Japan with the Royal Swedish Ballet, at the last performance practical jokes on stage (see Chapter 5) were extended further backstage: some zestful men had exchanged the signs on the doors to the showers saying 'ladies' and 'gentlemen'. From the corridor outside, I heard the surprised yelling from unexpected encounters. Although dancers are used to the physical closeness in the ballet world, it sometimes becomes problematic for them anyhow. One way to handle too much bodily contact between people who are attracted to each other, who could be attracted to each other – or who hate each other – is thus to joke about it. There are sexual and erotic jokes of reference and jokes of address. To the latter kind belongs flirtation: soft, sensual, hardly detectable on the one hand, and openly tantalizing, brazen jokes on the other, often accompanied with light touching. Cruel jokes can of course be both addressing and referential. The fact that there is a certain amount of acting of love in dancing adds to this. Teams who work very well together, perhaps even become famous together, are bound to be the targets of speculations and rumours, whether joking and/ or envious. Heterosexual men sometimes joke about the fact that 'we are supposed to be gay', occasionally by way of roles. A heterosexual male dancer who was dancing one of the ugly sisters in *Cinderella* (the ugly sisters are traditionally danced by men in Frederick Ashton's production) dressed in a woman's costume acted a woman flirting with men in the wings before performance. On another occasion, I was having coffee with a gay dancer and we were talking about favourite roles. He was in a joking mood, so he suggested that he would like to dance Kitri, the leading woman in *Don Quixote*, to indicate his gayness.

Male homosexuality, as well as assumptions about male homosexuality and gay relationships, were thus often handled through jokes. But male homosexuality also occasionally led to embarrassments and surprises, as well as to disappointments; women who were attracted to men they then learnt were gay usually had to find other romantic involvements. This also applied to gay men who were infatuated with heterosexual men. The latter may take it lightheartedly and inform the gay men of their sexual orientations, but reactions of horror and dismay also occur.

Early in my field study I was having lunch in the canteen with a number of the male dancers in the company. They were joking about the erotic side of ballet and 'dancing as a way to keep one's erotic impulses at bay'. Then they became more serious and started to inform me quite assertively, without my having asked about it, 'We are not gay!' They talked about the belief that male dancers are gay, while in fact most male dancers in this company were not. They were concerned about this and about making sure I realized that they were 'like any ordinary guys who are interested in technical stuff. The only difference is that we're interested in ballet.' One of them even showed me a picture that he kept in his wallet of his cherished car as a proof of his 'normality', as he phrased it. I was repeatedly told that there are in general more male gay dancers in contemporary than in classical companies, and less in those than there used to be. Yet male gayness is present as one feature of ballet culture as well as in the ballets, and increasingly also in contemporary choreography suggesting homoeroticism. One manifestation of the gayness in the ballet world is the large number of special terms and expressions to designate male homosexuality, such as 'feminine men', to 'be on the other side', or 'in the other department', which I frequently heard heterosexual men and women use when there were no gay men around. The Swedish term *fikus* is still common in the Swedish ballet world (but not outside it any more), not necessarily used deprecatorily. As with any form of persecuted subculture, male homosexuality in the ballet world may supply the grounds for sticking together and helping another gay man, like an invisible bond that is activated from time to time. In a large organization, however, where people are in competition, such solidarity cannot be taken for granted. Unexpected support may appear, of course, from heterosexual men and women who accept male homosexuality as just another way of life.

Not only do dancers feel that their colleagues are very close to them, but they are also exposed to each other in various stages of undress and nakedness. Between rehearsals dancers move around dressed in bath-gowns, shawls and warm slippers, even when they are running errands in the office. To shower every day without curtains between the showers may, however, become trying in the long run. ('You learn to shower at home', as a dancer said.) The physical closeness also makes many masks and attitudes fall off. It becomes impossible to disguise personal circumstances or pretend to be someone else in the long run, which leads to intimacy but also to conflicts and social dramas, which however are characteristically nonetheless resolved in the long run.

A case from a tour finally illustrates the ambiguity of the gender boundary in the ballet world: the dancers had all been presented with green bags with a label displaying their company name as a way of creating community and for promotional purposes. It did not take long for these seventy identical bags to get mixed up with each other. Once before a performance, I was in a dressing-room for women when one of them opened her bag, and then broke out into an excited giggle, yelling: 'There's a *susp* [man's suspensory] here!' Soon the whole dressing-room was shrieking with laughter. It was a matter of gender and context, since these women not only had seen suspensories many times, but had also felt them when they were dancing. But they had not expected a suspensory in their dressing-room, let alone to find one among their private belongings, as the woman who opened the bag initially thought she was doing.

Notes

1. Mewett (1982) makes these connections in his study of a Lewis crofting community where nicknaming of people is one aspect of belonging to the area. Through nicknaming, people with the same name are distinguished. Morgan, O'Neill, and Harré (1979) argue that children's nicknaming is a way for them to generate and maintain their social order.

2. Within a Marxist framework, Paul Willis (1977) has depicted a counter school culture formed by English working-class boys, which can be said to oppose society at large in class terms. Wulff (1988) deals with an ethnically mixed group of teenage girls in an inner-city area of South London who more or less openly rebelled against formal and informal rules at school and a youth club.

3. It took a long time before theories on the body and embodiment were treated more systematically in social theory, but they surface already during antiquity (like

the four temperaments) where thinkers sort out bodies, count them, and divide them into different kinds (Synnott 1993). The anthropological and sociological literature on embodiment has grown during recent years into an ample collection of general works on the whole body (Featherstone *et al.* 1991), as well as on specific aspects like the senses (Howes 1991) and the emotions (Lutz and White 1986). Mary Douglas (1970, 1978) early wrote anthropological landmarks about the body as social symbol and natural symbol. The article 'The Mindful Body' by Nancy Scheper-Hughes and Margaret M. Lock (1987) is widely cited as an agenda for research on the concept of the body in medical anthropology. The authors argue that body and mind are connected when it comes to health and sickness. With ethnography about ritual practice (healing and ritual language) in a contemporary Christian religious movement in North America, Thomas J. Csordas (1995) has discussed embodiment phenomeno-logically as a paradigm in anthropology for the study of culture and the self. He concurs with the view that body and mind are linked together in terms of embodiment. Feminist anthropologists like Martin (1987) have analysed the body in terms of reproduction in a patriarchal order.

4. Pierre Bourdieu's (1977) seminal notion of habitus explains how the practice of dancing inscribes dispositions, in the form of perceptions and actions, into the dancer's body, and how these are at work both in the actual dancing and in the social life of dancers.

5. Leach (1997) reports on psychological studies of dancers' average intelligence in Britain, Canada and the United States, on all of which they scored high points.

6. See Wacquant (1992: 247) on how boxers characterize their trade as '"a thinking man's game" which they frequently liken to chess'. And Palmer (1996: 140) relates how the body-centred skill of road cycling is yet depicted as 'chess on wheel' by the cyclists.

7. Cass (1993: 224) remarks that Noverre had in fact already requested an expressive kind of dancing that 'reflects nature'.

8. Koutedakis *et al.* (1996: 115) did not find any 'major differences between ballet and modern dancers' in their study on fitness and injury in dancers. See also Koutedakis (1996) on injuries, fitness and nutrition in professional dancers. In the wake of sports medicine, dance medicine has emerged as a new medical specialty. There are for instance orthopaedic surgeons who specialize in dance injuries.

9. In her study 'A Life of its Own: The Social Construction of the Tour de France', Catherine Palmer (1996: 123) mentions the 'battle scars' of a Belgian cyclist Leon Scieur, who won the Tour in 1921 in spite of the burden of a spare wheel on his back that left a permanent mark.

10. For further discussions on pain as embodiment see Jackson (1994) on chronic pain among patients in a pain treatment centre in New England who formed a community of meaning, E.V. Daniel (1994) on the individuality of terror and the pain of torture in Sri Lanka, and Csordas's (1994b) cultural phenomenology of the narrative of a young Navajo man's attack of pain from a tumour. A medical anthropological perspective on pain is provided by DelVecchio Good *et al.* (1992). See also the British report on dancers' health and injury by Brinson and Dick (1996).

11. See also Hall's (1963) 'A System for the Notation of Proxemic Behavior'.

12. Daly (1987, 1997, [1987–88]), Adair (1992), Wolff (1983), Hanna (1988), Novack (1993) and Foster (1996a,b,c) are but a few examples; and for debate see Jordan and Thomas (1994) and Thomas (1996, 1997).

13. The exact numbers of members of ballet companies keep changing somewhat, but during the time of my field study there were forty-eight women and thirty-one men at the Royal Swedish Ballet, forty-nine women and thirty-nine men at the Royal Ballet and forty-three women and thirty-two men at the American Ballet Theatre. At Ballett Frankfurt, the sexes were almost equally represented, with twenty-one women and twenty men.

5

Producing Performance

Ballet performances come about through the management of different perspectives and their frames by a number of agents occupying different positions in the ballet world. This chapter considers how the frames may be explored choreographically, and the fact that sometimes they need to be repaired, as well as maintained. When frames are broken, new ones are inevitably being created. Observations of performances from the auditorium, as well as backstage ethnography around performances, like that in the narrow liminal zone in the wings, will anchor the production of the framed illusion on stage socially in the companies. The audience, especially critics, are also taken into account. Many critics operate transnationally in the sense that they review performances abroad and foreign companies that come on tours. Since critics are there when the performance happens, they are more or less involved in its making. After commenting on the concepts of ritual and revelation in relation to ballet performance, I discuss the creation of ballet art from the dancer's point of view, looking at three different levels: frame maintenance, audience awareness and acting. Finally, a discussion on the significance of last performances will tie in with the notion of ballet as a short, intense career.

Reframing Ballet Performance: Manipulation

At the world première of the short ballet *Firstext* by William Forsythe in collaboration with Dana Caspersen and Antony Rizzi at Covent Garden, the stage was opened up and the stage manager and stagehands could be seen at work in the backstage area, as the audience slowly moved into the auditorium. Suddenly, at half-past seven sharp, when the performance was scheduled to start, the House lights were turned off. A large part of the audience stumbled about in the dark. When they finally found their seats, the auditorium was lit up again, brighter than the stage, and this is how it stayed for the rest of the ballet. On stage, the line 'The Organisation of Culture' was projected on the backdrop, and below it a fire spread in a groove along the entire stage, finally to be extinguished by a lid that was placed over the groove.

A woman dancer entered in silence, dressed in short trousers, sleeveless shirt, and socks. Down on the floor, she started to bend her legs seemingly beyond human imagination and capacity. A cracking sound illustrated that her legs really were breaking. Then a side curtain slammed down. There were false starts of Bach music and fire-cracker sounds. Except for a few scattered laughs, the audience seemed to be in a state of shock.

Framing Ballet Performance: Conventions

Most anthropological studies on theatre, dance and performance have dealt with traditional societies and are associated with ritual. Many rituals contain sequences of dancing, which are thus examples of performative behaviour. Since such behaviour can also be found in everyday life, the concept of performance has been applied quite extensively in a transferred sense.[1] For my purpose here in analysing the social production of ballet performances, I find Richard Bauman's (1992: 41) definition of performance as 'an aesthetically marked and heightened mode of communication, framed in a special way and put on display for an audience' appropriate.

The idea of frame in social acts is often linked to Gregory Bateson (1972: 177–93) and his metacommunicative message 'this is play', which may be challenged more or less explicitly. Erving Goffman (1974) analyses framing in theatrical performance (and even mentions ballet in passing), yet when it comes to ballet performances Barbara Myerhoff's (1990: 247) suggestion 'Let's pretend' is more accurate than the idea of play. As much as play is used as a metaphor in performance studies, its joyous connotation does not cover the range of existential themes around life, love and death in the plots of ballets. And, as my opening vignette suggests: framing as well as reframing may be fragmented in ballet performance – the audience at Covent Garden reacted in different ways to Forsythe's new frame.

The 1994–5 ballet season at Covent Garden opened with a gala performance of a new production of *The Sleeping Beauty*.[2] Choreographed by Marius Petipa to music by Pjotr Tchaikovsky, *The Sleeping Beauty* had its world première at the Maryinsky Theatre in St Petersburg in 1890. The performance at Covent Garden took place in the presence of Princess Margaret, president of the Royal Ballet. The Princess has been an ardent ballet lover from many years back, and can be seen incognito at performances. She is reputed in the ballet world to be quite knowledgeable about ballet. This November evening, as the audience – in tuxedos and evening dresses in the stalls, or in blue jeans on the higher balconies – made its way to the seats, the expectant atmosphere was building up. A low murmur of voices and the discordant sound of musicians tuning up their instruments in the orchestra pit mixed with the sweet smell of theatre make-up.

The stalls circle was decorated with flowers to honour Princess Margaret. When the auditorium was filled, there was a pause, the audience rose – and the Princess entered. The orchestra played *God Save the Queen*, and the audience sang. And then the performance started with the Prologue, the christening of Princess Aurora.

In the first interval, the audience streamed out to the foyers, under the huge sparkling crystal chandeliers: families with children, young and old couples, groups of friends, gay men. In the bars theatre-goers, balletomanes, critics, and ballet people mingled, standing in lines, talking in groups, exchanging greetings, meeting and avoiding glances. Those in the boxes remained seated, as salmon and champagne would arrive to order.

Three hours later, when Princess Aurora had married Prince Florimund in the glorious *grand pas de deux* in the third act, the applause exploded. There were loud 'Bravos!' and stomping feet. After the curtain calls, Princess Margaret rose. The audience applauded her, she had been given a small bouquet of flowers. She waved and left.

Ballet Performance Backstage

As in any theatrical stage performance, what can be seen of a ballet performance from 'up front', or 'out there', in the auditorium, is only half of it. Even experimental dance, which breaks boundaries and plays with the frames of illusion (sometimes extending beyond the stage by dancing among the audience, and even in the foyer during intermissions) originates from backstage, from what is mostly hidden from the audience. When backstage areas are exposed in performances, everyone knows that they have been cleaned up beforehand, and many of the ordinary activities that would usually go on in the wings have been moved away.

Not only does the polished illusion on stage appear totally different for dancers when they are in it compared to what they see of the same production from the auditorium the next evening, as they kept telling me emphatically; there is also an intense world backstage, producing the performance before, during and after 'the show'.

Many theatres get the dancers to sign in before performances, so that they can be called if they are late, or an understudy can be notified in time if someone is ill or injured. When I was on tour with the American Ballet

Theatre I discovered that sometimes it happened that some of the dancers signed in for each other before performances. As they explained to me: 'He's on his way, he just has to wake up' or 'She's having a bath.' At Covent Garden, the stage manager 'goes around the rooms [the dressing rooms] at half [half an hour before performance]' to check if someone is missing.[3] The dancers are also supposed to inform the ballet management or a coach if someone is not present in time.

The dancers are usually in the theatre about one hour and a half before performance, taking a temporary refuge in the dressing-rooms or hovering in the canteen. Some can be found doing warming-up exercises in a studio, or going over variations that they are soon to perform on stage. Messages are transmitted over the Tannoy system: 'Teresa to stage door. You have a visitor!', 'Joaquín, please call 154!' or 'Camilla, please contact Sophie Soloviev!' can be heard over and over again addressing different people, mostly dancers. Assisted by make-up artists, dressers and wig-makers, the dancers are putting on make-up and costumes, and have their hair done or wigs put on. As the stage manager announces: 'Ladies and gentlemen! This is your half-hour-call!', which in fact is called thirty-five minutes before the performance is scheduled to start, the dancers are dropping down to the stage. With full stage make-up and dressed in warm practice clothes such as worn woollen sweaters, leg-warmers and plastic trousers over their often aerial costumes, they walk towards the rosin box to make sure they will have a good grip, which they try on stage right away by doing some combinations of steps behind the closed curtain. There is already an indistinct humming from the other side of the curtain, as the audience is on its way into the auditorium. Outside the stage area, the stage manager is calling 'the quarter' – fifteen minutes left to performance. The dancers are nervous, but focused. A young corps de ballet dancer asks her colleague about the exact ordering of the steps in a section she is not sure about. Now the stage manager summons 'the fiver' and the ballet directors and coaches, dressed up in dark suits and ties, black silk and velvet dresses and high heels, come down on stage to see that everyone and everything is ready and to show their presence and support. As they hasten to their seats in the auditorium, the House manager who is 'up front' tells the stage manager through the interconnected speaker system to start the performance by turning the House lights down. The humming in the auditorium is lowered; then it stops. In breathless silence, thousands of people are waiting for the conductor to arrive. He is greeted by applause, and bows to the audience. Then he turns around and starts the orchestra. The curtain rattles to the sides – and there it is: another world for the audience to discover and recognize.

In classical ballets, the ballerina is welcomed by applause on her first entrance. So are guesting dancers who perform leading roles. As the performance progresses into the first interval, 'the red light is on' over doors leading to the backstage area in order to keep people out of the way when big heavy sets are moved quickly on and off stage. This is stressful for the stage-hands, who groan as they lift and push Renaissance stairs and court columns. (On other occasions, I heard stage-hands complain over their lack of influence in the theatre.) There are signs of class conflict in their loud shouts, as they warn each other to watch out, carrying pieces of sets together and putting them down with a bang that echoes through the auditorium, thereby attracting some attention from the audience. It becomes even more evident when such 'mishaps' happen during performances. After the curtain call, when the leading dancers have received flowers, and taken their bows, the curtain is closed. Then the ballet management comes on stage to give compliments and corrections to dancers who have done leading roles or solos, or who have had a début. And then it is over – the dancers rush to their dressing-rooms, tired now, with smeary make-up and wet through. The tension has usually been replaced by relief, but also many nagging thoughts about mistakes such as a crooked *pirouette* and lack of rapport between dancers. For even if the audience have seemed to enjoy the performance, the dancers and the ballet management have another scale of judgement. Dancers are rarely completely pleased with their performances – not even top dancers at the peak of their careers.

Ballet Performance and Risk

Every performance is unpredictable. So much (dancing, sets, light, music, costume) and so many people (including dancers and orchestra, about two hundred people are working front- and backstage during a full-length classical ballet) have to function for a performance to run smoothly. In order to handle the risk that a performance may not be successful, let alone the risk that it may leave dancers injured, many dancers follow a special routine on 'pre-performance days', by resting, meditating, praying, dieting, or taking drugs of one kind or another. The stage fright reaches its peak minutes before the performance: then the dancers appeal to supernatural powers in order for the performance to go well. This behaviour may for example entail knocking three times on the floor (for it to hold), or the scenery, or touching a special spot backstage (in the opera house in Frankfurt some of the dancers touched a red box that covered electrical appliances) while the curtain is still down, though the music may have started. I have seen dancers from Catholic or Greek Orthodox families, who declared that they had nothing to do with religion, cross themselves in the wings seconds before they go on stage. Certain accessories, like a pair of leg-warmers that one happened to wear on a 'pre-performance day' when the performance went really well or a pair of pointe-shoes (as long as they last), may be preferred after that. This can be explained by an awareness that chance or randomness may turn the performance one way of another. At the same time, this theatre behaviour functions as a kind of concentration cues. Although these tricks are mainly learnt from older ballerinas in the company, new habits are also picked up from foreign dancers who come guesting. There are special good luck expressions such as *'merde!'* or *'toi-toi-toi!'*, which must not be answered back (especially not close to or on the stage), since that is believed to bring bad luck.[4] So it is to say 'thank you' for *'toi-toi'* cards and faxes that also come from friends and colleagues abroad, or for presents, usually small dolls, soft toy animals or sweets.[5] Apart from verbal expressions, cards are the most common way of wishing good luck, especially before débuts and premières, when dancers (the popular ones) often get quite a lot of them. Although they are all supportive, the tone varies from friendly to sweet to brazen. Before a revival of *La Bayadère* at the Royal Swedish Ballet a woman dancer (of American origin) who was going to dance Nikia, one of the leading roles, received a small white card from a Dutch couple who both worked in the theatre, the woman as a corps de ballet dancer and the man as a physiotherapist. They had written in English: 'You're *very* beautiful in this part, the only thing to do is to enjoy the performance! TOI TOI TOI.' Two dancers who are going to perform together in a team also wish each other good luck by way of cards. The one-act ballet *La Ronde* by Canadian choreographer Glen Tetley is about the decadence of *fin-de-siècle* Vienna. When it was performed by the British Royal Ballet during my field study one of the women dancers gave her partner a postcard with a picture of a lady dressed in well-to-do nineteenth-century clothing. On the back of the postcard, the dancer had written: 'Lots and lots of love and luck for your debut as "the count" – It has been such fun working with you – I've enjoyed every minute!! See you out there (we'll show em!!) Lots of over the topness –'. The bond between dancers who are cast for the same role in different casts comes across in the following card (quoted with wordplay and all), from a male dancer who had already had his début as Bryaxis, the pirate chief, in *Daphnis and Chloë* by Frederick Ashton (after the Greek story by Longus), and therefore knew what it was like, to a dancer who was about to do it for the first time: 'Wishing you all the very best of Brutish Good Luck for Bryaxis tonight and "La Valse" too. You'll be fucking exhausted by the end of it all but I promise It'll be worth it and you'll feel a real sense of triumph. Go for it PIRATE CHIEF!'

In the Wings: Watching, Working, Waiting

In the obscurity of the wings, with the heat from the spotlights close by and a smell of dust and old paint, there is a vibrant zone of intense social activity structured by the happenings on stage and the transformations of the dancers going back and forth on stage. But other things are also going on in this narrow passage. There is a lot of waiting, not least for dancers between entrances, but also by technicians for their cues, and by dressers for dancers. They all learn the particular rhythm of a production and follow it through the music. So do dancers and dressers who happen to be in the dressing-rooms and the corridors, where the music can be heard over the Tannoy system (in important places like the stage door, the ballet director's office and the make-up rooms there are monitors of the stage as well) for those with later entrances.

On their evenings off, dancers sometimes watch from the wings because they have nothing else to do, or because they have a friend in the performance. They may also be in a different cast than the one that is on, or in the process of learning a role that is danced by someone else. Spouses and friends, whether they are dancers, ex-dancers or non-dancers, may watch from the wings. Groups of dancers and other people from the House come there to give support to a young dancer who is doing a début or who has been asked to dance at a short notice because of an injury. Such support is expressed through good luck wishes, applause and compliments when the dancer comes back to the wings, as well as consolations when things have not gone so well.

All watching, however, is not benevolent. It sometimes happens that dancers who define colleagues as threatening take to a subtle but deeply stressful way of harassment; when the competitor is dancing a difficult variation of steps on stage, the rival tries to disturb her or him by standing in the wings on a spot where the dancer on stage has to look – and making faces or waving. Established dancers moreover watch younger colleagues from the wings, to check on their potential as competitors. Between entrances dancers judge each other, discuss how their colleagues are dancing, and compare them with themselves. Envy is mixed with admiration and camaraderie.

The wings are also a place for intimate conversations between close friends, as well as soft flirtations between dancers: two boys, or a boy and a girl who do not know each other too well. Other forms of play occur, such as verbal and non-verbal joking. The non-verbal, bodily jokes often take the form of imitation of a dancer who is on stage, producing suppressed giggles that spread along the wings. This is a space offering temporary shelter from the exposure on stage, where muscles and facial expression have to be controlled, and any physical pain must not show. In the wings, on the other hand, there is room to scream it out (since the music is so loud), and also for weeping over an ugly *arabesque* or a bad day in general.

Repairing the Frame: Mistakes

In the transnational ballet world, William Forsythe is regarded as one of the innovators of contemporary ballet. In a fax to the British Royal Ballet he described how he was sharing authorship with his dancers in Ballett Frankfurt: 'Not only are the dancers fluent in a movement coordination that evolves outside of the classical norms, but now they are also responsible for the co-construction of the movements and the phrases and the counter-points thereof.'

In *Firstext* he was making fun of the frames of ballet performance, breaking them on purpose in his endeavour to create new ballet art. This strategy is of course more common in experimental dance and theatre, with already converted, knowledgeable audiences.[6] At Covent Garden the audience seemed to be particularly uncomfortable with Forsythe's use of silence. The audience remained silent, however, out of politeness. Yet the silence was undoubtedly diversified, containing different attitudes and stances: next to the reactions of horror were both amazement and wonder.

The conventional framing of ballet performances enacted beyond the time and place of the theatre room can easily be disturbed by technical errors. Both ethereal and dramatic atmospheres on stage may evaporate through a heavy bang backstage, or a mishap with costumes or sets. It can be a dancer who loses a shoe, or a door that does not open, that turns a magnetic flow of feelings into awkward comedy. The spell is broken – and everyone present is painfully reminded of the fact they are at a dance performance.

As a part of the reframing (cf. V.W. Turner 1982: 79) of ballet perform-ances, and his boundary-breaking aim, Forsythe does not really distinguish between rehearsal and performance: at his base in Frankfurt he continues to change steps during performances. Technical errors do, however, occur also in William Forsythe's open form. At the world première of a new ballet programme *Six Counter Points in 1996*, Ballett Frankfurt presented six short ballets. The performance the day after the première went well until the fourth ballet. When the curtain went up for (*Approximate Sonata*), everyone who had been watching the rehearsals saw that a spotlight that was placed to light up a flag that projected a '*Ja*' on the backdrop, was far too strong. The small white light dominated the stage. The dancer, an American man, started his 'improv' (improvisation), a jerky walk along a straight line towards the audience. He probably did not see the spotlight. Then everybody could hear William Forsythe's voice, calling the stage manager on his microphone from his seat next to composer Thom Willems on the first balcony. Irritatedly, he demanded that the ballet should start over again. The audience giggled amusedly. The curtain went down, not only once, but twice, before the spotlight was corrected and the ballet could really start. Was this then planned? That the spotlight was too strong was not planned, but since Forsythe could in fact communicate with the stage manager without anyone hearing, he obviously chose to turn this technical error into another kind of 'improv'.

Curtains that unexpectedly go up and down have actually become one of Forsythe's trademarks. What would count as a disaster in many, if not most, other ballet productions has become one way for Forsythe to explore and manipulate the frame. He unleashed these *coups de théâtre* on purpose in *Firstext*, albeit with a side curtain, and he does it time after time in *Artifact*, a full-length ballet that was first performed in 1984 and since then has been hailed as a masterpiece. When Ballett Frankfurt danced *Artifact* in Stockholm, the Swedish critic Gunilla Jensen (1994) described the curtain that went up and down here and there in the performance as 'a twinkling eye that sharpens the attention of the viewer'. When I did my field study in Frankfurt, Forsythe's stage manager told me that this curtain trick had in fact occurred to begin with because she once pushed the wrong button, causing the curtain to go down in the middle of a performance. And Forsythe had kept it in as a gimmick.

It is, in fact, more common than not for something to go wrong during a performance. Most of the time, however, the audience does not notice. A dancer missing a step or two does not really belong in this category, partly because they can be 'rescued' by partners. I both observed and heard many stories about dancers falling on stage, but then getting up and dancing even better than before, knowing that they had the attention – and the sympathy – of the audience. It is expected to happen to everyone at some point; yet it is often an upsetting experience.

Timing is crucial in ballet performance; entrances and exits have to be coordinated with the music. The dancer stands in the wings, listening to the music, waiting for his or her cue to enter. And then it is a matter of seconds. On stage, leading dancers can communicate with the conductor: at least they are able to see each other, and if things are at their best there is rapport between them. A late entrance may confuse succeeding cues for the music, sets or dancing. Some cues themselves consists of dancing: for instance, 'the vision of Aurora' in the second act in *The Sleeping Beauty* is a short variation danced by a corps de ballet girl, but is itself also at the same time the cue for the dancer who dances Aurora to enter. In one performance at Covent Garden, the vision was forgotten: the corps de ballet girl was there, but there was no light on her, so that the principal dancer who did Aurora that evening missed her entrance. Some cues are called for by the stage manager, communicating with stage-hands over the electronic system; others stage-hands are responsible for themselves.

Entrances are sometimes missed because a dancer just forgets. In a perform-ance of *The Sleeping Beauty*, one of the women principals was waiting in the wings for her solo in the third act, when she discovered that one corps de ballet woman, who was to take part in a *pas de trois*, was not there. On the spur of the moment the principal woman got into the costume – and did it! Meanwhile the missing dancer was found in the shower, with wet hair.

There are also comic effects in stage errors that can make the audience and/or the dancers laugh. A male dancer at American Ballet Theatre was wearing a wig with long black hair like the other boys in a group in *The Red Shoes*. In a fast movement his wig flew off. Because of the speedy tempo, and to the amusement of the audience, he had to finish the variation displaying a stocking that covered his hair. And in a performance of *Danses Concertantes* by Kenneth MacMillan at Covent Garden one of the soloist women nearly lost her balance, stumbling as she was entering with two other women dancers. The next day she asked me if I had seen it. 'We were hysterical after that!', she assured me.

The ballet management in Stockholm was, however, not amused when the magnificent diadem worn by Gamzatti, the daughter of the rajah in *La Bayadère*, kept falling down over her face at the end of the first act. The make-up artist had not fastened it well enough. In a sense it was a kind of luck, anyway, that it started falling down in Gamzatti's fit of jealous temper against her rival, Nikia, a temple dancer, over a warrior, Solor, whom they both loved. The dancer seemed to emphasize her fury as she kept pushing her diadem back up.

Major injuries that happen unexpectedly on stage can cause actual dramas. An American principal was dancing Prince Siegfried in *Swan Lake* on a tour with the British Royal Ballet in Washington, DC. Suddenly, in the first act 'my knee collapsed, I had snapped a ligament'.[7] The stage manager also told me spontaneously about this incident. She said that the dancer had fallen with his back towards the audience, which meant that it did not see his grimacing. At moments like that, the stage manager is responsible for deciding whether to close the curtain or not. This time, it was closed, and the dancer was carried off stage. In the idiom of 'the show must go on' that structures the ballet world, a male dancer who was watching from the wings was asked to continue the performance. He had danced Prince Siegfried before, so the dressers put the injured dancer's costume on him – and fifteen minutes later he was on stage.

Ritual and Revelations

In the extensive debate over connections, similarities and influences – and the lack thereof – between religious and secular ritual, and theatre and performance in traditional societies and in the West, ballet may appear far removed, like a very special case of Western high culture entertaining a small segment of the population. It is, however, not devoid of ritualistic aspects that can be detected already in its Renaissance origins in peasant folk-dancing and court processions. There are traces of them in ballet productions, like the folk-dances in *Swan Lake* and the court procession in *Romeo and Juliet*. The behaviour around Princess Margaret at the première of *The Sleeping Beauty* at Covent Garden also brings ritual to mind.

Ballet performances at Covent Garden are not rituals in the strict sense of the term, solving social conflicts and crises through communications about transformations that temporarily reveal central social structures, as do for instance a Hindu funeral in Trinidad (cf. Gerholm 1988) or the West Indian carnival in Notting Hill (cf. A. Cohen 1993; Wulff 1988). Yet ballet performances nevertheless fit into Victor Turner's (1964 [1957]: 20) original definition of ritual as 'prescribed formal behaviour for occasions not given over to technological routine, having reference to beliefs in mystical beings or powers'. For even if there is reframing going on by manipulation as well as repairing of mistakes, the framing of ballet performances is very much 'prescribed formal behaviour.' A 'technological routine' is indeed regarded as desirable, but is seldom realized during a performance: minor or major technical errors happen all the time. And there are certainly 'beliefs in mystical beings or powers' connected to ballet performances: not only is there pre-performance supernatural behaviour, but the plots of the Romantic classical ballets often feature 'mystical powers' of witches, magicians and fairies as crucial for the course of events. Drawing on themes from folk-tales the classical ballets present universal human conditions, but present them steeped in a highly specialized cultural idiom.

The transformative quality of rituals is to be found in the liminality of the wings, where the dancers go in and out of their roles, some during a split second, while others are already inside them when they come from the dressing-rooms to the wings. This temporary transformation of the dancers provides the stuff of 'Let's pretend' for the audience. There may be spectators in the audience who experience transformations, as well, but of a different kind.[8]

Creating Ballet Art

Acting in dance performance is not as elaborate as in theatre performance, even if the leading roles have to be created quite carefully, not least when they are supposed to display some kind of development. Except for William Forsythe's interest in theatrical theorists, I never came across any systematic discussion of theories of acting in ballet in line with Stanislavsky's system, for instance. The system seemed to have informed coaches and other choreographers, however, especially Stanislavsky's idea that actors should use their 'emotional memory' (1967: 53–5) when they are on stage. Choreographers and coaches told me how they tried to get dancers to use their memories, and dancers did talk about how they applied their personal experiences when they were acting. A male principal who was dancing Romeo just days after his girlfriend had broken up with him confessed that, in the scene where Romeo finds Juliet thinking she is dead – he had shed real tears. And a male corps de ballet dancer was pondering over the fact that they were 'required to rape and kill – most of us have not raped or killed anyone'! Yet a woman principal in her early thirties, who had danced most of the leading roles in classical ballet, revealed that she did use her own experiences, and mostly those of pain, when she was dancing. At one point when she was dancing Manon: 'In the *pas de deux* towards the end, when she is dying', the dancer said 'I was such a mess, I was just hysterical, because I felt as if I was really there. It took me about twenty minutes to recover afterwards!'

Otherwise, there is a kind of double consciousness, or 'double agency' (cf. Hastrup 1998) in performing ballet roles: it does not consist of a dual awareness of technique and artistry, since dancers say that ballet art comes about when they forget the technique. At the same time as they 'become' certain characters, they are aware of the audience, of the fact that they are acting, however. Once, when *Romeo and Juliet* was played in Stockholm and the balcony scene was about to end with Romeo and Juliet kissing each other: as they parted a string of saliva grew longer and longer between their mouths. This the audience did not see. Instead, it was overwhelmed by the touching emotions on stage, while the dancers had to concentrate very much on not bursting into laughter by the breaking of style in the situation. Here a third level in the double consciousness on stage appeared: on top of the acting and the awareness of the audience, the dancers had to make an extra effort to maintain the frame.

Most of the time, dancers on stage do not see the audience – it is all dark out there. And since there are not that many comic ballets, the audience usually does not laugh. Yet the dancers say that they can 'feel' whether the audience responds or not. The frequency and strength of applause is important in this, but there is also a more subtle sign: after ethereal sections featuring exquisite emotions, when the music has stopped – 'there is a pause, it's as if they don't want to break that mood' dancers told me 'before they start clapping'.

There is a widespread belief in the ballet world that people come to watch ballet performance as a way to escape personal problems and the general drudgery of life. This may partly be explained by dancers' own experiences of getting into a role and forgetting personal hardships while they are dancing. They are usually not at the top of their dancing capacity, however, during difficult periods in life.

Audience: Balletomanes and Theatre-goers

As was suggested in Chapter 2, ballet dancers define themselves above all as artists, feeling alienated among people who go to ballet performances for social prestige, not out of interest. Although there are members of ballet societies that are more drawn to the social life they provide than to ballet itself, true balletomanes can also be seen at their meetings. For balletomanes, ballet is an absorbing hobby. There are balletomanes who after years of admiration at a distance get to know their stars personally. Balletomanes are also known for taking dance editors and critics to task if their stars have suffered bad reviews.

Dancers make an important distinction between good and bad balletomanes. One bad variety of balletomanes are those ballet fans who, I was told by dancers, choreographers and ballet directors 'go to the ballet because they lead distorted lives, they are fanatics who pursue dancers' by way of dirty telephone calls and obscene or pathetic love letters. There are also more conventional fan letters, like this one from a male fan to a principal woman dancer: 'I hope you will excuse my liberty in writing to you . . . you are a Goddess, sheer poetry in motion . . .'. Another genre of fan letter comes from teenage girls who would like to become dancers. This long letter (which has been cut here, but otherwise is reproduced with original spelling and grammar) was addressed to another principal woman dancer:

> Hello. I understand this letter might come as a shock to you, but I have always wanted to write a fan letter to you since I saw you dance the role of Kitri . . . I do

hope you don't mind that I write to you, for I have admired you immensely for
your beautiful dancing and for your superb acting . . . I started at the age of 10,
quite old, I think to start ballet, but. anyway I had fulfilled my wish . . . Now I
have trained for only 2 and a half years, almost 3 and I feel that ballet is the most
sacred and the most beautiful art in the world . . . I want you to know that I love
your dancing and that I admire the effortless grace you put into your dancing and
the feeling of weightlessness, so beautiful and haunting . . . Thank you very much
for reading my letter and for making me feel like I could someday dance as
beautifully as you for you have inspired me in my confidence! Again thank you
for your time and consideration. I know you are extremeley busy with rehearsing
the ballets for the spring season, so I do not expect you to write back, and I do
hope you do not feel that you have to write back, for I am happy enough when I
am writing to you.

Ballet fans can also be found in the groups of people who wait for colleagues,
friends and family outside the stage door after performances. Most ballet
fans just stand there to get a glimpse of their star, perhaps an autograph
(often written on the picture of the star in the programme), or a short
opportunity to offer compliments. Ballet students, usually girls around ten
years of age, can be seen waiting for a woman star. They are innocent and
cause no harm, by contrast with the adult fans who have nothing to do
with ballet on an everyday basis and are talked about inside the theatre in
terms of 'the nuts at the stage door'. Dancers often find it strange that people
they do not know thank them for the performance in person outside the
stage door or through mail. When the dancers leave the theatre, tired and
without stage make-up, carrying their practice clothes and other belongings
in 'five shopping bags', as a female corps de ballet dancer described it, 'you
don't feel particularly glamorous'. And if the performance did not go so
well, from the dancer's point of view, but the audience still loved it, the
encounter becomes even more problematic. The contrast between how the
dancers feel and look and the illusion of fairy-tale courts that the audience
is still absorbed by tends to make it difficult for dancers to relate to admirers.
The dancers cannot hide in their roles any more. And occasionally, ballet
fans have trouble forgetting that the dancers are not Manon or Julia, but
someone completely different that they do not in fact know.

Especially after premières with famous dancers and on tours, there can
be quite a mass of ballet fans blocking the way out, screaming and taking
opportunistic photographs. A few times, when even I was stopped and asked
to sign my name, I realized that they did not know all that much about their
idols. But some obviously do, at least those that follow their stars abroad.
Dancers may be quite surprised when the fans make themselves known, like
a Japanese woman fan who gave a napkin with an embroidered 'for you

only' on it to a Swedish male dancer at the stage door of one of the theatres on the tour to Japan. She had seen him dancing at the ballet competition in Lausanne five years earlier. Dancers who just receive flowers on a foreign tour from fans who have seen them dance before, but whom they do not know, may feel less embarrassed. Once on the Royal Swedish Ballet's tour to Japan, a group of girl fans of one of the male principals was allowed to watch a rehearsal. Overwhelmed by meeting her star in person, one of the girls started to cry.

'Followings', on the other hand, keep a respectful distance from the stars they admire, and tend to limit expressions of their appreciation to the auditorium by applauding, shouting 'Bravo!' and throwing flowers on stage. Ordinary theatre-goers without a special interest in ballet keep a low profile in the auditorium.

Some balletomanes, even ballet fans, have the same seat in the theatre for long periods of time. Sooner or later, however, they usually discover that watching a single production over and over again from different seats in the auditorium will reveal new patterns, forms and accents. Habitual ballet-goers, who know the ballets, can sometimes be seen leaving the theatre in the last intermission, when the best variations have already been danced. Having watched *Swan Lake* for two or three consecutive evenings, they may leave after the third act when the famous thirty-two *fouettés*, whipping turns, by the leading woman dancer have been safely performed. Or they sneak out of the theatre before the last piece in a triple bill has started.

Islands of different kinds of audience are revealed through the applause: regular ballet-goers know when there is a pause in the music to applaud solos, and do not interrupt the music unless an exceptional accomplishment is taking place on stage. They also see to it that they are informed about débuts, so that they can support the dancer who does a role for the first time with applause and cheers. If the dancer who is making a début is unknown, family and friends, often other dancers, who say that they 'know what it's like' will start the applause. Dancers also watch from the auditorium in order to encourage friends and colleagues who feel low, because of personal problems or a recent bad review. They initiate applause that may spread and become louder or they put new force into an acclamation that seems to be fading away too soon.

Critics: The Evaluating Gaze[9]

The day after the gala of *The Sleeping Beauty* at Covent Garden, there was a happy relief in the rehearsal studios. The première had gone very well.

The dancers were pleased with their achievement, and they had felt the audience responding well to them. The ballet management was quite content. Then the reviews started coming in. On the whole, the critics were not impressed, especially not by the lavish pastel set and costumes.

The profound tension between the artistic and the critical attitude is explained phenomenologically by Bensman and Lilienfeld (1973) as generic and as consisting in the artist's aim being to hide technique in order to create a 'natural' world of artistry, which the critic however then demolishes by analysing the technique.[10] This becomes especially evident in non-verbal and non-textual art forms that use images, since the critic is confined to words. Those dance critics who are skilled writers and are able to create depth and other dimensions through their texts still tend to deal with one component of a performance after another, since there is a certain linearity about a text that cannot be avoided. (Neither can the particular size and form of the page.) In the article 'On Your Fingertips: Writing Dance Criticism', Sally Banes (1994) delineates four operations that dance critics perform in different combinations: description, interpretation, evaluation and contextualization.[11]

Unless something exceptional had occurred, many dance reviews from my field study started with a general description of the choreography, the plot, if there was one, or an interpretation of the emotions that the steps could be said to signify. Evaluations may be built in, or come afterwards. Then came a remark about the music, and perhaps towards the end costumes, lighting and sets may be mentioned. Some critics made a point of contextualizing dance pieces in dance history, the history of ideas or the wider art world, as well as in social conditions. But again, in contrast to a performance, which offers a *combined* experience of different visual and aural components, a review usually only has room for one component at a time because of its textual nature. Critics often feel constrained by their short deadlines and the limited number of words they have at their disposal.

Comparing dance reviews, I noticed how some critics switched from focusing on the choreographer's intentions in one review, to the social context in another, and the dancing in a third – all this depending on what kind of work they were reviewing and the nature of the occasion, whether it was a première of a contemporary piece by a choreographer who was regarded as a ground-breaker by critics, a fund-raising gala for research on AIDS presenting short sections from different productions, or a revival of a classic featuring the début of a budding star, for example.

The New York reviews were the most intertextual, presupposing a certain local knowledge about the New York ballet scene and previous reviews. *The New York Times* has at least one dance review or article every day, which is far more than the daily papers in London, Stockholm or Frankfurt-am-Main. The London reviews were less intertextual and at times more arrogant, but also entertaining, while the reviews in Stockholm and Frankfurt-am-Main had a pedagogical slant. Vail (1985) has suggested that context-oriented criticism relating to the social and political world outside the theatre is more common in Europe than in the United States, where the dance itself and the codes of its choreography are what is in focus. This makes sense, since it could be said to reflect the European tradition of story-ballets versus the American abstract style (cf. Chapter 2 on national styles). Recently Vail (1995) has reported on a change in American dance criticism, however: influenced by feminist theory, literary criticism and an ethnological perspective, a generation of dance writers construct writing and movement as instances of cultural performance. Incidentally, this is also happening in Europe.

In general, older critics in my study relied on their experience of having watched and reviewed vast numbers of performances of the classical productions, performed by many different companies, while there was a tendency among younger critics to prefer contemporary work. Defining classical ballet in terms of a 'museum' portraying an 'ideal' but unattainable and undesirable femininity, they held the view that classical ballet is 'always the same' and 'the choreography is rigid'. They found the aims for straight lines and refinement in classical ballet restraining, and usually noted that they were not achieved. There was a certain contextual variability in this stance, however: I observed both critics and contemporary choreographers moving back and forth between dismissing classical ballet or contemporary dance, as well as embracing both genres in general, but not every single production or performance of them.

The distinguished critic and editor of the British dance magazine *Dancing Times*, Mary Clarke, pointed out in an interview, however, that reviewing classical ballets is more demanding than reviewing contemporary dance. The critic needs to know the classical ballets very well, she told me, and this detailed knowledge can only be gained by watching a ballet many, many times. Dance scholar Sally Banes, who used to be a critic, comments that since classical choreography is already known, classical ballet criticism is more evaluative than criticism of contemporary dance, which tends to be characterized by description. Banes brings out the creative possibility in dance criticism, the fact that critics may be able to formulate things that the choreographer has not yet seen (Wulff 1996). Another critic told me that choreographers sometimes asked him for advice in their work, but that he also had received his 'share of hate-letters', which seems to be a part of a critic's job.

In the conflict over interpretative authority between dancers and critics, the critics' stance tends to be 'it's none of dancers' business to read reviews!', since 'I'm not writing for the dancers, but for the readers of the newspaper.' To this dancers comment ironically that 'we also read this newspaper', but despite the fact that they are the people who did the dancing and are evaluated in the reviews, they are not supposed to read them. This becomes even more paradoxical when terms like 'breakthrough' provide dancers with the recognition they have been striving for. Reviews also serve to confirm positions and add to loss of recognition. There are dancers who decide to stop reading reviews, but since they live in a social context where other people – mothers, friends, competitors and ballet directors – read reviews, they may find themselves in a situation where someone unexpectedly comes up to them and starts consoling them, or congratulating them. It is also rather difficult to avoid reading reviews when they are posted on the notice-boards next to the schedules in the theatre. Some seasoned leading dancers have learned to avoid getting upset or euphoric as a result of reviews by asking someone else to collect reviews for them during a season or set of performances; the dancers then read them afterwards.

One or two critics were singled out by dancers and choreographers as knowledgeable and sensitive, even useful to read (most of the time). On the whole, however, critics were feared but not always respected in the ballet world. After having had a major breakthrough, a choreographer ran into one of the critics who had praised his work. Pleased with her review and to have been among the first critics who had identified this talent, launched him, as it were, the critic seemed to expect him to thank her. Instead the choreographer went into a fit, taking her to task for her claim. After all, he was the one who made the piece! Another example of a choreographer defending his integrity against a critic was performed by Bill T. Jones when he entitled a dance piece *Fever swamp*, which was the headline of a negative review of one of his earlier pieces by the eminent critic Arlene Croce (1994–5).[12] She talks about Jones and William Forsythe among other choreographers who 'had fun heckling the critics – anticipating or satirizing reviews' (1994–5: 58). Choreographers and dancers of a certain fame may be in a better position to get back at critics than unknown ones; yet the damage is usually done by then.

The *asymmetry* of the relationship between critics and dancers, where critics *de facto* have more power, is thus quite obvious. Dancers are vulnerable, since critics review them in public and have an impact on their professional identities and careers, but not the other way around (unlike what happens with academics and writers who review each other). Dancers review critics backstage, however, and then they can be quite annihilating, and explain bad reviews by 'she's not very beautiful' or 'she's drunk at performance'. Scornfully they also take critics to task at a distance for mixing up dancers with each other, writing about dancers who were injured and replaced at a short notice by others on stage.

Dancers often felt called upon to state, firstly, that 'critics don't understand how much power they have' and, secondly, that 'critics don't know anything about ballet'. Dancers' knowledge is an absorbing, bodily one, the knowledge of an insider. Many dancers have performed various roles in certain productions over a long period of time. Critics know other things: they tend, for example, to be more versed in dance history than dancers. Many critics have moreover seen a larger number of companies in different productions than the dancers have. After all, since the latter have to concentrate on their own dancing all the time, they do not have very much time to go to other performances in their city or abroad. Those critics who used to dance on one level of course remember what it was like, but are now involved in a different kind of career project.

It is the discrepancy between *doing ballet* and *watching ballet* that is at work again (see Chapter 1). Although dancers and critics are all versed in ballet literacy, dancers may best further their careers by presenting an image of success, while critics usually acquire *their* recognition among editors and fellow dance writers by writing mixed reviews, more negative than positive, at least with regard to established choreographers and companies. Dancers often point out that critics have their favourites (not necessarily the same dancers), and that there are dancers that particular critics obviously just do not like. The ambiguity of mixed reviews allows them, furthermore, to be read in different ways. Some reviews contain contributions to internal debates among critics, or on art and society, and even personal communications of various sorts. Personal alliances and animosities between ballet people and critics add to the layers of meaning and subtexts in dance reviews. In the review essay 'Dancers and Dance Critics', Arlene Croce (1977) criticizes fellow dance critics in her characteristic authoritative tone of voice for not watching carefully enough, for mixing up their personal tastes in dancers with their actual dancing, and for avoiding to 'be cruel even to be kind' (1977: 334). After all, a bad review can also be an incentive for the ballet management to improve things.

Even though ballet people and critics on the whole constitute different camps, they both contain diversified experiences. The same performance appears quite differently to leading dancers who are responsible for solos, on the one hand, and corps de ballet dancers on the other. Established critics tend to be more negative than young critics who are writing their very first reviews, although this does vary.

Neither do habitual balletomanes and ordinary theatre-goers register the same features of a particular performance. And even if they all happen to be touched by an unexpected creation of ballet art on stage, thereby sharing an intense presence, they will reflect upon this state in fragmented ways afterwards, depending on their earlier experiences of ballet, art and life.

Frequently critics work transnationally in the sense that they travel abroad to watch new productions, attend dance festivals and cultivate transnational networks of colleagues. Almost all critics see to it that they are informed about transnational ballet events and news. There are dance correspondents who cover their country for the dance magazines in the ballet centres; and critics also review foreign productions for their native newspapers or dance magazines. In London and New York, there are some full-time dance critics and writers; in Stockholm only a couple. Few dance critics stay on for decades, unlike the older generation of critics, who often worked for the same newspaper for many years. Recently, with expanding dance studies and programmes at universities in the United States and Great Britain, and even in Sweden, there is a growing professionalization of critics (as of many other professions). Yet the autodidact 'gentleman critic' who has been around for a very long time and seen a considerable number of performances of the classics and the birth of many contemporary productions possesses a knowledge and an experience that is highly respected, especially when it is combined with a stylistic talent.

From a transnational comparative point of view, the dance review climate was in general tougher in the United States than in Britain, and even milder in Sweden and Frankfurt-am-Main for both critics and dancers. The market had more influence over the content of newspapers and magazines in the United States than in Europe, and hence on dance criticism, as well. In Britain the situation grew more competitive for dance critics, however, during my field study, because of the 'newspaper war'. British newspapers used to be owned by families; but Rupert Murdoch's entrance into the market and the fact that he radically lowered the prices of newspapers led to a generational shift among critics in London: some of the older established critics were fired, and others left major newspapers. Dance reviews were suddenly required to be 'gossipy and controversial', a renowned critic told me, in order to attract readers and hence buyers of the newspaper.

The most conspicuous case of a dancer's reaction to a negative review during my field study concerned an upcoming young woman dancer who kept getting good reviews. Suddenly she was said to have 'chunky legs' by a critic. In response to this, the dancer developed anorexia. She was certainly in the risk zone for this condition before the review; but the review did trigger the onset. Critics, especially those who work full-time as critics and dance writers and hence write a great many reviews all the time, do not remember exactly what they have written about individual dancers and choreographers after a while – and they may even prefer to acquire a habit of forgetting. The dancers remember, however; they can go on brooding over a negative adjective for decades.

On the other hand, dancers are seldom aware of how critics may have to negotiate with editors about space and formulations in reviews. Few dancers know anything about the extent to which some critics are involved in continuous battles for dance *per se* at newspapers and magazines, battles that not only go beyond their own career projects but at times even risk jeopardizing their reputations. Dancers do not necessarily agree with good reviews (about their colleagues), however, or disagree with bad reviews. One ex-dancer with the Royal Ballet in London told me how a critic had complimented a gesture that Margot Fonteyn had made, and how this had made her so aware of it, that she was unable to repeat it in the same delicate way. Some critics make a point of cultivating a detached integrity, others seek actively to get to know ballet people personally. There are certainly ballet people who work on charming critics, and vice versa. They all share a love of ballet, and genuine friendships do develop, although the dancer who married a critic is an exception.

If there was often an ambivalence toward critics in Stockholm, London, New York and Frankfurt, I noticed a totally different attitude among the Russian dancers I talked to and interviewed in the companies. Having lived through the period of political oppression in the Soviet Union, where dance reviews had to be in line with the party mood – and hence were always positive – these Russians found the reviews in the West refreshing and interesting to read. Horst Koegler (1995) mentions how critic Vadim Gayevsky wrote a book in which he condemned Yuri Grigorovich, then chief choreographer at the Bolshoi Ballet: the book was withdrawn and the editor was fired.

Last Performance: Jokes and Trauma

There are various kinds of last performances in the ballet world: of a tour, a season, or a production (for the foreseeable future), and a dancer's last performance. Dancers who 'have an audience', those with fame, give a farewell performance at which they bid goodbye to their admirers. Last performances of unknown corps de ballet dancers are acknowledged back-stage: the ballet director usually comes on stage after the curtain call and gives a speech behind the closed curtain to the dancer who is about to retire or leave the ballet world to study or take up another job. Not even thirty years old, one male corps de ballet dancer decided to leave and go to university instead. He had pursued a career as a ballet dancer against his parents' will and had been trying to stop dancing for quite some time, and even worked as a travel guide for three years. When his last performance day came, he was presented with flowers from the ballet management and the company in his dressing-room. At the final curtain call he was given the largest amount of flowers, although he was standing at the back among the other corps de ballet dancers. As the ballet director gave a speech in his honour, thanking him for his work with the company, the momentousness of the situation overtook him – still in his costume, and carrying the large bunch of flowers, he rushed off stage in tears.

Occasionally, dancers with long, outstanding careers, are asked by the ballet management to do a performance to celebrate twenty years with the company, for instance, although they continue to dance for a while after that. The curtain calls may then last for a very long time. Despite the fact that the dancers are prepared for it, the force of a standing ovation that lasted for nearly twenty minutes still came as a surprise shock to a celebrated woman principal. 'I had no idea . . .', she told me, 'that they liked me so much.'

There is a tradition in the theatre world, and also in the ballet world, of insiders' practical jokes. In her study of actors in the Stockholm theatre world, Marika Lagercrantz (1995) notes that actors take to practical jokes aimed at slightly disturbing colleagues on stage. The loss of concentration that may result – even the giggling – usually pass by the audience unnoticed. This also applies to the tradition among artists and technicians in the theatre world of surprising each other by making minor changes in the procedure of last performances. At the last performance of a theatre production that Lagercrantz had followed from the beginning at the Stockholm City Theatre, the technicians added a buzzing noise to a microphone that amused everyone involved.

Also in the ballet world, last performances of a tour, a season, or a production are highlighted through the custom of practical jokes that the dancers come up with. This can be seen as a kind of safety valve, a ritual of rebellion, (Gluckman 1982 [1956]), a release after a long period of hard work when dancers on the whole have to do what they are told. This tradition of making fun of colleagues and choreographers is one opportunity for agency: for a change, dancers are let loose to do exactly what they please.

The jokes are usually internal, symbolically reducing the power, success, and sex appeal of colleagues and choreographers, or well-meaning compliments saying something about how a person may appear to others on stage or in the social dynamics of the company. One common trick is to surprise a dancer on stage by making changes in the set, or exchanging roles and costumes, perhaps adding dancers to classical solos like that of the beneficent Lilac Fairy in *The Sleeping Beauty*, who appeared as triplets one year when the American Ballet Theatre danced the last performance of their annual season at the Metropolitan Opera House in New York.

This kind of joking is usually a subtle and harmless manipulation of the frame, the dancers' own manipulation. Yet everyone is expecting it to happen, so some dancers take extra precautions. During the last performance of *Cinderella* on the Royal Swedish Ballet's tour to Japan, one of the seam-stresses, an attractive woman, while she was waiting for her entrance in the wings checked the box she was supposed to open on stage. She found a plastic worm in it.

The Swedish one-act pantomime ballet *Opportunity Makes the Thief*, choreographed by Regina Beck-Fries, features a scene where a young boy kisses a shy pretty young girl in the market crowd in a Swedish village in the eighteenth century. During the last performance of a tour to a provincial town in Sweden, which also was the last time this production was scheduled to be played for a while, the shy pretty young girl found herself kissed by an inelegant old lady, who was danced by one of the men. In the same performance, another lady was supposed to whip her daughter, but instead of the birch the lady was given a baguette from the wings. There was nothing she could do about it, and the audience did not notice; but everyone else did.

Sometimes the audience is likely to wonder what is going on, however – supposing they are unaware of the custom of making practical jokes at last performances. When the Royal Swedish Ballet danced Jiří Kylián's comic *Symphonie in D* for the last time at the end of a season in the month of June, the women dancers were dressed in leotards with legs covering half their thighs, like old-fashioned swimming costumes. Four of them entered in a square formation, three of them wearing sun-glasses . . .

A Star Bows Out

In its turn, however, the last performance of a dancer is no joking matter, but fraught with emotions. When the contract of a renowned principal woman was terminated without warning, her last performance was a major event in the theatre. Her dismissal had upset many of the dancers especially, and in the weeks before her last performance, her situation came up frequently in conversations in canteens and dressing-rooms. On the day of her last performance flowers were sent in immense quantities to the theatre from her family, friends and following. When I watched the performance from the wings, I caught glimpses of desperation while she danced one of the leading roles in classical ballet with her long-time partner. In the last intermission, as the final act was about to start, I noticed that one of the directors came backstage from the auditorium and sneaked off into a corridor leading away from the backstage area. He may have had an errand to run; but it is more likely that he wanted to protect himself from this dancer's very last curtain call. It was bound to be very emotional. As the final act moved on, dressed up dancers came to the wings to support their colleague in her distress. Pressing together in small groups, there was soon a crowd in the wings. A male principal announced 'Fifteen minutes left!' Some of the corps de ballet girls were in tears, saying 'It's so sad' over and over again to each other, and to me. A small group of women principals dressed up in hip style were clinging together with slightly triumphant airs. *They* had not been fired. Then the applause burst. It rose to an almost deafening level, triggered by loud 'Bravos!' that soon melted into a chorus. The dancers in the wings joined in the applause. And there the dancer was, taking her last bows on her own, in a rain of tulips and daffodils that soon covered the stage like a carpet. Then it was over – and she hastened, controlled, without flowers now, to her dressing-room to change for the reception that was going to be held in her honour at the bar in the foyer.

I went to the reception with one of the male soloists, who was very upset on the dancer's behalf, and kept saying 'it's all about taste, you know'. The guests at the reception included balletomanes from ballet societies, some sponsors, the family and friends of the leaving dancer, a large part of the company, the ballet management, the press department, technicians. Then the dancer entered, dressed in a black mini-dress: everyone turned to her and broke into applause. One of the other women principals gave a short speech handing over presents from the company: diamond earrings and a photo album with pictures of the dancer in every role she had danced. She seemed genuinely happy over the presents. This was followed by a short speech from one of the technicians, who, touched, also gave her a present 'from us backstage.' The dancer bowed in gratitude, managing to say 'I love you all!' She had not shed a visible tear during the whole day, which must have been one of the worst days of her life. Perhaps this was a part of the decision to fire her – the management probably knew that she would behave like a true professional, not causing any dramas in public.

The next day, the rest of the company took class as usual, and then there was a stage call for an upcoming première. In the canteen, over lunch, the conversation soon circled around the events of the previous evening. One woman principal did not seem to care: shrugging her shoulders she looked the other way, and started to talk about the pain she got from rehearsing a new ballet. When she went back to the rehearsal, the partner of the dancer who had been fired revealed his depression to me: 'It's a matter of taste, really. Our whole career is like that – so much depends on the taste of the director!' And since directors are changed more often than dancers, the same dancer may go up and down with different directors.

Notes

1. The concept of performance has a linguistic history to which Dell Hymes's (1975) definition relates when he points at the communicative competence of both performer and audience in performance, as well as the responsibility that the performer takes on in relation to the audience. Erving Goffman (1959) early identified aspects of everyday life as performance behaviour. Singer (1972) and Fabian (1990) are examples of anthropological monographs on theatre performance in non-Western societies. Hanna (1983) is a survey of performer intention and audience response to ethnic, contemporary and tap dance performances in Washington, DC.

2. This new production of *The Sleeping Beauty* had world premièred on a tour in Washington DC, USA, in April 1994.

3. The stage manager is in charge of the technical side of performances backstage. This is called 'being on the book', and means that he or she follows the score of the ballet in order to know when to signal cues. Since technical errors do happen, and may be potentially dangerous, the stage manager is asked to do a 'show report' after performances; preferably this should then be a 'clean show report'.

4. Significantly, the French expression '*merde!*' was common in the United States and the German '*toi-toi-toi!*' in Sweden, even though '*toi-toi-toi!*' was indeed used in Germany as well. Although good luck expressions in one's native language are used, avoiding them may, however, be another way to call for some extra supernatural ballet power. This can be related to the widespread belief in many societies that mentioning the proper names of desirable conditions or objects will prevent them from happening or coming into one's reach. The Arabic custom of precaution around the notion of the 'evil eye', which includes a taboo on praising loved ones or desirable possessions, since that may mean that one loses them, is also an example of this. Strange as it may seem in the ballet world, I also heard (and saw written) the expression 'Break a leg!' used for good luck before premières by British dancers in Sweden and Britain. '*Chukkers!*' or '*Chukkas!*' was another expression I picked up at the Royal Ballet in London. (A *chukker* or a *chukkar* is a polo period of seven and a half minutes when the ball is in play. It is derived from the Hindustani word *chakkar* and the Sanskrit word *chakra*, meaning 'wheel': *Dictionary of the English Language* 1963). The Swedish *Spark!*, or 'kick' in English, was quite prevalent at the Royal Swedish Ballet, as it is in larger Swedish society, for good luck, often combined with a physical kick in the behind of the person whom one wishes well. Although *toi-toi* behaviour

was commonplace, especially before premières but also before regular performances, there was in particular one coach who dismissed it as 'superstition' when I interviewed her about it, arguing that dancers should learn mental training instead. I suspect, however, that when this coach was still dancing she did one or two *toi-toi* tricks now and then. Just in case. The custom is simply very widespread in the ballet world.

5. Whistling backstage is another old theatre taboo that is still avoided, or at least commented on as potentially harmful for an upcoming performance. Swedish ethnologist Kerstin Koman (1996) describes the folk rule against whistling on sailing ships, because it was believed to stir a wind, or even a storm, in the old days. Koman notes that there is still a resistance against whistling on board many contemporary merchant ships.

6. An interesting case of layers of framed illusion is provided by Carmeli's (1990) analysis of travelling circus performances in British towns in the late 1970s. They evolved around a play on the notion of the real, when the presenter kept claiming that the performers and the tricks were real and at the same time impossible for anyone else to do.

7. It took him two years to recover, but the fact that he did recover and is now dancing leading roles again is considered something of a miracle by himself as well as his colleagues and coaches.

8. Experiences of ballet art can be phrased in terms of transcendence (cf. Fernandez 1986), even if this concept tends to illustrate the state of mind of the performer (cf. Zarrilli 1990 and Myerhoff 1990), not the audience.

9. In the ethnography of critics that follows here, my aim is to give an account of *both* 'the critic's point of view' and 'the dancer's point of view' about dance criticism. Since they are by nature basically in conflict this is not an attempt to even things out, but just to suggest what a social analysis of this minefield might look like.

Interestingly, there is an idea of *the critic as ethnographer* (Vail 1985, 1995; Banes 1994; Gere 1995) in dance studies, since critics and ethnographers can be said to make cross-cultural interpretations between stage and society, not least in recent times, with almost all dance becoming ethnically mixed into what is sometimes termed world dance. In the article 'Criticism as Ethnography', Sally Banes (1994) also considers the fact that ethnographers have avoided evaluating the people we study, whereas evaluation is in fact the main task of critics. Others have rejected the idea of the dance critic as ethnologist (Jowitt, Acocella and Siegel 1995) and anthropologist (Siegel 1995) on the grounds that most dance critics are not fully trained in ethnographic methods, nor do they spend as much time learning another culture as professional ethnographers do. As a professional ethnographer and anthropologist who has studied critics, but not written journalistic dance criticism, I sympathize with the idea of the critic as ethnographer. This is really a matter of cultivating a cross-cultural awareness where the Western canon is not taken for granted and dance pieces are situated in social, cultural and historical contexts. This awareness also includes a reflexive stance as to the critic's own cultural identity.

10. Walter Sorell (1981) traces the history of art criticism back to the contests of Aeschylus and Aristophanes and other classical Greek dramatists, who were ranked

by ten judges. Plato, had of course, an opinion about this, accusing the judges of conceding to the reactions of the audience. The announcements of the prizes in these contests were recorded on stone tablets. With the invention of the printing press in the fifteenth century, the opportunities for spreading criticism, like so many other kinds of texts, became immense. When Giorgio Vasari, who lived in Florence, had his *Lives of the Artists* (1963) printed it became a Renaissance best seller, the beginning of modern art criticism. Sorell remarks that, because of the wide influence of Vasari, his adjectives inevitably defined artists thenceforth: Michelangelo was divine and Rafael eclectic, and that would not change, neither would the reputation of those artists who were Vasari's pet hates. For centuries to come, art criticism was virtually non-existent. Then in the eighteenth century English periodicals that mainly dealt with literature featured scattered comments on the modest dance life in England. Reflecting the music scene in Germany, music journals throve there. When Marie Sallé danced *Pygmalion* in London in 1734, it was reported on – but not evaluated or discussed – in the *Mercure de France*. In his famous *Letters on Dancing and Ballet* (1983), which were published in 1760, dancer and choreographer Jean Georges Noverre discussed and criticized ballet. The forerunner of modern dance criticism, Théophile Gautier, did not appear until Romanticism in the 1830s and 1840s in Paris, when ballet blossomed, as did the commercialization of press and journalism.

11. Applying Roman Jakobson's classic diagram of the communicative act (where a coded message is transmitted from sender to receiver) to dance criticism, June Adler Vail (1985) identifies four models: choreographer performer-oriented criticism, viewer-oriented criticism, context-oriented criticism, and dance/codes-oriented criticism. Vail adds a fifth, interactive, orientation model in order to acknowledge that the dance and the writer create each other in a process that is also reflexive.

12. Arlene Croce (1994–5) mentions this in passing in the article she wrote instead of reviewing Bill T. Jones's dance piece *Still/Here*. The main topic of the article is the problem of reviewing 'victim art' (1994–5: 55), as she calls it, pointing at the fact that Jones was HIV-positive and used video clips of people with mortal illnesses, cancer and HIV in the piece. Croce's stance was that 'victim art' cannot be evaluated on the same premises as other art. Her article caused much controversy in the dance world, both among writers and dance people.

6

Moving and Mixing

The focus on transnational connectivity in the ballet world is sharpened in this chapter by an exploration of how dancers move around in particular on tours, and communicate by way of media and technology across long distances. Ballet notation, scores and video, are also sent around between companies in different countries. Since new technology such as computers and video is increasingly being used in contemporary ballet and dance productions, the last ethnographic case in this book is drawn from the making of a technological ballet at Ballett Frankfurt.

Touring Culture of the Company

One prominent aspect of the mobility of the ballet world is touring, especially transnational touring, which meant from my point of view that the field was moving.[1] On a few occasions I was able to move with it, as when I went with the Royal Swedish Ballet on the three-week tour to Japan. This part of my field study thus included participant observation on jetplanes, Shinkanzen (the Japanese bullet train), company buses, sightseeing tours and hotels, on top of my usual field habitat backstage and frontstage of the theatres.

National ballet tours tend to go just to one site for a few days, while transnational tours go to one site or several in a number of countries. They last between one week and anything up to two months. American Ballet Theatre, the touring company, used to be on tour for four months per year, but this has been reduced to about two months. The British Royal Ballet, the American Ballet Theatre and Ballett Frankfurt all tour both nationally and transnationally every year. The touring schedule of the Royal Swedish Ballet is more irregular. Ballett Frankfurt has an exchange programme with Nederlands Dans Theater in the Hague: the companies visit each other's theatres once a year. Ballett Frankfurt also has an agreement with the Théâtre du Châtelet in Paris to perform there every spring. Tours usually come about because a company is invited, or asked to come back, to a number of theatres that are combined on the same tour. Impresarios and agents make a large part of the arrangements, connecting people in different countries, as well as fund-raising: tours are very expensive and extra sponsoring is needed. Transnational tours are often set up as a part of cultural exchange programmes between two countries; hence the custom of receptions and dinners at the embassy of the country a company is going to before the tour, and at the embassy of the home country of the company when it is on tour. Negotiations for transnational tours take a number of years; much work turns out to have been in vain when tours do not materialize or are postponed. Like everything else in the ballet world, tour schedules are subject to continuous change.

Although there are many circuits in transnational ballet touring, some carry more prestige than others. Apart from the traditional ballet centres, Japan and Brazil are current noteworthy stops on tours. Impelled by a combination of economic capital coupled with a perceived lack of Western cultural capital, Japan has been active since the Second World War in inviting Western ballet and dance companies. The old indigenous Japanese theatre dance forms such as Kabuki and Gagaku are still practised, and academic dance was introduced at a modest level in the early 1900s; but it was a tour by Anna Pavlova's company in the early 1920s that laid the foundation for a more substantial interest in ballet. After the Second World War ballet schools were established teaching the Russian style, later producing ballet companies such as the Tokyo Ballet Company, which came into being in 1960 (Koegler 1987).

Tours are a kind of intensive communitas that accentuates certain structures such as the company-as-family quality, with older dancers taking care of younger dancers by feeding them at restaurants and comforting those who are upset because of homesickness, stage-fright or conflicts with coaches. But structures are also revealed on tours that are hidden in the everyday life at home in the theatre: the division between men and women, as well as the separation into three age groupings, becomes more articulated on tours. Yet new structures and personal links are also created, some temporary, others continuing afterwards. Tours may be an opportunity for love affairs that can develop into long-term relationships. There is, however, a certain touring culture of each company that is structurally similar to those of other companies, yet distinct from them because of the current castings and combinations of dancers, the company climate and local circumstances on the tour site. A company touring culture is reactivated and renegotiated on every tour. The time-limited, liminal character of touring culture allows some room for late-night partying, which normally has to be avoided because of the intensity of schedules and other personal commitment. On tours, especially, young corps de ballet men, who are very fit and do not dance such demanding roles as soloists and principals, relax by partying in hotel rooms and clubs on the town. Older dancers that took part in these bouts, when I asked how they managed to dance when they had been drinking and were living on very little sleep, told me that 'you know your limit'.

Ballet productions, both the choreography and the set, need to be adjusted to go on tour. Set and costumes must not break during transportation, and are usually brought along in smaller quantities than in the original production. (Costumes and set are also sometimes shipped between countries as loans between companies.) The choreography usually has to be accommodated to a larger or a smaller stage than the one it was originally made for.

We were around seventy people, including dancers, dressers, technicians, administrators, producers and directors from the Royal Opera House in Stockholm, who went on the tour to Japan. Changing planes at Heathrow Airport, the feeling of tour community was established when 'the Royal Swedish Ballet' was called to the gate over the loudspeaker. Accommodated at a large hotel in Tokyo for the première of the tour, we were greeted by posters saying 'Welcome Royal Swedish Ballet'.

Senior corps de ballet dancers, soloists and principals had single rooms. Young corps de ballet dancers were sharing double rooms with someone they had chosen back in Stockholm, and eleven male–female couples who were married, engaged or living together in Stockholm were also staying in double rooms. (In one of the other companies in this study, gay men and heterosexual women who were long-time partners on stage or just friends shared room on tours as a matter of course.)

Although dancers often say that they enjoy the travel of tours, mentioning that 'getting to see other countries' is one of the advantages of being a dancer, they were hit by attacks of homesickness in Japan. Towards the end of the tour, there were obvious signs that living and working even more close to each other than at home was hard, causing irritation and social dramas. Chaperoned around most of the time, the dancers had very little direct contact with Japanese society, especially as the schedule was extra-intense, with seventeen performances in twenty-one days in five cities (Tokyo, Fukuoka, Hiroshima, Osaka and Nagoya).

On one of the first evenings, the Japanese sponsor of the tour, a cigarette company, invited the company to a lavish banquet at the hotel including a performance by a local theatre group. The première of *The Sleeping Beauty* was sold out and was quite successful. Swedish Princess Christina, the patron of the Royal Swedish Ballet, had flown in for it, and so had the director of the Opera House in Stockholm. Six members of the Japanese imperial family were also present. One of them, a prince with a young family, was said to be a ballet enthusiast. They came to a second performance and then went on stage afterwards to thank the dancers, as it is customary for dignitaries to do.

The Japanese hosts, the agent and the theatre managements had asked for traditional classical ballets. So the Royal Swedish Ballet danced *Cinderella*, as well as *The Sleeping Beauty* and the short modern *Miss Julie* by Birgit Cullberg. *Cinderella* and *The Sleeping Beauty* were very well received by both audience and critics. *Miss Julie* was less appreciated. This Swedish midsummer drama about a young noblewoman who seduces her father's servant and is then so overtaken by regret that she kills herself, aided by the servant, was reviewed by Nobuko Hara (1994) in the *Asahi Evening News* as: 'the most disturbing and erotic ballet I've seen: A servant rapes his mistress and helps her commit suicide'.

After travelling around Japan for nearly two weeks, we came back to Tokyo for the last set of performances. By then everyone was exhausted and one of the dressers I was working with was counting the hours that were left of the tour. The very last day was a marathon, with two perform-ances of *Cinderella*, one matinée and one in the evening. In the final curtain call, the applause accelerated and the dancers made their bows, touched by the poignancy of the situation. Suddenly they were drenched in colourful confetti, gold stars and paper streamers falling down from the ceiling of the stage, glittering in the spotlights. The dancers cheered jubilantly at this surprise present from the sponsors.

They all rushed backstage, shouting and jumping, overjoyed that the tour was over. Now they could indulge in all-night partying. First they had to dress up, however. There had been a notice on the notice-board urging them to dress up, since we were invited to a reception at the Swedish Embassy. 'No jeans!' was the instruction. So the dancers appeared in suits, jackets and ties, dresses, mini-skirts and high heels. The Swedish Embassy, is located in the middle of Tokyo, with a terrace encircling the house and a stunning view of a city landscape of skyscrapers. Entering the house, the dancers were all of a sudden intimidated, overtaken by shyness. We signed our names in a guest book. Then, we had to make our entrance, which indeed is a skill that is a part of the dancers' job – that is, when they are dancing. In this setting, they clung together, hesitating before entering a large room where the Ambassador was making conversation with the ballet management. There was a buffet, and a group of us sat down in a small room next door. The wife of the Ambassador told us about the house and life in Tokyo. When she had left, the atmosphere relaxed and, as spirits ran higher and higher, the jokes and stories became increasingly daring. Back at the hotel, the party continued in the room of one of the dancers. Someone called the ballet director: 'Come and celebrate with us!' But he was reluctant to join his dancers at this hour. The room was crowded with ecstatic dancers and loud music. The dancer who had called the ballet director tried again, and this time he appeared. Then a man from the hotel staff knocked on the door, complaining about the noise. The party moved to another dancer's room, I was told by the dancers the next day on the bus to the airport. One of them, a woman soloist who had danced Cinderella, had been very nervous before the performance. And then she danced as never before, surpassing herself. She had celebrated more than most of the other dancers.

Dance Media and New Technology

Media and new technology have been pivotal in the growth of transnational connectivity in the ballet world. Yet old, established media like dance magazines are still important. The American *Dance Magazine* mostly covers the United States, and the British *The Dancing Times*, founded in 1910, focuses on classical ballet in Great Britain, with regular reports from St Petersburg and New York. *Dance Europe* is a recent bimonthly addition from Britain that deals with classical and contemporary dance all over Europe. The biannual British *Dance Theatre Journal* provides an intellectual approach to contemporary dance. The monthly *Ballett International*, published in both an English and a German edition, discusses especially and quite substantially the German contemporary dance scene. The new *Dance Now* is a British quarterly journal concentrating on articles about people and topics in British ballet and dance, and has a section reviewing dance books, videos and compact discs. The Swedish bimonthly *Danstidningen* reports on dance and dance people in Sweden, but has a transnational outlook as well.

Among the new media, documenting videos are sent abroad as a way of promoting companies for touring as well as individual dancers for guesting. Dancers and companies are also promoted with artistic commercial videos. Dance videos have developed into a distinct art form, manifest in the annual dance video competition, Carina Ari Grand Prix International Video Dance Award. Videographed by Lovell Bacogh to music by Thom Willems, William Forsythe's six minutes and sixty seconds black-and-white *Solo* won the 1996 award for best video dance and music. Later Forsythe was invited to create a new dance piece, *Hypothetical Stream*, for Daniel Larrieu's troupe in France. He then started the work process via video and fax while he was still at work on *Sleepers Guts* (see below) before he was able to arrive himself.

Video and computers (and also slide and film projectors) are integrated into choreography on stage in a growing number of contemporary ballet and dance productions. In contrast with most traditional stage properties, new technology tends to be mobile in one way or another. Video is used extensively in rehearsals to learn steps or as a reminder of steps, even after premières. Documenting videos of performances might show why a combination of steps went wrong on stage, even though what is registered on the small video screen might not have been distinguishable for the audience – and vice versa. Dancers thus spend a lot of time watching themselves on video, critically objectifying their own bodies.

Digital technology has renewed work practices backstage, where marketing, administration, lighting, sound and scenography are now computerized. Internet's World Wide Web offers information about dance companies, repertories and time and place for performances and tours all over the world. Some choreographers are making choreography on computer programs such as 'Lifeforms'.

Video dance has the potential of reaching people, locally and also transnationally, who do not normally go to dance performances. So does dance on television, whether it is filmed stage dance, dance productions that are choreographed for television, or dance transposed to television from the stage; it has become an aesthetic genre in itself (cf. Cullberg 1992; Jordan and Allen 1993). This Walter Sorell (1981: 399) has called 'the triumph of technology'. During my field study, six of the dancers at the Royal Swedish Ballet were filmed for American Channel 13 in *Dancing on the Front Porch of Heaven: Odes to Love and Loss*, choreographed for them by Ulysses Dove in 1993. It was later broadcast both in the United States and in Sweden. Dove died of AIDS in June 1996. He was commemorated at a gala in the New York State Theater at Lincoln Center just days later. The six Swedish dancers were flown in and danced *Dancing at the Front Porch of Heaven* in his honour. The British Royal Ballet were filmed by the BBC dancing their new production of *The Sleeping Beauty* at Covent Garden (see Chapter 5). It was broadcast by the BBC and also made into a commercial video.[2]

Both choreography in video dance and dance on television can utilize the special technology and format of video and television choreographically: slow motion, close-ups and different camera angles creating new lines, colours and distances. Even depth, such as landscapes or an interior other than the studio where the filming took place, can be inserted afterwards with chromakey technique.

CD-ROM technology is reaching into the ballet world. My informants who were working with choreography on computers told me about the possibility of making CD-ROMs where the spectator/user can make his or her own choreographic choices, and influence the narrative or the ending of a dance piece. *Mirrors*, by English choreographer Mark Baldwin, is a dance

CD-ROM where this is already happening. As Jann Parry (1996–7: 74), critic and dance writer, has said, these technological opportunities, which are often collaborative work, will change the meaning of 'performance' as well as the notion of 'authorship'.

Zentrum für Kunst und Medientechnologie in Karlsruhe has a homepage on the Internet (http://www.zkm.de/) advertising a CD-ROM that William Forsythe and Thom Willems produced there as: 'a digital school of dance' and a 'revolutionary advancement on all previous methods of analyzing and documenting dance... Now a first ever "tangible" document is available. For the use of present and later generations of dancers and dance-lovers...'.

Entitled *Improvisation Technologies or Self Meant to Govern*, this CD-ROM, or 'installation' as it is also called, was made in 1994, in collaboration with Nik Haffner, a Ballett Frankfurt dancer (Haffner 1997; Ziegler 1997). The CD-ROM won a prize at the New Voices–New Visions digital art competition in New York in 1996, and has been exhibited in New York and Paris, among other cities. It is thus an example of how interactive multimedia can contribute to the development of dance culture (cf. S.J. Norman 1996): anyone who knows basic computer skills can easily operate it (as I did while watching it in Karlsruhe). When the dance piece *Self Meant to Govern* was created for the stage, and later revived as one act in the technological full-length *Eidos: Telos*, the CD-ROM was used by the dancers to learn and rehearse steps, and also by new dancers as one way to understand how Ballett Frankfurt worked. For a while, a computer was brought into the studio with the CD-ROM for the dancers to use when they wanted. It consists of one hundred theoretical lessons lasting between thirty and ninety seconds, where Forsythe goes through his choreographic principles on a video film. Each step is illustrated by video sections danced by a dancer, sections from rehearsals with several dancers and performances. It is obvious that Forsythe is addressing his own company on the CD-ROM. It was made to be understood from the dancer's point of view. While demonstrating one step at a time, Forsythe urges the dancers: 'It's important to remember the shape of your hand in relation to the rest of your body!', 'Use the surface of your body' and 'You draw a line like this!' In order to illustrate the last call, he made a circular movement with his arm that became even clearer as a white line was inserted on the screen.

This CD-ROM is both a piece of art in itself and a pedagogical catalogue of Forsythe's dance style that at the same time contributes to Forsythe's position as a renowned choreographer. It took seven months to produce the CD-ROM, and it was quite expensive. This is an obvious limitation to its distribution; yet when it is exhibited anyone has access to it. It is also probable that CD-ROMs, like other computer technology, will become cheaper with time, both to produce and to buy.

One medium can be used in many different ways. The idea that mediated ballet is inaccurate is always close at hand in the ballet world; but for dancers, ballet media may also have a direct impact on their careers. The same ballet medium, whether it is a dance magazine, a video or a fax can serve as a source of new information, a supply of reminders of steps, and/or a means of getting into contact with another person or a company abroad. Dance reviews in daily papers, dance magazines and culture programmes on television and the radio not only serve as information for the general public, but at the same time provide ballet people with news about each other. Reviews are one way of keeping track of friends, colleagues and ex-students, as well as rivals, one has not seen for a while. Ballet people in my study, from ballet students, mothers, and professional dancers to choreographers and ballet directors who were looking for ideas and dancers to recruit or jobs to apply for, kept up with repertories, casting, and other transnational ballet news about appointments and dismissals by reading transnational monthly dance magazines. They were also read by critics and dance writers and/or correspondents, some of whom were contributors to them.

Popular media that feature ballet and ballet dancers for the general public, such as biographies, ballet films, commercial videos and ballet performances made for television, stage work filmed for television, and television document- aries about dancers and choreographers, as well as recordings of ballet music on tape and CDs, are thus used differently by ballet people than by other people that is the audience.

Often I heard dancers and ballet people complain about the negative portrayals of the ballet world in ballet films or television documentaries: either they concentrate on the pain and hardships of ballet or they present a silly over-romantic view – 'airy-fairy', as a dancer said – failing to convey the many facets of love of ballet, from the hardships of constant practice and injuries to the wonder of progress and the unpredictable zone where ballet art is created on stage: in short the reasons for pursuing a career as a ballet dancer. An extraordinarily precise representation of ballet and ballet culture is, however, Fredrick Wiseman's television documentary 'Ballet', featuring the American Ballet Theatre in the early 1990s.

Talking to dancers who take photographs or make dance videos, I asked how their photographs and videos differ from those made by non-dancers. I was then told that since dancers, or ex-dancers, know the steps of the ballets, they can adjust timing and angles 'to what comes next in the choreography', that is after the photograph has been taken, or the filming is finished. In the sensitive rehearsal work, it seems probable, however, that it was also the fact that the dancers knew the dancers–photographers that made the dancers relax in front of the camera.

Yet another media habit, in the transnational ballet world where people work together for shorter or longer periods of time, is to present colleagues one is leaving with signed photographs of oneself in rehearsal or performance, saying 'with gratitude, love and admiration', or something similar. These photographs are often framed and put on walls in collections displaying crucial events in transnational careers and networks.

Ballet Notation: Preservation, Revival, Copyright

How to document and preserve the elusive art of dance is a problem as old as dance itself. Many notation systems have been developed over the centuries.[3] One early treatise on dancing technique originates from just after the year 1400, before printing had been invented. Guest (1988) mentions that the ballet master Domenico of Piacenza, who taught at Renaissance courts in northern Italy at the time, wrote down about twenty of his dances. Nearly two hundred years later, when Beaujoyeulx mounted *Ballet Comique de la Reine* in Paris, he also wrote a libretto describing and illustrating the ballet. This he sent around Europe. The success, fame and historical prominence of this ballet production thus came about in large part because of the written record. In 1700, Raoul Auger Feuillet published a system for notation that according to Sorell (1981) was in use until the French Revolution. Labanotation was created in 1928, and the Benesh system originates from 1955 (McGuinness-Scott 1983). These two systems are now computerized and are the most used today. They take two years to learn and are taught at schools in London and New York. Most dancers and choreographers cannot read them, so when a new ballet is being created, a trusting and respectful relationship has to be built between the choreographers and the choreologist. Since the formal dance notations are complicated and take such a long time to learn, coaches and choreographers develop their own individual notation systems, as do some dancers for the ballets they are learning. They take notes, in other words, more or less systematically.[4]

I never saw choreologists (or notators as they also are called) write down ballets as they were being created in the studio on computers: they still wrote the first score with a pencil in big books during the time of my field study. The Royal Swedish Ballet and the Royal Ballet in London have resident Benesh choreologists; the American Ballet Theatre was looking for a choreologist when I was there; and Ballett Frankfurt managed without one.

With ballet notation, laws on copyright[5] of choreography emerged. It is usually the theatre, or the ballet company (sometimes a foundation) that commissioned a production that owns the score, whereas the choreographer has the performance rights of his or her productions. (Another consequence of this is the fact that dancers, and coaches, do not have any legal right to the steps they know, 'to steps that are in their muscular memory'.) When choreographers die, these rights are in most cases inherited by the leading dancers for whom the choreography was first created. They often go on coaching new generations of dancers in the company and abroad in their old roles. Many of the vast number of George Balanchine's ballets are managed by the Balanchine Trust.

At the Benesh Institute in London, attracting students from many different countries, students have to sign a disclaimer saying that they will not claim any copyright on work they write. There is a certain transnational trade in ballet scores, involving both commercial and more or less informal exchanges.[6]

When a ballet production is revived or recreated and the coach and/or the dancers would like some changes to be made in the choreography, they have to ask the choreographer for permission – that is, if he or she is still alive; otherwise his or her foundation, or those who have inherited the rights of the ballet, have to be approached. They may then accept the changes and get a royalty for them. Changes may be called for because a leading dancer is good at a particular step that he or she would like to display in perform- ance, but bad at one that is in the score. Some sections may be written down in variant versions, which is often an advantage. Yet many changes are made without permission, and changes do happen all the time in ballets, from one performance to the next. Two performances are never exactly the same. The fact that two choreologists might notate the same production differently adds to the space for interpretation and creativity.[7]

Most choreologists are ex-dancers, and I was told by choreologists that it was useful because 'you have a shared knowledge of the dance world' and that they are 'treated with proper respect' by the dancers. Choreologists also pointed out that 'those of us who have lived in dance, look at this in a different sort of way – like pictures in space'. This feel for form may, however, also be a talent that certain non-dancers possess. But the experience of 'sitting late at night correcting an *arabesque* to a long *attitude* – I would feel it in my leg' clearly occurred because this choreologist used to be a dancer. A non-dancer would not 'feel' an *arabesque* moving into an *attitude* through the body (cf. Chapter 4 on ballet body work). The fact that ballet scores are made 'from the dancer's point of view', not the spectator's, probably matters as well.

A choreologist has to be at ease in the studio. I observed one choreologist who had not been trained as a dancer. She behaved in an uncomfortable way, not melting into the rhythm and spaces of studio work. Choreologists are present at rehearsals of new ballets in order to write down the steps, learning the ballet with the dancers. Then they go on to rehearse the dancers 'through their bodies', they said to me. Some are appointed ballet masters by the director of the company they have worked with for a number of years.

It sometimes happens that the relationship between the choreographer and the choreologist fails, and then there will not be any score. Some choreographers prefer their own choreologists in the long run. There are coaches who do not have enough confidence in a particular choreologist, or may question the idea of this cooperation. Ex-dancers for whom certain leading roles were once created, or who created them, are then called in to rehearse young dancers for revivals instead. This, however, is not always appreciated by the young dancers, who tend not to like to be compared with those who once were stars.

Dance notations are meant to preserve the visual and mobile three-dimensional art of dance, but as Goodman (1981) points out, there are nuances that cannot be grasped through drawings on a paper. They can still however be accurate enough to produce a performance that will be recognized as one of its kind. Taking Labanotation as his example, Goodman notes that it leaves room for a certain openness, such as is to be found in most musical notation as well.

Video and film are increasingly used as complements to dance notations; but just as choreologists may make mistakes when they write down ballets, dancers when they are videoed may forget a step or do a section in a way that was not intended by the choreographer, both in rehearsal and in performance. In her comprehensive study on dance notation, Ann Hutchinson Guest (1984) argues for the advantages of notation over film or video in learning new productions for dancers. Since her book was published in the early 1980s, the use of video has exploded, however, not only in society in general (where a VCR is commonplace in homes as well as at places of work), but also in the ballet world. Videos for documentation or rehearsal have not made notation obsolete; but video has become a necessary item of equipment, alongside notation, in the ballet world of the 1990s. During the almost three years of my field study, I noticed an increase in the use of videos, as well as in the quality of the tapes. Rehearsal videos that have been recorded in a studio or on stage are often of better quality than those that record performances, since the lighting is poor in performance, and not adjusted to filming.

Unless a studio is equipped with a VCR on the wall, or on a table, VCRs are brought into the studio; some of them are portable miniVCRs. At Ballett Frankfurt, when one of the pieces was new, the coach offered the dancers an opportunity to watch the video of the performance immediately afterwards.

Videos are thus nowadays used frequently in studio rehearsals, in video rooms at the theatres, and in the homes of the dancers and the choreographers. There are also educational videos for ballet students, and videos featuring classes for professional dancers. Dancers learn new productions and are reminded of steps in revivals by watching video together, on their own, or with their coaches. After all, video is a medium they can learn from directly, as opposed to notation, which requires an intermediary choreologist. Hutchinson Guest (1984: 11) suggests that one of the reasons that notation is superior to film or video is that 'Copies of the score can be handed out and referred to in the train, at home, on the beach.' This does not take account of the fact that, again, most dancers have VCRs at home nor, even more importantly, of the fact that dancers would need a choreologist to decipher the scores – bringing along a choreologist on the train, at home, or to the beach does not seem to be a feasible idea. Furthermore, those dancers who are at work in the 1990s have grown up watching videos (as well as television and films), which means that they have acquired a more elaborate sense of pictures, of 'reading' pictures in motion, and are thus undoubtedly able to grasp many more details on dance videos than the previous generations of dancers were. If a dancer who is watching a video misses a step, the video can always be stopped and rewound. Dancers watch videos over and over again during the different stages of learning or rehearsing a ballet production. A disadvantage with video, however, is that the tapes become worn out after many viewings. It is thus important that they are recopied in time.

One of many transnational aspects of ballet videos is illustrated by the case of an American and a Russian dancer with the American Ballet Theatre: the Russian dancer had learnt about the company when he was still in Russia by watching videos of Mikhail Baryshnikov, whereas the American dancer, who grew up in Minneapolis and went to North Carolina School of the Arts as a teenager, had not heard of the company before one of his friends suggested that they went together with a group of friends to New York to audition for it.

All this watching of themselves on video is not particularly enjoyable for the dancers. They are rarely pleased with what they see, but at least they know that they are being filmed. It did happen, time after time, that dancers were filmed for documenting videos or clips for culture programmes on television, or that they were photographed for newspapers, but that they themselves never got to see the pictures. During my field study, I often commented on something I had seen on television or read in a newspaper, and the dancer it was about was upset: his or her body had been put out for public view without the dancer's being told about it. This reaction was also evoked by reviews, which the dancers had not always seen, or other forms of dance writing or journalism. Still, they were strikingly flattered by media attention – if they were prepared for it, and on form. I would have thought that people who have been photographed so much and performed for many thousands of people for a number of years would be fed up with, or at least used to it. One of the definitions of success, it turned out, was to have an advance feature article written about oneself.

Several times when I went backstage in intermissions and happened to bring the programme of the evening's performance with me, dancers flocked around me to see if they were in the pictures, and, if so, what they looked like – and of course to keep an eye on how their rivals were presented. It seemed as if the programmes were withheld from the dancers, but this is not so – they just happened to be the last people to see them, if they ever got to see them at all.

Coming Together to Make a Ballet

When the technological ballet production *Sleepers Guts* was made at Ballett Frankfurt in the autumn of 1996, steps, set and sound were worked out without much contact.[8] For about a year, William Forsythe had exchanged drafts on scenographic ideas with an American video artist on e-mail. Months before the production was scheduled to start, Thom Willems knew that he wanted to combine woodwind and percussion instruments with live sampling: he held auditions to get two oboe-players, one cello-player, and one percussionist (two of whom were still students). All of them were German. Then an American sound designer was contracted, together with a German assistant, as well as an American assistant of Willems. They began working in August at the Studio for Electro-Instrumental Music (STEIM) in Amsterdam, building the electronic equipment,[9] which they brought to Frankfurt-am-Main in the middle of September, when the rest of the production was getting started.[10]

At a company meeting, Forsythe explained that he wanted modules, nine times nine minutes. He suggested themes around nature, movement flow, hierarchy, organization; then he added death. He was eager to 'unimagine', as he said, rising from the chair he was sitting on and walking a few steps as if he was leaving something behind. He wanted to find a new form, and referred to earlier pieces where the dancers had moved on the floor, and said that one idea would be to get up from the floor, to do light jumps. This would later materialize in an act of the production called 'the ballet scene' that also included one neoclassically inspired *pas de deux* and a solo by a woman dancer. 'The ballet scene' was, however, taken out of the production after a few performances.

The first days and weeks were defined by what Forsythe had termed 'open door'. This meant that the dancers were supposed to get together in groups and make steps on the themes that he then would 'edit', as he said. Books and articles on avant-garde art and postmodern architecture were circulated for inspiration. The dancers spent a lot of time sitting on the floor in the studios discussing steps, making drawings and taking notes. Forsythe went between the groups, but mainly he stayed in one studio working with those who happened to be there. He wanted to give the dancers freedom to develop their own ideas on choreographing, inserting agency in a shared authorship. At the same time he hoped to be inspired by the dancers' work. There was a notion that 'a second generation of Forsythe choreographers' was coming up.

The making of steps was sometimes interrupted by company meetings about the progress of the production or lectures by the sound designer on the technology (computer programs and a video camera)[11] that it was planned to use in the production. The technological staff were eager to present the variety of ways there was of performing the same technological tricks, whereas the dancers who were interested in contributing choreography tried to get more focused information that they could apply in this particular production.[12]

The sound studio (or 'the tonstudio', as it was called in German–English colloquial) in the Opera House was a well-insulated windowless room with good acoustics. For this production it had been furnished with three computers, a synthesizer, a harmonizer, a CD-player, a tape-recorder, a laser disc, a monitor, a video camera and loudspeakers. There were additional laptops and a printer. Everyone in the technologically trained staff had written music and worked with technology as artists in other contexts.

In the sound studio, Thom Willems and Joel Ryan collected layered samplings of Renaissance, modernist, popular and ethnic music. A number of sessions with the musicians provided them with material to work with. The two oboists, the cello-player, and the percussionist, who had been equipped with an electronic drum set and a small steel drum, as well as one of the dancers, who had brought an Australian didgeridoo, played different scales or short scores by Willems. As the music went into the computers by way of microphones the sound designer and his assistant processed it by changing the time, pitch and colour of it. They changed sections second by second, every beat, or every bar. Sometimes they added colouring with the cello, or doubled the number of oboes. The sections that came out of it were named as a means of distinguishing between them. There were thus, for example, 'HighLow', which consisted of high and low notes, 'Figaro', which sounded like wedding music, and 'Smoke', which came about as a light dust was released from the cello when the cello-player used his bow to scratch the strings. Later, in performance, Willems would 'conduct' the musicians on the side of the stage through wireless communication to play live music that the dancers heard on stage. The music then went into computers that were placed in the orchestra pit and was processed by the sound designers into electronic sounds for the audience to listen to.

The dancers related in various ways to the technology on stage (a big, tilted video screen, a camera, projectors): some were indifferent, others irritated because of the risk of injuries if they stumbled on it. Yet other dancers were excited by the technology and saw new choreographic possibilities opening up. Although dancers have grown up with television and video, these technologies have not been part of their dance training. They have learnt to dance with other dancers, not with machines. Some dancers may therefore, at least in the beginning, be made uncomfortable by having to share the stage with video screens, monitors and film and slide projectors. Traditional set and stage properties might also break, be in the way or fall down over them; but the feeling that the behaviour of machines is strange and unpredictable may produce distress, at least initially. Yet many dancers are fascinated by technology in dance performances – especially those who have a special interest in choreography. They regard technology as a tool for creating new choreographic effects.[13]

After four weeks of work on steps, music and text in different studios, it was all put together on stage for two weeks of stage calls leading up to the première. Because of an awareness that steps look different and music sounds different on stage than in the studio, there was a readiness for changes. This was also the phase when most people involved found themselves working twelve hours per day. Just like touring, the making of a new ballet takes the form of an intensive short-time communitas that makes the outside world temporarily unreal. (This often put a strain on relationships with family and friends who are not in the production and not in the theatre, let alone those not in the country.)

The entire work process was defined by changes. Dancers, music and choreographic sections were taken out of the production by Forsythe as a matter of course, and some put in again and taken out again. Stuck in the creativity block that seems to be a necessary phase in all artistic (as well as intellectual) projects, the voyage from chaos to order was not over when the day of the première came. The production was still in progress, and it would take a number of performances before it suddenly came together: a beam of light was floating across and to the sides of the video screen (on the backdrop) projecting the words 'one flat thing', as it was falling, to magnetic, heart-piercing music. When the curtain went down after the first act, there was a pause – and then the applause exploded like thunder.

The piece opened with a woman dancer standing in front of the big tilted video screen, which was placed facing outwards, displaying video clips of landscapes and abstract patterns mixed with live pictures of the dancer's face, sometimes from the side. Across the clips expressions like 'the rules are never stated', 'fiction and wish', 'substitute glue for puppies', and 'even if the lights go out' were projected, sometimes moving. The dancer was talking into a microphone: she was telling a story, line by line, about a liar, while bending and turning her arms and legs around her body. Three other women dancers went up to one microphone each and started reciting Forsythesque lines. The different speeches, the words, the voices and the accents of the dancers all came together like music. They followed a rhythm that was displayed by way of numbers inside the proscenium arch. Two white women danced a duet, two black women danced another duet. One of them went up to a microphone and started chewing gum while a part of her face was being filmed by a small live camera that was attached to the camera and simultaneously projected on the screen. Two small mirrors helped illuminate the dancer's face and also allowed her to see that she was in the right place. The video screen moved up and down, dancing, as it were.

The second act, mostly choreographed by Antony Rizzi, who also danced in it, did not include any visible new technology. With the scene looking like a battlefield after the battle has been lost, distorted bodies were lying around and others slowly moved up and down, seemingly in pain: the atmosphere was melancholic. The final short act was choreographed by Jacopo Godani, one of the two male dancers who did a duet while filmed by a video artist from the wings. The film was projected on the video screen or on the side of it as they were dancing, switching between the dancers and other objects, like a close-up of one of the oboes, a bow, or a turning doll, and abstract pictures from an art book that were placed on a table in the wings. One of the dancers was dancing behind the video screen. In the centre of the stage again, he jumped. While he was in the air – the light went out. There was a loud bang. It was all over.

Coda and Conclusions

Starting out all the way back in the fourteenth century when ballet was born at Renaissance courts in northern Italy, this book ends with digital technology in dance, thereby foreboding the next millennium. The tension between tradition and change runs through this anthropological analysis of the transnational ballet world, concerned with dancers and the making and unmaking of their careers. Ethnographic cases have illustrated the connections between transnationality and national culture, learning the bodily skill of dancing, notions of the body, time, including age and gender, frames in ballet performance, tours as travelling culture, and the aesthetic and cultural implications of new technology in the ballet world. Dancers think of themselves primarily as artists, not as participants in the 'high culture' of front stage. Although dancers want as many people as possible from all walks of life to come to see them dance, they also want their audience to react to what they see, to be 'touched', 'mesmerized' and 'to go home and really remember'. There is a fear in the ballet world that such experiences of ballet art will not come about if ballet people cooperate too closely with the market, turning ballet into light entertainment.

A Slowly Changing Ballet World

Even though there is a lot of contact between different places in the transnational ballet world, this does not mean that it is exactly the same everywhere. The transnational ballet world contains homogeneous work practices and heterogeneous national employment laws and funding systems. Dancers move across borders, not only between classical companies, but also back and forth between classical and contemporary companies, for longer or shorter periods of time. National and artistic borders become significant when they are crossed. The notion of place, in the form of classical ballet centres that are associated with ideas of national ballet styles, as well as centres of contemporary ballet and dance, is thus crucial in the reproduction of the transnational ballet world.

Although mediated communications in the ballet world, through fax, video, e-mail and telephone, have grown in usage they cannot replace face-to-face encounters. Mediated communications can complement direct contact and keep it up to date, but they are of a different social quality. This is why ballet people make an effort to travel far away to watch a dancer or a performance while it is happening, or to meet with people for negotiations about tours. This also concerns artistic creativity, as the case from the making of the new ballet at Ballett Frankfurt shows. The acclaimed video artist who had worked with Forsythe over e-mail for many months only made two short visits to the company during the seven weeks of rehearsal and performances. His suggestions and contributions were hardly used in the end. Instead the work of a couple of aspiring young video artists who were around all the time was incorporated in the production.

Although there have been influences between the national classical ballet styles, the increased moving around in the ballet world has now intensified the mixing of national and choreographic styles, as well as of the nationalities and ethnic identities of members of ballet companies. For even though William Forsythe keeps making choreographic points of ethnic mixture, the classical companies are *de facto* becoming ethnically mixed – as a reflection of society at large in Sweden, Britain and the United States. There is still a certain resistance in the classical world against ethnic and racial mixture on stage; but this is bound to change with time. In one of the companies, a male dancer with one black and one white parent used 'light make-up' in order to pass for white on stage, although two Japanese male dancers were used in a ballet flanking a woman, which accentuated their ethnicity. Classical companies outside the United States still seem to be reluctant to hire black dancers; but Japanese dancers are readily accepted in classical as well as contemporary companies in the West. Latin American dancers are usually in a better position than black dancers in classical companies in Europe and North America.

Coming from Balanchine's abstract American neoclassical style and Merce Cunningham's fragmented postmodernism, William Forsythe has also been relating to the German dance theatre tradition developed by Pina Bausch in the country where he is now working. In that respect, Forsythe's contemporary ballet style has national traits, albeit more eclectic than those in classical ballet.

The pyramidal appointment hierarchy of classical companies, with a few dancers on top and a mass of corps de ballet dancers at the bottom, is also likely to change. This structure was established before social reforms and welfare programmes increased the Western middle class. Contemporary companies have equal ranking, at least formally, and make efforts to include dancers in decision-making about repertory, tours and choreography, as well as shared authorship in the making of choreography. At the Royal Swedish Ballet the dancers have a say through voting about the appointment of the ballet director every sixth year. Otherwise it is customary that the board of a ballet company controls this appointment.

Reflecting Swedish culture at places of work, there was a much larger number of parties for the whole company at the Royal Swedish Ballet than at the other classical companies in this study – on tours, after premières, in connection with Swedish holidays and at the end of annual seasons. These last served as rituals of rebellion (Gluckman 1982 [1956]), while the Lucia party was a social initiation of young members, who were asked to do a Lucia procession for the ballet management and their colleagues, to the company. Lucia is celebrated on 13 December in Sweden, both in the private and public sphere. Traditionally a young woman, 'Lucia', wearing a white gown and a crown of candles, is followed by an entourage of male and female attendants. They all sing Christmas songs. The formal atmosphere, the gender roles and the text of the songs are often changed into parody, and this was the case at the Lucia party that was held in a studio at the Royal Swedish Ballet. It started in a ceremonial atmosphere with one of the young women dancers entering dressed as 'Lucia' with three female attendants and three little brownies. They had notes with the text of the songs. One of the male soloists of the company accompanied them on a piano. Suddenly 'Lucia' and her entourage broke into club dancing steps, jazzing up one of the traditional songs. It was funny, and we laughed. But they could not keep up the jocular atmosphere. It became a bit embarrassing as it went along. The event can be said to include a slight element of desecration, a ritualized hazing. It was an opportunity to give a bad performance (including using their voices, which they were not trained to do), and then be accepted socially as the new dancers in the company.

Ballett Frankfurt also had many parties for the whole company, both on tours and in Frankfurt, cultivating a sense of community among these foreigners in Germany. There was for example the exhilarating annual Halloween party, arranged by one of the Americans in the company. Most guests were not dressed up, but there were those who had taken the opportunity to borrow costumes from the costume department in the theatre. Dancers thus appeared at this masquerade in nineteenth-century outfits and dresses from the 1920s and 1930s. Someone came dressed in autumn leaves; but there was also an American dancer wearing his Japanese kimono, complete with make-up and wig, and men in drag.

In studies on transnationality generally, it is often assumed that the United States is especially responsible for producing a Western hegemony. In the ballet world, the situation is more complex. Classical ballet is not an American invention, nor did it, like many other expressions of culture, grow in fame and into recognition when it reached the United States. Classical ballet has a long and well-established European history. It is, however, admittedly Western. The 'ballet boom' in the 1970s and 1980s in the United States can be attributed to economic growth in combination with the Cold War. This was the time when ballet could make sensational political news as dancers from the Soviet Union defected to the West.

Transnational connectivity in the ballet world does not always mean that things click culturally, however. There are also cultural clashes, both personal and artistic ones. The highly regarded Russian heritage of dancers, choreographers, and coaches, but also in the Russian ballet style and an old-fashioned authoritarian idiom, has caused a lot of tension in the West in the 1990s.

The reproduction of cultural power in the classical ballet world is often criticized, even from within its own ranks. Yet it is still there, supported by an ideology of exclusion. Dancers sometimes perform outside the ballet world in advertisements for magazines and newspapers and commercials on television, in churches and in operas, plays and films. In the long run the classical ballet world will have to open up to the outside world and incorporate modern ideas of pedagogy that recognize individuals into its routine work practice.

There has been an expansion of the number of dancers during the last decades, and consequently also of dance schools of many different kinds. According to Leach (1997) this has not yet produced enough advances in teaching methods and in the international coordination of the many types of training that are being practised. This is important, since the rate of injury has reached unacceptable levels. Dancers are pushed much more technically nowadays; they are indeed on the average better in that respect than just a few decades ago. But they are also injured far more often than the previous generation of dancers. During my field study, the National Ballet of Canada in Toronto was mentioned as a company that is in the forefront of healthy training. It seems obvious that ballet students and dancers need regular medical examinations and individual training programmes in order to avoid injuries that cause immense personal suffering and have become a monumental threat to ballet. The hard physical training of dancers furthermore has to be supported by mental training in order to work. Mental training has helped many dancers to continue dancing, to dance better and to go back to dancing after an injury. It is a way to improve the low self-esteem of dancers (through goal-ladders and their own accounts of what they can influence and what they cannot influence), and to teach them concentration cues and relaxation techniques and how to handle stage fright and setbacks in casting and promotion, as well as negative reviews. If mental training is included already in ballet schools as a part of the early dance training, the stigma that is still attached to it ought to disappear. In order to facilitate the transition to a second career, dancers could use longer and broader general schooling than most have at present. Leach (1977) suggests that ballet students should complete secondary education.[14] After all, not every ballet student becomes a professional dancer, and others may want to stop working as dancers earlier than they at first thought because of injuries. There are also dancers who realize after a while that they do not like dancing as a career as much as they had thought they would, and leave the ballet world because of new professional interests.

Although there are centres for the transition of dancers to a second career in a few countries, and others are in the making, there is still a lot to do in this area. One idea might be to establish more formalized collaboration between ballet companies and career officers in order to find and create jobs for ex-dancers outside the ballet world, although extra funding would be needed for this (Wulff 1997–8). At the moment, the dominant view is that ex-dancers need to learn how to find jobs for themselves. Some companies make a certain effort to help dancers in transition, but the responsibility is with the individual dancer, not with the company or the theatre where they have worked, or even the unions they have belonged to. With dancers working not only in different companies, but also in different countries, the situation becomes even more complicated.

Despite the fact that the idea of Nederlands Dans Theater 3, Jiří Kylián's company for five older dancers, goes against the conventional aesthetics of classical ballet, it is likely to set an example. The movement quality of older dancers is a whole new landscape to explore, not least in combination with the depth of their artistic expression. Older dancers can create other lines and spaces than young dancers. There are thus both social and artistic reasons to form more and even bigger companies of older dancers (Wulff 1997–8).

The increased moving and mixing in the ballet world, by both famous and unknown dancers, choreographers and coaches, is changing the centre–periphery structure. This leads to more crossovers between classical and contemporary styles, as well as between dance and other art forms. Contemporary choreographers and dancers thus work with other transnational artists like sound designers, computer musicians, video artists, movie-makers, fashion designers and architects. In the growth of transnational connections, the occupational linkages are particularly obvious. The world of dancers is a case in point.

Notes

1. In 'Traveling Cultures' and 'Spatial Practices: Fieldwork, Travel, and the Disciplining of Anthropology' James Clifford (1997) discusses the implication of mobile lives for anthropological fieldwork.

2. To the dancers' custom of dancing at memorial services and funerals for dance people has recently, by way of new technology, been added the possibility of – dancing at one's own funeral. When Keith McDaniel, who used to dance with the Alvin Ailey American Dance Theater, died of AIDS at the age of thirty-eight there was a memorial service at the Alvin Ailey headquarters in Manhattan. As his ex-colleagues danced a section from *Revelations* in which McDaniel had taken part, they were being videoed.

Then video clips of McDaniel dancing different roles were shown on a monitor, and after that a tape with him singing was played on a tape-recorder.

3. On the philosophical problems and possibilities of notating dance, see Goodman (1981). Another application of dance and ballet notations is the medical rehabilitation of handicapped and deaf people and athletes (Hutchinson Guest 1984; McGuinness-Scott 1983).

4. Dance theoretician Betty Redfern (1983) discusses dance notation and laments the absence of one universal notation system for dance. There is in fact a rivalry between the Laban and the Benesh systems, but there have also been points of cooperation between them.

5. Copyright on folk-dance is confused, I was told at the Benesh Institute, as well as on tribal dance: 'there are families who say that they own the steps'.

6. Ballet scores are expensive. A desirable score can cost up to $4,000.

7. On copyright, intellectual property, new technologies and multiple authorship see Lury (1993) and Born (1995, 1996). See also Baulch (1996) and Williams (1996) on copyright on technological dance specifically.

8. This way of working is influenced by Merce Cunningham and John Cage, who created choreography and music independently and then put them together in performance. William Forsythe and composers Thom Willems and Joel Ryan developed the choreography and the music for *Sleepers Guts* quite separately (with Forsythe making visits to the sound studio now and then in order to listen to sections they had made). Much synchronizing work was also being done at stage calls. Chance is not only used for unpredictable connections between choreography and music in performance, however. There is also choreographic chance, and this is different from improvisation. Susan Foster (1986) notes that choreographic chance operations are usually made before performances – it is a method for making dance pieces; whereas improvisation occurs on stage by way of spontaneous choices of certain sections of steps and the ordering of them. Foster exemplifies with Merce Cunningham's pioneering work with chance choreography in the early fifties, especially *Suite by Chance*. The fact that Cunningham was tossing coins and throwing dice as ways of making random choices (among already existing sections) has also been commented on by Banes (1994), Copeland (1983) and Franko (1995), among others. A Japanese interpretation of Cunningham has been critiqued by Nagura (1996).

9. The fact that part of this computer technology that now unleashes aesthetic forms was first developed by American defence programmes is indeed an ironic footnote.

10. The making of *Sleepers Guts* coincided with a public debate over recent budgetary cuts in municipal funding of the arts in the city of Frankfurt-am-Main. In the strained economy of Germany after the reunification, the arts, in this case the new Opera House, were among the first institutions to suffer setbacks in support. This produced a huge conflict between the Opera Company and Ballett Frankfurt over money that Ballett Frankfurt had made on tours and that the Opera Company wanted to get access to. Although William Forsythe did keep a low profile in this conflict, he was said to have threatened to leave Frankfurt if he were to lose this

money. A few months later, the director of the Opera Company resigned, and Forsythe renewed his contract.

11. The so-called 'Big Eye' is a video that is connected to a computer. The colours and movements that the 'Big Eye' is filming make sounds that can be processed in the computer.

12. With the use of high technology in multimedia dance performances, collaboration between different occupational specialists has become even more important (cf. Kozel 1995). The division of labour between technological knowledge and artistic vision creates a mutual dependency. Respect and trust become particularly significant, since the involved partners are not in complete control of each other's domains. It is a sensitive collaboration, especially when it is being enacted between two individuals regardless of whether they have been a team for many years or just for a short period of time.

13. Haraway (1991) and Kozel (1994, 1995) discuss fear versus euphoria in relation to technology, as well as notions of incompatibility and continuity between humans and machines.

14. This is being done in Austria, Belgium, Canada, France, Sweden, Britain and the United States (Leach 1997).

Bibliography

Adair, C. (1992), *Women and Dance*, New York: New York University Press.

Adshead, J., Briginshaw, V. A., Hodgens, P., and Huxley, M., (1988), *Dance Analysis*, London: Dance Books.

Alford, R. R. and Szanto, A. (1996), 'Orpheus Wounded: The Experience of Pain in the Professional Worlds of the Piano', *Theory and Society*, vol.25, no.1, pp.1–44.

Altorki, S. and Fawzi El-Solh, C. (eds) (1988), *Arab Women in the Field*, Syracuse, NY: Syracuse University Press.

Amit-Talai, V. and Wulff, H. (eds) (1995), *Youth Cultures*, London: Routledge.

Appadurai, A. (1988), 'Putting Hierarchy in Its Place', *Cultural Anthropology*, vol.3, no.1, pp.36–49.

—— (1996), Modernity at Large, Minneapolis: University of Minnesota Press.

Banes, S. (1987), Terpsichore in Sneakers, Hanover, NH: Wesleyan University Press.

—— (1994), *Writing Dancing in the Age of Postmodernism*, Hanover, NH: Wesleyan University Press.

—— (1998), *Dancing Women*, London: Routledge.

Barnes, C. (1977), *Inside American Ballet Theatre*, New York: Da Capo Press.

Bateson, G. (1972), 'A Theory of Play and Fantasy', in idem, *Steps to an Ecology of Mind*, New York: Ballantine Books, pp.177–93.

Baulch, L. (1996), 'Copyright', in H. Trotter (ed.), *Is Technology the Future for Dance?*, The Green Mill Dance Project Papers 1995, Canberra: Australian Dance Council, pp.128–32.

Bauman, R. (1992), 'Performance', in idem (ed.), *Folklore, Cultural Performances, and Popular Entertainments*, New York: Oxford University Press, pp.41–9.

Becker, H. S. (1963), *Outsiders*, New York: Free Press.

—— (1984), *Art Worlds*, Berkeley: University of California Press.

Bensman, J. (1983), 'Introduction: The Phenomenology and Sociology of the Performing Arts', in J. B. Kamerman and R. Martorella (eds), *Performers and Performances*, South Hadley, Mass.: Bergin & Garvey Publishers, pp.1–37.

Bensman, J. and Lilienfeld, R. (1973), 'The Artistic and Critical Attitudes', in eidem, *Craft and Consciousness*, New York: John Wiley & Sons, pp.15–31.

Blacking, J. (ed.), (1977), *The Anthropology of the Body*, ASA Monographs 15, London: Academic Press.

Bloch, M. (1992), 'What Goes Without Saying: The Conceptualisation of Zafimaniry Society', in A. Kuper (ed.), *Conceptualising Society*, London: Routledge, pp. 127–46.

Born, G. (1995), *Rationalizing Culture*, Berkeley: University of California Press.

—— (1996), '(Im)materiality and Sociality: The Dynamics of Intellectual Property in a Computer Software Research Culture', *Social Anthropology*, vol.4, no.2, pp. 101–16.

Bourdieu, P. (1977), *Outline of a Theory of Practice*, Cambridge: Cambridge University Press.

—— (1984), *Distinction*, Cambridge, Mass.: Harvard University Press.

—— (1993) *The Field of Cultural Production*, New York: Columbia University Press.

Bourdieu, P. and Passeron, J. C. (1977), *Reproduction in Education, Society and Culture*, London: Sage.

Brinson, P. and Dick, F. (1996), *Fit to Dance?* London: Calouste Gulbenkian Foundation.

Brown, P. and Levinsson, S. C. (1987), *Politeness*, Cambridge: Cambridge University Press.

Browning, B. (1995), *Samba*, Bloomington: Indiana University Press.

Burt, R. (1995), *The Male Dancer*, London: Routledge.

Carmeli, Y. S. (1990), 'Performing the "Real" and "Impossible" in the British Traveling Circus', *Semiotica*, vol.80, no.3–4, pp.193–220.

Carter, A. (1993), 'Contemplating the Universe', *Dance Now*, vol.2, no.1, pp.60–3.

Cass, J. (1993), *Dancing through History*, Englewood Cliffs, NJ: Prentice Hall.

Clarke, M. and Crisp, C. (1992), *Ballet*, London: Hamish Hamilton.

Clifford, J. (1997), *Routes*, Cambridge, Mass.: Harvard University Press.

Cohen, A. (1993), *Masquerade Politics*, Berkeley: University of California Press.

Cohen, A. P. (ed.) (1982), *Belonging*, Manchester: Manchester University Press.

Copeland, R. (1983), 'Merce Cunningham and the Politics of Perception', in R. Copeland and M. Cohen (eds), *What Is Dance?*, Oxford: Oxford University Press.

Cowan, J. K. (1990), *Dance and the Body Politic in Northern Greece*, Princeton, NJ: Princeton University Press.

Crisp, C. (1995), 'Rudolf Nureyev', in Programme for the Royal Swedish Ballet, *Don Quixote at the London Coliseum*, pp.9–11.

Croce, A. (1977), *Afterimages*, New York: Alfred A. Knopf.

—— (1994–5), 'Discussing the Undiscussable', *The New Yorker*, 26 December–2 January, pp.54–60.

Csikszentmihalyi, M. (1990), *Flow*, New York: Harper Perennial.

Csordas, T. J. (1994a), *Embodiment and Experience*, Cambridge: Cambridge University Press.

—— (1994b), 'Words from the Holy People: A Case Study in Cultural Phenomenology', in T. J. Csordas (ed.), *Embodiment and Experience*, Cambridge: Cambridge University Press, pp.269–90.

—— (1995), 'Embodiment as a Paradigm for Anthropology', *Ethos*, vol.18, no.1, pp.5–47.

Cullberg, B. (1992), 'Television Ballet', in W. Sorell (ed.), *The Dance Has Many Faces*, Pennington, NJ: a capella books, pp.137–43.

Daly, A. (1987), 'The Balanchine Woman: Of Hummingbirds and Channel Swimmers', *The Drama Review*, vol.31, no.1, pp.8–21.

—— (1997 [1987–88]), 'Classical Ballet as a Discourse of Difference', in J. C. Desmond (ed.), *Meaning in Motion*, Durham: Duke University Press, pp.111–19.

Daniel, E. V. (1994), 'The Individual in Terror', in T. J. Csordas (ed.), *Embodiment and Experience*, Cambridge: Cambridge University Press, pp.229–47.

Daniel, Y. (1995), *Rumba*, Bloomington: Indiana University Press.

DelVecchio Good, M.-J., Brodwin, P. E., Good, B. J., and Kleinman, A. (eds), (1992), *Pain as Human Experience*, Berkeley: University of California Press.

Denby, E. (1986), *Dance Writings* (ed. R. Cornfield and W. Mackay), New York: Alfred A. Knopf.

Desmond, J.(ed.) (1997), *Meaning in Motion*, Durham: Duke University Press.

Dictionary of the English Language (1963), International Edition, New York: Funk & Wagnalls Company.

DiMaggio, P. and Useem, M. (1983), 'Cultural Democracy in a Period of Cultural Expansion: The Social Composition of Arts Audiences in the United States', in J. B. Kamerman and R. Martorella (eds), *Performers and Performances*, South Hadley, Mass.: Bergin & Garvey Publishers, pp.199–225.

Douglas, M. (1970), *Natural Symbols*, New York: Vintage.

—— (1978), *Purity and Danger*, London: Routledge & Kegan Paul.

Edelman, B. (1997), *Shunters at Work*, Stockholm Studies in Social Anthropology, no.37, Stockholm: Almqvist & Wiksell International.

Ericson, D. (1988), *In the Stockholm Art World*, Stockholm Studies in Social Anthropology, no.17, Stockholm: Almqvist & Wiksell International.

Evans-Pritchard, E. E. (1928), 'The Dance', *Africa*, vol.1, pp.446–62.

Fabian, J. (1990), *Power and Performance*, Madison: University of Wisconsin Press.

Featherstone, M. (ed.) (1991), *Global Culture*, London: Sage.

—— Hepsworth, M. and Turner, B. S. (eds) (1991), *The Body*, London: Sage.

Federico, R. C. (1968), 'Ballet as an Occupation', unpublished Ph.D. thesis, Northwestern University.

—— (1974), 'Recruitment, Training and Performance: The Case of Ballet', in P. L. Stewart and M. G. Cantor (eds), *Varieties of Work Experience*, New York: John Wiley and Sons, pp.249–61.

Fernandez, J. W. (1986), *Persuasions and Performances*, Bloomington: Indiana University Press.

Finnegan, R. (1989), *The Hidden Musicians*, Cambridge: Cambridge University Press.

Foster, S. L. (1986), *Reading Dancing*, Berkeley: University of California Press.

—— (1992), 'Dancing Culture', *American Ethnologist*, vol.19, no.2, pp.362–6.

—— (ed.) (1995), *Choreographing History*, Bloomington: Indiana University Press.

—— (ed.) (1996a), *Corporealities*, London: Routledge.

—— (1996b), 'The Ballerina's Phallic Pointe', in S. L. Foster (ed.), *Corporealities*, London: Routledge, pp.1–24.

—— (1996c), *Choreography and Narrative*, Bloomington: Indiana University Press.

Foucault, M. (1973), *The Order of Things*, New York: Vintage.

—— (1979), *Discipline and Punish*, New York: Vintage.

Franko, M. (1995), *Dancing Modernism/Performing Politics*, Bloomington: Indiana University Press.

Gamson, J. (1994), *Claims to Fame*, Berkeley: University of California Press.

Gardner, H. (1993), *Creating Minds*, New York: Basic Books.

Garsten, C. (1994), *Apple World*, Stockholm Studies in Social Anthropology, no.33, Stockholm: Almqvist & Wiksell International.

Gere, D. (1995), 'Introduction', in D. Gere (ed.), *Looking Out*, New York: Schirmer Books, pp.1–7.

Gerholm, T. (1988), 'On Ritual: A Postmodernist View', *Ethnos*, vol.53, no.3–4, pp.190–203.

Gherman, B. (1994), *Agnes de Mille*, New York: Collier Books.

Gilman, R. (1982),'The Actor as a Celebrity', *Humanities in Review*, Cambridge: Cambridge University Press, pp.106–24.

Gilpin, H. (1993), 'Static and Uncertain Bodies: Absence and Instability in Movement Performance', *Assaph*, no.9, pp.95–114.

Gladstone, V. (1995), 'Nureyev Auction Breaks Records', *Dance Magazine*, May, vol.LXIX, no.5, p.21.

Gluckman, M. (1982 [1956]), *Custom and Conflict in Africa*, Oxford: Blackwell.

Goellner, E. W. and Murphy, J. S.(eds) (1995), *Bodies of the Text*, New Brunswick, NJ: Rutgers University Press.

Goffman, E. (1959), *The Presentation of Self in Everyday Life*, Garden City, NY: Doubleday Anchor Books.

—— (1974), *Frame Analysis*, New York: Harper & Row Publishers.

Goodman, N. (1981), *Languages of Art*, Indianapolis: Hackett Publishing Company.

Gordon, S. (1983), *Off Balance*, New York: Pantheon.

Grau, A. (1993), 'John Blacking and the Development of Dance Anthropology in the UK', *Dance Research*, vol.25, no.2, pp.21–31.

Gross, L. P. (1973), 'Modes of Communication and the Acquisition of Symbolic Competence', in G. Gerbner, L. P. Gross, and W. H. Melody (eds), *Communications Technology and Social Policy*, New York: Wiley, pp.189–207.

Guest, I. (1988), *The Dancer's Heritage*, London: The Dancing Times.

—— (1996), *The Ballet of the Enlightenment*, London: Dance Books.

Guilbault, S. (1983), *How New York Stole the Idea of Modern Art*, Chicago: University of Chicago Press.

Gupta, A. and Ferguson, J. (1992), 'Beyond "Culture": Space, Identity and the Politics of Difference', *Cultural Anthropology*, vol.7, no.1, pp.6–23.

Haffner, N. (1997), 'The Dancer as Medium', *Ballett International*, no.8–9, pp.11–12.

Hall, E. T. (1959), *The Silent Language*, Garden City, NY: Doubleday & Company.

—— (1963), 'A System for the Notation of Proxemic Behavior', *American Anthropologist*, no.65, pp.1003–26.

—— (1966), *The Hidden Dimension*, Garden City, NY: Doubleday & Company.

Hamilton, L. H., Brooks-Gunn, J., Warren, M. P. and Hamilton, W. G. (1988), 'The Role of Selectivity in the Pathogenesis of Eating Problems in Ballet Dancers', *Medicine and Science in Sports and Exercise*, vol.20, no.6, pp.560–5.

Hanna, J. L. (1979), *To Dance is Human*, Austin: University of Texas Press.

—— (1983), *The Performer–Audience Connection*, Austin: University of Texas Press.

—— (1988), *Dance, Sex and Gender*, Chicago: University of Chicago Press.

Hannerz, U. (1983), 'Tools of Identity and Imagination', in A. Jacobson-Widding (ed.), *Identity*, Atlantic Highlands, NJ: Humanities Press, pp.347–60.

—— (1992), *Cultural Complexity*, New York: Columbia University Press.

—— (1996), *Transnational Connections*, London: Routledge.

Hara, N. (1994), 'A Touch of Erotica from Sweden', *Asahi Evening News*, 30 January.

Haraway, D. J. (1991), *Simians, Cyborgs, and Women*, London: Free Association Books.

Haskell, T. L. and Teichgraeber III, R. F. (eds) (1995), *The Culture of the Market*, Cambridge: Cambridge University Press.

Hastrup, K. (1985), *Culture and History in Medieval Iceland*, Oxford: Oxford University Press.

—— (1993), 'Native Anthropology: A Contradiction in Terms?', *Folk*, no.35, pp. 147–61.

—— (1998), 'Theatre as a Site of Passage: Some Reflections on the Magic of Acting', in F. Hughes-Freeland (ed.), *Ritual, Performance, Media*, ASA Monographs 35, London: Routledge, pp.29–45.

——, *A Place Apart*, Oxford: Clarendon Press (Forthcoming).

Howes, D. (ed.) (1991), *The Varieties of Sensory Experience*, Toronto: University of Toronto Press.

Hutchinson Guest, A. (1984), *Dance Notation*, London: Dance Books.

Hymes, D. (1975), 'Breakthrough into Performance', in D. Ben-Amos and K. S. Goldstein (eds), *Folklore*, The Hague: Mouton, pp.11–74.

Jackson, J. (1994), 'Chronic Pain and the Tension between the Body as Subject and Object', in T. J. Csordas (ed.), *Embodiment and Experience*, Cambridge: Cambridge University Press, pp.201–28.

Jensen, G. (1994), 'Koreografi som Genetiska Tecken: Vidunderlig Variationsrikedom i Frankfurtbaletten under William Forsythe', *Svenska Dagbladet*, 3 November.

John-Steiner, V. (1985), *Notebooks of the Mind*, New York: Harper & Row Publishers.

Jordan, S. and Allen, D. (eds) (1993), *Parallel Lines*, London: John Libbey & Company.

Jordan, S. and Thomas, H. (1994), 'Dance and Gender: Formalism and Semiotics Reconsidered', *Dance Research*, vol.XII, no.2, pp.3–14.

Jowitt, D. (1988), *Time and the Dancing Image*, Berkeley: University of California Press.

Jowitt, D., Acocella J., and Siegel, M. B. (1995), 'Coming to Grips with the "Other": A Discussion among Writers', in D. Gere (ed.), *Looking Out*, New York: Schirmer Books, pp.181–95.

Kaeppler, A. (1978), 'Dance in Anthropological Perspective', *Annual Review of Anthropology*, no.7, pp.31–49.

Kealiinohomoku, J.(1983 [1970]), 'An Anthropologist Looks at Ballet as a Form of Ethnic Dance', in R. Copeland and M. Cohen (eds), *What Is Dance?* Oxford: Oxford University Press, pp.533–49.

Kendall, E. (1979), *Where She Danced*, Berkeley: University of California Press.

Kirstein, L. (1994), *Mosaic*, New York: Farrar, Straus & Giroux.

Kisselgoff, A. (1983), 'There Is Nothing "National" about Ballet Styles', in R. Copeland and M. Cohen (eds), *What Is Dance?*, Oxford: Oxford University Press, pp.361–3.

Koegler, H. (1987), *The Concise Oxford Dictionary of Ballet*, Oxford: Oxford University Press.

—— (1995), 'A Life between Art and Politics', *Dance Now*, vol.4, no.3, pp.88–93.

Koman, K. (1996), *Mynt under Masten och Vissla på Vind*, Stockholm: Rabén Prisma.

Koutedakis, Y. (1996), 'Nutrition to Fuel Dance: A Brief Review', *Dance Research*, Winter, vol.XIV, no.2, pp.76–93.

Koutedakis, Y., Pacy, P., Sharp, N. C. C., and Dick, F. (1996), 'Is Fitness Necessary for Dancers?', *Dance Research*, Winter, vol.XIV, no.2, pp.105–18.

Kozel, S. (1994), 'Spacemaking: Experiences of a Virtual Body', *Dance Theatre Journal*, vol.11, no.2, pp.12–47.

Kozel, S. (1995), 'The Virtual World: New Frontiers for Dance and Philosophy', Paper for the Fifth Study of Dance Conference 'Border and Tensions: Dance and Discourse', University of Surrey, 20–23 April.

Lagercrantz, M. V. (1995), *Den Andra Rollen*, Stockholm: Carlssons.

Lassalle, N. and Burgess, A. (eds) (1995), *School of American Ballet*, New York: School of American Ballet.

Lave, J. and Wenger, E. (1995), *Situated Learning*, Cambridge: Cambridge University Press.

Leach, B. (ed.) (1997), *The Dancer's Destiny*, Lausanne: International Organization for the Transition of Professional Dancers.

Lewis, J. L.(1992), *Ring of Liberation*, Chicago: University of Chicago Press.

Lury, C. (1993), *Cultural Rights*, London: Routledge.

Lutz, C. and White, G.(1986), 'The Anthropology of Emotions', *Annual Review of Anthropology*, no. 15, pp.405–36.

McGuinness-Scott, J. (1983), *Movement Study and Benesh Movement Notation*, Oxford: Oxford University Press.

McRobbie, A. (1991), 'Dance Narratives and Fantasies of Achievement', in idem, *Feminism and Youth Culture*, Boston: Unwin Hyman, pp.189–219.

Manning, S. (1997), 'The Female Dancer and the Male Gaze: Feminist Critiques of Early Modern Dance', in J. C. Desmond (ed.), *Meaning in Motion*, pp.153–66.

Marcus, G. E. (1989), 'Imagining the Whole: Ethnography's Contemporary Efforts to Situate Itself', *Critique of Anthropology*, vol.9, no.3, pp.7–30.

—— (1995), 'Ethnography in/of the World System: The Emergence of Multi-Sited Ethnography', *Annual Review of Anthropology*, no.24, pp.95–117.

Marcus, G. E. and Fischer, M. M. J. (1986), *Anthropology as Cultural Critique*, Chicago: University of Chicago Press.

Marigny, C. de (1990), 'Is Dance an International Language?', in B. Schønberg (ed.), *World Ballet and Dance 1990–1991*, London: Dance Books, pp.2–7.

Martin, E. (1987), *The Woman in the Body*, Boston: Beacon Press.

Meisner, N. (1995), 'The Improbable Dream Team', *The Times*, 6 July.

Merton, R. K. (1972), 'Insiders and Outsiders: A Chapter in the Sociology of Knowledge', *American Journal of Sociology*, vol.78, no.1, pp.9–47.

Mewett, P. G. (1982), 'Exiles, Nicknames, Social Identities and the Production of Local Consciousness in a Lewis Crofting Community', in A. P. Cohen (ed.), *Belonging*, Manchester: Manchester University Press, pp.101–30.

Mills, C. W. (1961), *The Sociological Imagination*, New York: Grove Press.

Morgan, J., O'Neill, C., and Harré, R. (1979), *Nicknames*, London: Routledge & Kegan Paul.

Morris, G. (ed.) (1996), *Moving Words*, London: Routledge.

Myerhoff, B. (1990), 'The Transformation of Consciousness in Ritual Performances: Some Thoughts and Questions', in R. Schechner and W. Appel (eds), *By Means of Performance*, Cambridge: Cambridge University Press, pp.245–9.

Nagura, M. (1996), 'Cross-Cultural Differences in the Interpretation of Merce Cunningham's Choreography', in G. Morris (ed.), *Moving Words*, London: Routledge, pp.270–87.

Narayan, K. (1993), 'How Native is a "Native" Anthropologist?', *American Anthropologist*, vol.95, no.3, pp.671–86.

Näslund, E. (1995), *Birgit Cullbergs Fröken Julie*, Department of Theatre and Film Studies, Stockholm University, Stockholm: Theatron.

Ness, S. A. (1992), *Body, Movement, and Culture*, Philadelphia: University of Pennsylvania Press.

—— (1996), 'Observing the Evidence Fail: Difference Arising from Objectification in Cross-Cultural Studies of Dance', in G. Morris (ed.), *Moving Words*, London: Routledge, pp.245–69.

—— (1997), 'Originality in the Postcolony: Choreographing the Neoethnic Body of Philippine Dance', *Cultural Anthropology*, vol.12, no.1, pp.64–108.

Norman, K. (1994), 'The Ironic Body: Obscene Joking among Swedish Working-Class Women', *Ethnos*, vol.59, no.3–4, pp.187–211.

Norman, S. J. (1996), 'Technology in the Performing Arts: Ways of Doing, Ways of Seeing', in H. Trotter (ed.), *Is Technology the Future for Dance?*, The Green Mill Dance Project Papers 1995, Canberra: Australian Dance Council, pp.53–60.

Novack, C. J. (1990), *Sharing the Dance*, Madison: University of Wisconsin Press.

—— (1992), 'Artefacts (The Empire after Colonialism)', *Women and Performance*, vol.5, no.2, pp.82–9.

—— (1993), 'Ballet, Gender and Cultural Power', in H. Thomas (ed.), *Dance, Gender and Culture*, London: Macmillan.

Noverre, J. G. (1983 [1760]), 'From Letters on Dancing and Ballet', in R. Copeland and M. Cohen (eds), *What Is Dance?*, Oxford: Oxford University Press.

Olsson, C. (1993), *Dansföreställningar*, Lund: Bokbox.

Ostrower, F. (1995), *Why the Wealthy Give*, Princeton, NJ: Princeton University Press.

Palmer, C. (1996), 'A Life of Its Own', unpublished Ph.D. thesis, University of Adelaide.

Pálsson, G. (1995), *The Textual Life of Savants*, Chur: Harwood Academic Publishers.

Parry, J. (1996–7), 'Dance on the Edge: Jann Parry Considers What Constitutes the Cutting Edge of British Dance Today', *Dance Now*, vol.5, no.4, pp.67–75.

Radcliffe-Brown, A. R. (1964 [1922]), *The Andaman Islanders*, New York: Free Press.

Ralf, K. (1979), *Operan 200 år*, Stockholm: Prisma.

Ramel, E. and Moritz, U. (1994), 'Self-reported Musculoskeletal Pain and Discomfort in Professional Ballet Dancers in Sweden', *Scandinavian Journal of Rehabilitation Medicine*, no.26, pp.11–16.

Redfern, B. (1983), *Dance, Art & Aesthetics*, London: Dance Books.

Robertson, R. (1992), *Globalization*, London: Sage.

Rödin, E. G. (1979), 'Operahusen', in K. Ralf (ed.), *Jubelboken Operan 200 År*, Stockholm: Prisma, pp.19–34.

Rosaldo, R. (1989), *Culture and Truth*, Boston: Beacon Press.

Royal Ballet School (1992–3), 'Annual Report', unpublished brochure.

Royal Ballet School, (undated), unpublished brochure.

Royce, A. P. (1980), *The Anthropology of Dance*, Bloomington: Indiana University Press.

Salaman, G. (1974), *Community and Occupation*, Cambridge Papers in Sociology, 4, Cambridge: Cambridge University Press.

Sandström, P. (1993), 'Operan/Kungliga Teatern: En Publikstudie', unpublished report, Stockholm.

Savigliano, M. E. (1995), *Tango and the Political Economy of Passion*, Boulder: Westview Press.

Schechner, R. (1995), *The Future of Ritual*, London: Routledge.

—— and Appel, W. (eds) (1990), *By Means of Performance*, Cambridge: Cambridge University Press.

Scheper-Hughes, N. and Lock, M. M. (1987), 'The Mindful Body: A Prolegomenon to Future Work in Medical Anthropology', *Medical Anthropology Quarterly*, vol.1, no.1, pp.6–41.

Schutz, A. (1967), *Collected Papers I*, The Hague: Martinus Nijhoff.

Sennett, R. and Cobb, J. (1973), *The Hidden Injuries of Class*, New York: Vintage Books.

Shami, S. (1988), 'Studying Your Own: The Complexities of a Shared Culture', in S. Altorki and C. Fawzi El-Solh (eds), *Arab Women in the Field*, Syracuse, NY: Syracuse University Press, pp.115–38.

Sherlock, J. (1993), 'Dance and the Culture of the Body', in S. Scott and D. Morgan (eds), *Body Matters*, London: The Falmer Press, pp.35–48.

Siegel, M. B. (1995), 'On Multiculturality and Authenticity: A Critical Call to Arms', in D. Gere (ed.), *Looking Out*, New York: Schirmer Books, pp.223–31.

Singer, M. (1972), *When a Great Tradition Modernizes*, New York: Praeger.

Skeaping, M. and Ståhle, A. G. (1979), *Balett på Stockholmsoperan*, Stockholm: Norsteds.

Solway, D. (1994), *A Dance Against Time*, New York: Pocket Books.

Sorell, W. (1981), *Dance in Its Time*, New York: Columbia University Press.

Spencer, P. (ed.) (1985), *Society and the Dance*, Cambridge: Cambridge University Press.

Stanislavsky, K. (1967), *On the Art of the Stage*, London: Faber and Faber.

Stokes, M. (1994), 'Introduction: Ethnicity, Identity and Music', in M. Stokes (ed.), *Ethnicity, Identity and Music*, Oxford: Berg, pp.1–27.

Strathern, M. (1987), 'The Limits of Auto-anthropology', in A. Jackson (ed.), *Anthropology at Home*, ASA Monographs 25, London: Tavistock, pp.16–37.

Sutherland, D. E. (1976), 'Ballet as a Career', *Society*, November/December, pp.40–5.

Synnott, A. (1993), *The Body Social*, London: Routledge.

Tajet-Foxell, B. and Rose, F. D. (1995), 'Pain and Pain Tolerance in Professional Ballet Dancers', *British Journal of Sports Medicine*, vol.29, no.1, pp.31–4.

Thomas, H. (ed.) (1993), *Dance, Gender and Culture*, London: Macmillan.

—— (1995), *Dance, Modernity and Culture*, London: Routledge.

—— (1996), 'Do You Want to Join the Dance?: Postmodernism/Poststructuralism, the Body, and Dance', in G. Morris (ed.), *Moving Words*, London: Routledge, pp. 63–87.

—— (ed.) (1997), *Dance in the City*, New York: St Martin's Press.

Traweek, S. (1988), *Beamtimes and Lifetimes*, Cambridge, Mass.: Harvard University Press.

Turner, B. S. (1984), *The Body and Society*, Oxford: Basil Blackwell.

Turner, V. W. (1964 [1957]), 'Symbols in Ndembu Ritual', in M. Gluckman (ed.), *Closed Systems and Open Minds*, Edinburgh: Oliver and Boyd, pp.20–51.

—— (1982), *From Ritual to Theatre*, New York City: Performing Arts Journal Communication.

Vail, J. A. (1985), 'Viewing and Re-viewing Dance', unpublished MA thesis, Wesleyan University.

—— (1995), 'What the Words Say: Watching American Critics Watch World Dance', in D. Gere (ed.), *Looking Out*, New York: Schirmer Books, pp.165–79.

van Nieuwkerk, K. (1995), '*A Trade like Any Other*', Austin: University of Texas Press.

Vasari, G. (1963), *Lives of the Most Eminent Painters, Sculptors and Architects*, New York: E. P. Dutton.

Wacquant, L. J. D. (1992), 'The Social Logic of Boxing in Black Chicago: Toward a Sociology of Pugilism', *Sociology of Sport Journal*, no.9, pp.221–54.

—— (1995a), 'The Pugilist Point of View: How Boxers Think and Feel about their Trade', *Theory and Society*, vol.24, no.4, pp.489–535.

—— (1995b), 'Pugs at Work: Bodily Capital and Labour Among Professional Boxers', *Body and Society*, vol.1, no.1, pp.65–93.

Weston, K. (1991), *Families We Choose*, New York: Columbia University Press.

Williams, M. (1996), 'Copyright: Legal Protection of Dance and the New Technologies – The Nutcracker Comes to Bits', in H. Trotter (ed.), *Is Technology the Future for Dance?*, The Green Mill Dance Project Papers 1995, Canberra: Australian Dance Council, pp.133–44.

Willis, P. (1977), *Learning to Labour*, Farnborough: Saxon House.

Wolff, J. (1983), *Aesthetics and the Sociology of Art*, London: George Allen & Unwin.

Wulff, H. (1988), *Twenty Girls*, Stockholm Studies in Social Anthropology, no.21, Stockholm: Almqvist & Wiksell International.

—— (1992), 'Young Swedes in New York: Workplace and Playground', in R. Lundén and E. Åsard (eds), *Networks of Americanization*, Stockholm: Almqvist & Wiksell International, pp.94–105.

—— (1995a), 'Introducing Youth Culture in Its Own Right: The State of the Art and New Possibilities', in V. Amit-Talai and H. Wulff (eds), *Youth Cultures*, London: Routledge, pp.1–18.

—— (1995b),'Inter-racial Friendship: Consuming Youth Styles, Ethnicity and Teenage Femininity in South London', in V. Amit-Talai and H. Wulff (eds), *Youth Cultures*, London: Routledge, pp.63–80.

—— (1996),'Att Tolka Tidens Rörelse', *Danstidningen*, no.2, pp.6–7.

—— (1997–8),'Das Leben nach dem Tanz: Der Wechsel zur zweiten Karriere', Parallax, December/January, no.5, pp.8–15.

—— (1998), 'Dans på Laddad Mark', *Danstidningen*, no.1,pp.3–6.

Zarrilli, P. B. (1990), 'What Does it Mean to "Become the Character": Power, Presence, and Transcendence in Asian In-body Disciplines of Practice', in R. Schechner and W. Appel (eds), *By Means of Performance*, Cambridge: Cambridge University Press, pp.131–48.

Zerubavel, E. (1981), *Hidden Rhythms*, Chicago: University of Chicago Press.

Ziegler, C. (1997), 'The CD ROM', *Ballett International*, no.8–9, p.13.

Index